Reading the Bible with Your Feet

Lucy Winkett

CANTERBURY
PRESS
Norwich

© Lucy Winkett 2021

Published in 2021 by Canterbury Press
Editorial office
3rd Floor, Invicta House,
108–114 Golden Lane,
London EC1Y 0TG, UK
www.canterburypress.co.uk

Canterbury Press is an imprint of Hymns Ancient & Modern Ltd
(a registered charity)

Hymns Ancient & Modern® is a registered trademark of
Hymns Ancient & Modern Ltd
13A Hellesdon Park Road, Norwich,
Norfolk NR6 5DR, UK

British Library Cataloguing in Publication data

A catalogue record for this book is available
from the British Library

978-1-78622-330-2

Typeset by Regent Typesetting
Printed and bound in Great Britain by
CPI Group (UK) Ltd

Contents

Introduction

A few years ago, a message flashed across my computer screen telling me that I was the victim of a malware ransom attack. All my Word files were now quarantined and inaccessible to me unless I transferred $1,000 within 48 hours. It was quite a moment. I like to think I'm just about competent on a computer but no more than that. And I hadn't backed up any of my files from the laptop that had all my sermons on it. It was a strangely cleansing experience, realizing that the words I had preached would no longer be recorded, that they would be lost for ever. After the initial shock, I became sanguine and thought to myself, well, if I've thought it once, I could think it again. And if I don't, then it wasn't important anyway. If the Holy Spirit had inspired words before, the future would be secure. A kind colleague retrieved some old sermons which had been uploaded on to the website, but others going back years were lost.

This year I realized I have been a priest for 25 years. Being ordained in those first couple of years of women's priesthood, and as the subject of very public, distressing and enduring opposition at the time of my appointment to St Paul's Cathedral in 1998, I found celebrating this anniversary poignant, overwhelming and astonishing in equal measure. To one family member who had been mildly appalled at my saying I had a vocation to be a priest back then, I remember saying that I couldn't convince them, so they would just have to see how it went. Watch me, I said. And here I am 25 years later.

That's a lot of sermons, in a lot of different places. And so, while this collection is necessarily from more recent years, I can detect themes that go back to the beginning, tracing a preaching history through Birmingham, Newham, cathedral ministry and now a city-centre parish. I have done some editing because

I've realized, with some chagrin, that some of my sermons have almost been all one sentence. Writing for others to read is a different discipline from writing notes to speak as part of the liturgy, and so some work has been needed to make them readable, not just hearable.

I feel extremely grateful to have been trained ecumenically at The Queen's Foundation, as an Anglican in the minority at a Methodist-majority college, and in preaching terms, immensely grateful for the year-long placement in a Black-led, Black-majority Pentecostal church in city-centre Birmingham. Both these contexts instilled in me the importance of preaching in the moment, however extensive the preparation or study beforehand. This ecumenical training, which placed me at a formative time as a preacher in the minority, in terms of denomination, gender and ethnicity, gave me a strong conviction that the sermon is preached together with the assembly, grown out of love for and with them. While the Holy Spirit can and does do her work in the weeks and days before preaching, with the commentaries and the computer, it is in the moment of connection in the context of worship that preaching becomes preaching, not just talking. The upshot of this is that I don't always say everything I've prepared.

It's a very curious thing to do, to read through things that you have said over years. There is not a little humiliation involved, as my hypocrisy and inadequacy call out from every page. Of course, anyone who dares to preach publicly about matters of the spirit and the heart, about a life of faith, must realize pretty quickly that the person they are preaching to mostly is themselves, realizing too their utter inadequacy in the face of the task. And so it is exposing, and rightly so, although hopefully within a liturgical context characterized by a level of trust. Nearly all of the sermons in this book have been preached in the context of the Eucharist, which also means that the breaking of the Word has been done only in the context of the imminent breaking of the Bread. As such, they are words offered at the crossroads between time and eternity where the sacramental life of the Church is expressed. There is some repetition, which I have not attempted to smooth out, taking my cue from John Wesley who apparently commented that if a sermon was worth preaching it was worth preaching at least ten times.

But the overwhelming sense I have had in putting these sermons together is one of huge privilege that I have been afforded the time and space by congregations to explore with them the meaning of Scripture in today's world. This is a very generous gift on their part. At times I have preached in situations of great pain for a church community, at funerals or in times of controversy. And in common with any preachers who are at least trying to speak honestly, I have been heckled and more than once people have walked out. This happened especially in a large cathedral where I spent 12 years preaching my way through some tough times when mine was the only female voice I could hear. I have never taken for granted the privilege of speaking publicly in church, remembering the silencing of women for much of Christian history in the UK, and the truth that the vast majority of the 2 billion Christians in the world today won't ever hear a woman preach a sermon in their church.

As women who preach, Black, Brown, white,[1] cisgendered or trans, whatever our hidden or visible disabilities, our voices matter. But women often find it hard to stay in the public space, contested as it is. In the spirit of the woman in Luke's Gospel (Luke 13.10–17) who moved from the side to the centre in response to the prompting of God, I hope that women from all backgrounds and experiences will continue to find strength and encouragement to move into the public spaces of religious practice and speak from there. We need to hear you. Please say what you have to say without fear.

I am also aware as a preacher that, for many people who identify as LGBTQ+ and who come into a church, the most they hope for is that the sermon won't contain something devastating for them, or that they won't hear something they later have to recover from. The bar is shamefully low. And for many others it's simply that sermons don't acknowledge their experience or identity at all. As a church, we must do better than this. Diversity is a fact but inclusion is a choice. And preachers, whatever our identity ourselves, must confront this every time we dare to speak, in season and out of season, as part of a community whose stated desire and purpose is to proclaim Good News.

Preaching as an activity asks that we read Scripture, not only with our heads in the commentaries or our hearts open to the promptings of the Spirit, but also with our feet.[2] This implies that we are invited to travel with it, step into it, and know, by that immersion in it, that Scripture itself is the story of the people travelling through life within the eternal mystery of God. Reading the Bible with our feet implies bodily as well as intellectual or emotional commitment. Not least because sometimes all we can do is turn up. And know again that those same feet have been washed by Christ who kneels before us to teach us a better way.

So for all the mistakes I make in preaching I ask constantly for forgiveness, and I pray for God's blessing on these offerings over the years. Most of all, I thank all the church communities of which I have been part, especially the people of St James's Church Piccadilly, who have shaped, challenged and held me as a preacher and a priest.

At the same time, I'm curious, and more than that, eager to see what the Spirit will ask us to say next.

Lucy Winkett
St James's Church Piccadilly
May 2021

Note

1 Taking part in a public debate in 2021 considering gender and race in Christianity, the participants, including me, agreed to capitalize the description of Black but not white. One of the participants, Chine McDonald, highlighted that this followed the example of the *New York Times* style guide who, when capitalizing the word 'Negro' in 1930, explained they wanted to 'act in recognition of racial respect for those who have been generations in the "lower case"'. As a white Christian writing today I choose to do the same, in recognition that different arguments are made about this and that decisions such as this will no doubt change over time.

2 Carlos Mesters, *God's Project*, quoted in Christopher Rowland and Mark Corner, 1990, *Liberating Exegesis: The Challenge of Liberation Theology to Biblical Interpretation*, London: SPCK, p. 13.

I

Why I am a Christian and How

St Luke Holloway, Lent 2019

Psalm 91
John 4

This is a story of muddling through.

Someone said to me recently that the trick to climbing a mountain was to put one foot in front of the other enough times.

And the key phrase for me is that last one: enough times.

I have been asked to speak as part of a series on 'Why I am a Christian and how'. For me, that has meant living my life as a priest. For many people, perhaps for most people who live their lives without reference to organized religion, that makes me into some kind of professional Christian. Paid to be nice to people, and somehow doing the Christian life in a more intense way.

But to me the central vocation I have is not to be a priest, however irreducible this seems for my life, but to be a human being fully alive. And for my humanity to become more Christ-shaped the longer I live. That has meant saying yes to being a priest, and, as I am now, in a parish.

But if I stopped doing the work of a priest, I would be left with the most important part of vocation: to be a human being called into becoming more and more closely aligned with Christ the longer I go on.

But what does that mean in practice?

For the most part I think I have sung myself into faith rather than argued it or talked myself into it. The practice of music, especially singing, has been an important way for me to find ways to express mysteries for which it is hard to find words.

In a broader way, the spiritual life has been, continues to be, a journey of finding my voice. And this has involved learning to breathe deeply, learning that repetition and practice are necessary in the spiritual life. Learning that this is both exhilarating and effortful. And learning that I am somehow – mostly – keen to put in that effort.

When I was a child, my mum put a poem on the fridge. It was quite a trite poem, but living beside it every day, somehow, it's gone in. And its sentiment has proved to be important in my life as I've tried to muddle along being a Christian.

God has not promised skies always blue
Flower strewn pathways all my life through
God has not promised sun without rain
Joy without sorrow
Peace without pain.

But God has promised strength for the day
Rest for the labour
Light for the way
Grace for trials
Help from above.
Unfailing sympathy
Undying love.

I think, to be truthful, my mum also found this sentiment helpful when combatting any childish complaint of 'It's not fair!' with a reposte – 'Whoever said it was going to be fair?' The implication being that not even God had said it was going to be fair. This has probably gone deeper than I thought.

Rather than take you through the Winkett years, I want to pick out some moments that might start to explain 'Why I am a Christian and how'.

I am 12 years old in the parish church choir. I have asked if I might be a server like my brother, in a high church with periodic incense and a sanctuary bell. The elderly man who is the head server kindly but firmly says that he will not have 'serviettes' in his church. So instead I learn British Sign Language and chat silently under the pew to my teenage friend throughout the sermons each Sunday.

I am 17 at the annual Greenbelt Festival with a large group of teenagers. Bernard and Sue, a couple who seemed really old to me then, but actually must have been probably my age now, have a bunch of us round to their house every Friday night. And for a few years they also take us to Greenbelt. I become a fan of the band Fat and Frantic and with some friends buy a washboard and start playing skiffle.

I am 21 and my world has fallen in. I'm sitting by the bedside of someone I love very much. He had fallen down a mountain and was in a coma. The nurses in the Geneva hospital have said we should speak to him. Apart from the inane chatter I continue with, I find myself reading him Psalm 91, suggested by someone else in his family. 'God will give his angels charge over you so that you dash not your foot against a stone.' Even as I read it, I remember saying to God: That's a lie. That's exactly what's happened to him. It was a stone and there were no angels. There was no saving. Despite our reading and sitting with him, despite our singing the classic Darts song 'Come back my love, don't go away' to the extent that we made one of the younger nurses cry, after eight days he dies, aged 22.

I've sung Psalm 91 many times since then. What happens these days is not that I accuse God of lying – although sometimes I do still do that. And I wouldn't be able to get past it if it was just about the words. What happens now is that I hold that poetic promise tenderly in my hands as a piece of Scripture that has sometimes, like the stone it describes, cut my hands and slashed my heart and hurt me. But, as another poem I know goes, the wind of my rage has smoothed it and the lashing of my tears has weathered it, so that the promise is beautiful once more, and I can hear its song. And I remember again that Jesus was confronted with that very promise in the desert. Christ resisted testing God with it; and so probably should I.

A few years later I am living in a L'Arche community where people with learning disabilities live with assistants like me. My whole world view is challenged and changed by the people I live with. By S, whose pain of years of rejection by her family and friends gives her a piercing gaze from which I am unable to escape. By A, who doesn't speak and who sings tunelessly as we sit together on a bench in the Kent countryside. Very suddenly, her tunelessness becomes something different. She starts to hum 'Mine eyes have seen the glory of the coming of the Lord'.

I look at her. 'A, do you know what you just sang?' A moment's recognition follows until she returns to rocking and the meandering tune only she knows.

In the 1990s, a couple of years later, I am living in Handsworth, Birmingham, training to be a priest; well, I was selected to be a deacon but the vote to allow women to be priests was passed at some point during my training. I am on attachment at a Black-led Pentecostal church and I hear the stories of the congregation during the testimonies every Sunday, and the everyday racism they experience. I am the only white-skinned person in the congregation for a year and I have to preach from time to time as part of my training. The generosity of this congregation overwhelms me as they accept my tentative rookie sermons, even though I find this terrifying as their expectation is for a much longer sermon than I am used to. Trying to preach for 45 minutes is hard. But I discover that the congregation will help me. I learn to let the church help me, as a young preacher. I can say 'Let God's people say' and they will reply 'Amen', and I am given courage to continue. And if I am really stuck someone at the back shouts sincerely and empathetically 'Help her Jesus.' I am accepted in this remarkable church, and loved, and taught. I learn in this church, more than I have ever learned before, that it's vital to connect faith with lived experience. In this formative and important year, I hear Black Christians reflecting on unemployment, worries about family, divorces, job hunts. I hear Black preachers preaching to Black congregations about the liberation and justice promised in the gospel. And I listen to the yearning for change. And sometimes I feel violent towards my own white skin which affords me such privilege and unacknowledged (by me at least) power.

I discover that, in these first years of the prospect of women being priests, I am, along with others, an object of interest for the media. I take part in a TV documentary at theological college.

And a highly formative period follows in Manor Park, east London, where I start to learn to live a life of public ministry. I get a call from my mum while away on holiday. She is in tears and says, 'You're on the front page of all the national newspapers.' My appointment to be the first woman priest at St Paul's Cathedral in London has been leaked and despite the cathedral's determination to keep it quiet for a week, it's all out. On returning from holiday, I couldn't go home but went to a safe house as my East London flat was besieged by satellite vans and reporters ringing the doorbell off the hook. Once I went to St Paul's, I was followed by a BBC TV crew for a year. At the broadcast of the programme I received thousands of letters, many supportive but many also telling me that I was going against the teaching of the Bible, that I was disgusting, that I shouldn't be taking communion services if I was menstruating, and that people certainly wouldn't receive communion from me if I was menstruating. I felt dirty, and I felt as if the Church to which I was trying to give my energy, my love and commitment was, more than ambivalent, actually vomiting me up. The institution convulsed, and retched. And the level of disgust that was expressed towards me personally, as a symbol of the change that had happened, was shocking.

One low point among many was when I was on a deserted train platform late at night and I had some of this unopened post in my bag. Foolishly, I opened some. An anonymous letter informed me that an election had recently taken place in the group the letter represented and, after Diana, Princess of Wales, and the BBC presenter Jill Dando, I had been elected a sacrifice and so I should watch where I went.

On Easter Day, a man approached me on the steps of the cathedral after the service. He was crying and angry, shouting that I had taken his church away from him. He was beside himself, begging me to stop what I was doing.

What I learned there is that in the heat of the day, in the harsh media spotlight, it is very, very lonely. And I feel that some of my spirituality has been forged in the white heat of those experiences: of years of 20-something grief; and of the invasiveness of a searchlight media that has sent me inwards.

In the years since, I have become much more aware of how people behave when they feel their whole church, or their faith itself, is in peril, as those people did who wrote such terrible things to a young woman they had never met. I have come to feel a deeper sense of empathy than is feasible if it were down to me. And I believe passionately in remaining resolute about the humanity of the people who hate you – even if they are hating you loudly, or violently.

And, for reasons I don't quite fathom or understand, I seem not to be able to help believing in God.

I picked this Gospel reading for a few reasons, but primarily because in my own faith journey I have discovered that conversation, like the conversation between Jesus and the woman, can be revolutionary. I believe in the power of conversation. It can deepen our own empathy for ourselves and for others. It can broaden our compassion for ourselves and for others, and it is a mode of praying that is essential when times get really tough.

The criticism I personally received when St James's Piccadilly worked with Israeli, Palestinian, Jewish, Christian, Muslim and Druse partners in highlighting the multiple injustices endured by the people of Bethlehem over Christmas 2014 would be another of those white-heat experiences, along with eight days' travelling in Syria that I did last year. And even relatively recently, after some broadcast or other, a blog had the rather pithy observation that: 'there were two words that sum up all that is wrong with the church today. Lucy and Winkett.'

I guess that also, as I've gone on, I've travelled through different emphases. I love Mark's Gospel with its breathless pace and say-it-how-it-is tone. As I get older, I love John's Gospel because of its mysterious richness in signs, philosophy, paradox and miracle; and also because I think that in John's Gospel conversation is revolutionary. Conversations, like this one in the fourth chapter, change people's lives, can even save them.

In terms of my own Christian faith, I've enjoyed and found meaning over the years in trying to put to use some of the study I've done. Christianity is a matter of the heart but the intellectual enquiry, endeavour and reflection is crucial too. For instance, in this Gospel story, right at the beginning, I've learned that it's not so much that Jesus demurely perches himself on a wall. In the original Greek text, the sense is that he flings himself down on the side of the well – just too tired to go with the others to get food. We're not very used to seeing this kind of Jesus: we often think of him with some kind of supernatural, or at least superhuman, energy, marching purposefully about with his group, transforming people wherever he goes, saying remarkable things, changing lives. That will come. But for now, he's thrown himself down, sitting by the well, and the last thing his disciples see, as they head off to see if they can get some food, is him resting there.

If I'm speaking personally about faith and how it is that I believe, then I must highlight that I love Scripture. I wrestle with it, and have come to accept that before I read the gospel, the gospel reads me. At the same time I have come to believe that taking the Bible literally and without close attention to its context is more than a mistake; it's incredibly damaging and misleading to do so, when individual verses are taken and amplified like a tweet or a slogan. Rather, I am learning to treat the Greek words like a portal in the universe that I can dive into, finding multiple layers and multiple meanings, letting Scripture be itself, not always understood or explainable by me. That Jesus has flung himself down and is at the end of his tether gives me the context for his conversation with the woman. And it teaches me more about how revolutionary conversations can go.

For me too, humour has been incredibly important in how I believe. To poke fun at myself, at the Church, at faith itself has become more and more important. And to acknowledge that, to be honest, church 'fun' is quite often not actual fun. This realization in itself has led me to learn to laugh more easily as I've gone along, even in some of the more difficult experiences I mentioned earlier.

This gospel is a case in point. I've heard many sermons and talks on this story told from Jesus' point of view, mostly highlighting the risks he is taking by speaking publicly with a woman from the hated Samaria, and encouraging congregations to do the same. And yes, he is clearly breaking a taboo by talking to her. I think that in my younger days this kind of sermon encouraged me to want to do good, to want to help people – especially people who were despised, whoever they were.

But nowadays, I don't want to think like that. It's patronizing. I want to hear the gospel the woman is giving life to on its own terms. Instead of always pivoting to the experience of Jesus of Nazareth, focusing on how brave he's being by even talking to her, I'd like to discover her personality as a rounded human being, as a fellow disciple, an example of an apostolic life. She's fun, not afraid to tease and challenge. Told from her point of view, in this conversation, she meets someone who tells her everything she ever did; and this truth-telling sets her free to be braver than she ever thought she could be.

'Give you a drink?' she says. 'You, a Jewish man, asking me, a Samaritan woman, for a drink – are you out of your mind? You can't do that.' Perhaps she goes back to her task.

I imagine that Jesus, who is exhausted and probably a bit less patient than he might otherwise have been, is a little taken aback. After a pause he might venture, 'Oh, well, you know, all I wanted was a drink.' I like to think that he kind of gets himself together a bit and remembers that he's got things to say, stuff to teach people, and this might be a really good opportunity: so he retreats into what you might call sermon mode. 'OK then, well, if you knew who it was asking you for a drink, you'd actually be asking him – not the other way round – and the water he would give you would be "living water".'

The woman roars with laughter 'OMG! Well, I don't know where you think you're going to get that water. You haven't got a bucket – what are you going to do?' As we are watching this scene unfold, I imagine her like Fleabag, turning directly towards the camera to comment, breaking the fourth wall. 'There you go,' she winks. 'I knew he'd never done a day's work in his life. No clue.'

Jesus tries again with his teaching. 'Everyone who drinks water from the well here will obviously get thirsty again eventually, but actually I'm talking about water that stops you being thirsty at all.'

This is too much for someone who spends hours each day fetching fresh water, whose chores done in the middle of the day suggest she is suffering a degree of social ostracization. 'Fantastic,' guffaws the woman. 'So I won't have to do that again – it's a different life! Let's have that water! Honestly, you couldn't make it up!'

I like to think of Jesus – who, we remember, started this conversation pretty exhausted, and just wanting a simple drink of water in the heat of the day – now getting a bit near the end of his tether. 'Go and call your husband,' he says.

'Well,' says the woman, perhaps defiantly now, being a little economical with the truth; 'I don't have one, so I can't.'

'Yes, you're right,' says Jesus. 'And I know that not only that, but you have had five, and the one you're living with now isn't your husband.'

And then the conversation starts to be of a different order: I see what Jesus says next as something that elevates both of them to speak on a different level.

Jesus says to her: 'What you have said is true.'

What you have said is true.

There is no explanation or comment on her personal circumstances, although people hearing the story might disapprove of her in some way. Jesus simply says, 'What you have said is true.' This truth-telling about her life sets them off on a different path. After that, they discuss God – and this woman is set alight by the conversation to such an extent that she moves from being a comedian to an evangelist. She is energized, articulate, generous. 'Come and see someone who told me everything I ever did,' she says to the others later.

No one is tired any more.

She is known, she is recognized. Her story is told as it is, unvarnished, without any hubris or embellishment, with all her life experience, a mixture of shame and fun, hope and playfulness, loneliness, hard work, and a not uncomplicated relationship history. In among all of this she says to her friends, 'Come and see someone who told me everything I ever did.'

I recognize this woman. Sometimes, I see that I am this woman, and by turning the story around like that, I guess I learn in terms of my own faith not to take from this conversation that my calling is to be nice to people who are rejected, but to be much more transgressive than that: to seek out the taboos of our own society and try to break them. To try to have conversations in the light – when the sun is high – at noon – and not allow them, however complex, to be held in the dark. We're asked, tenderly as Jesus does for the woman, to contemplate the shame that we carry, and know that it is known, acknowledged, held by God; and we're asked to believe that even when the shame is venomous, sulphurous, silencing, there is always, in encounter with God, the possibility of transformation and peace. Where no one is tired any more, and no one is thirsty.

Another of the Samaritan stories that has seared itself into my spirituality and which keeps me faithful is the parable of the man beaten up on the road to Jericho. Others hurried past but the hated Samaritan was the only one who stopped.

There is a story within L'Arche communities that has been transformational for me in terms of the gospel lived out, not just read in a book. In L'Arche it's common to act out the Gospel readings from time to time. In one such drama, the actor with learning disabilities who was playing the Samaritan followed the action as rehearsed until she was to tend to the man's wounds. She took the towel and gently wiped his face. The audience thought she'd finished. But she carried on. She went and found the priest who had been too busy to stop and wiped their face too. She found the Levite who had hurried past and washed them. She went over to the innkeeper and wiped his face. And lastly, she went deliberately and found the robbers hiding behind a rock. And she gently wiped their faces too. This is truly reading the gospel with your feet because she walked right into the meaning of this beautiful gospel, revealing it afresh and teaching others in the walking. New real-life questions are provoked by this gospel if it is read with our feet.

What is the part of me that is beaten up, bleeding, left for dead at the side of the road, that the busy successful me wants to ignore and hurry past? Where is it that I am being asked by God to pay attention and realize that I have violent tendencies within myself too, that convince me, like the robbers, that I am not safe until I am armed?

This gospel, irrigated by the Spirit, is good news for the whole of creation whose voices are lifted in thanksgiving every time we gather at the altar for Eucharist. And it is at that altar that I have found my place as a Christian, on the boundary between time and eternity, as a priest administering the sacraments that bring hope and joy to the bleakest of days.

Eleanor Roosevelt famously said that a woman is like a tea-bag: 'You never know how strong she is until she is in hot water.'[1] For me, similarly, faith is like a teabag. I haven't known how strong it is until I've been in hot water, or until I've been out of my depth.

And so I'll close with a prayer that I wrote for the feast of the Presentation – when Jesus was taken to the Temple and Simeon and Anna told Mary and Joseph who he was. I was reflecting on the story as a moment when God became wordless in this baby, unable to speak, vulnerable and dependent. The God who chose to be poured out in this way, in the hubristic, violent, competitive world as it is, is the kind of God I want to walk with and believe in.

Holy God, show me myself as I am. Help me to name the fantasies I construct and the hiddenness of the truth. Show me where I am wordless and give me people who can give me words. Show me myself even when I resist you, when I fight myself, when I wish I were someone else. Show me myself, that I can recognize again that I am loved and for-given and free, whatever mess I've got myself into, however frightened I am of change and whatever the unknown future holds. Give me back to myself as I really am, which, I am willing to learn, is often much more surprising and beautiful than I think. Amen.

Note

1 M. Weishan, 'A woman is like a tea bag': Eleanor Roosevelt and radical women of the 20s and 30s, article on the Franklin Delano Roosevelt Foundation website, fdrfoundation.org, 6 March 2018.

2

Advent Sunday 2020

This and the following sermon, along with some others in this collection, were preached during the Covid-19 pandemic.

Isaiah 64.1–9
Mark 13.24–37

Advent begins. The altar cloth and stoles are purple: the colour of a suffering king. Advent (meaning 'waiting') is a four-week season in which to take some time, not so much to prepare for Christmas as to contemplate some fundamental questions of living in preparation for the end of time.

It's a season too in which the Church listens most especially to the Hebrew prophets.

Today we hear from the 64th of the 66 chapters of the prophet Isaiah, written at least 27 centuries ago. Scholars differ over whether there were two or three or more authors of the book of Isaiah, but in any case this comes towards the end of the prophecy and it is written from a context that has some resonances for us today.

The people of Israel have been in exile in Babylon. Some have now returned from exile to Jerusalem (from 538 BCE onwards). But despite their longing to go home, they find that their homecoming isn't smooth. There are arguments that break out with the ones who stayed: arguments about rebuilding the Temple, and who should have the power to define what happens next. The ones who stayed are criticized by the ones who've come home. Meanwhile other prophets, Haggai and Zechariah, plead with the people to get on with rebuilding the Temple, for while it is not rebuilt there is no place to signal Yahweh's presence among the people.

There has been huge disruption in society, and opinions are polarized. The voice of the prophet is that of the returning exiles who, rather than triumphantly returning to Jerusalem, are coming back only with Persian permission, having very recently been enslaved. In the heat of all this fractiousness, it might be easy for any of us reading this at some distance to feel impatient with all the arguing, before we remember that these are the conversations, debates and prayers of a people who have been colonized and controlled. There is a political context to the people's fractiousness with each other and their pleading with God, which means that this scripture demands to be heard politically as well as personally.

The prophecy is given from a place of societal disruption, from a post-colonial context. Yes, freedom has been won, but the freedom and homecoming are not what the people had hoped for. The destructive power of colonization and enslavement is clear; and in listening to their urgent prayer, asking God, among other things, to destroy their enemies, it's important to hear these prayers as those of traumatized victims of exile and coercive control.

The prophecy is given, the prayer is crafted, when a long-held hope is not being realized. Perhaps this could be described as prayer from a place of deep disappointment.

So what is the prayer crafted from this place of disruption and disappointment?

God is being pleaded with. First, to appear at all in order to fix things. But not only that, to appear to make sure that the enemies (and at this point it is not really clear who these enemies are; they could be Babylonian or Persian or internal groups) are 'as when fire kindles brushwood and the fire causes water to boil – to make your name known to your adversaries, so that the nations might tremble at your presence' (Isaiah 64.2). After this plea to God to come and destroy the adversaries, there follows an equally strong and powerfully honest expression of sorrow and contrition, recognizing the iniquity of all, rather than concentrating on the iniquity of others.

And then comes a more personal plea of distress, which could be paraphrased as: 'God, you're hiding – I don't know where you are – I can't see you. And I know deep down that my life is not for ever. That I will fade like a leaf; that my iniquities too will fade away. But, thank God, I am still mouldable; I am in your hands, my potter God – and I am still, thank God, a work in progress' (Isaiah 64.6–8). The prayer ends with a calmer collective statement of trust and recognition: 'Consider we are all your people' (Isaiah 64.9).

The emotional rollercoaster that is this reading may be recognizable in different ways for our own context.

In other years, the Church is out of step with the rest of society during its fasting and waiting season of Advent. The traditional themes are apocalyptic: Death, Judgement, Heaven and Hell. While in church services these themes of the 'end times' are shaping our prayers, meanwhile, out there, the loop tape of Christmas carols and songs about snow has been running in department stores from October onwards.

The 'out of step'-ness doesn't end there. Because as soon as Christmas Day is over, the rest of the world starts 'dry January'. But the Christmas season goes on for another 12 days. In the Christian year, four weeks of austerity are followed by 12 days of festival. In society, it is normally exactly the other way round.

But those traditional themes of Advent seem to have been closer, as the sickness of Covid-19, and the sickness endemic in our society of racism and inequality highlighted again by the Black Lives Matter movement, have meant that the Advent themes of judgement, of searing truth-telling by the prophets, of consideration of the fundamentals of life and death, have been with us acutely in these days. In some ways, Advent spirituality turns out to be suitably resilient for a pandemic.

There have been some obvious secularized expressions this past year of those traditional themes: Death, Judgement, Heaven and Hell.

Death has stalked, is still stalking, our families, our social interactions, our church gatherings, our schools. Judgement has been quick and brutal in a 24-hour social media frenzy, often very, very harsh, fearful and unkind. For some with financial security the restrictions have meant a taste of a gentler life, with more time, more fresh air, and less social pressure once the Zoom quizzes died down: something of a taste of how life could be, a heavenly listening to the birds in the middle of the city. And for some, this has been, still is, hell: the persistent and relentless stress of being unemployed, the constraint of furlough, the weight of making life and death decisions, the horror of being trapped in lockdown domestic violence.

Death, Judgement, Heaven and Hell have been given new expression in daily life on the faultlines exposed by the contagion of Covid and the sickness of racism.

We gather as church not only to name our sicknesses but, along with the post-exilic audience of Isaiah, to search for, to beg for, healing.

And Advent Sunday is also the day when the Church begins its New Year. Each year, we read a different Gospel. This year it's the Gospel of Mark: the shortest and oldest of all the Gospels, arguably the starkest too.

In today's thirteenth chapter of Mark, Jesus makes a long speech – one of the longest in the Gospels. It's a sermon. Mark has temporarily turned aside from his often fast-paced recounting of Jesus' actions, and puts into his mouth a strongly worded sermon. This form of preaching is known as *parenaesis*, that is, a form of communication that is urging its hearers to do something. Fervent and urgent, *parenaesis* is a form of speech designed to persuade, to convince, to urge us who hear it to do a particular thing. And characteristically it's full of the poetic brilliance that we come to expect from the energetic, enigmatic Marcan Christ, with his eyes set on the end times: 'after that suffering, the sun will be darkened and the moon will not give its light, and the stars will be falling from heaven, and the powers in the heavens will be shaken' (Mark 13.24–25). Echoes of the prophetic, poetic spirit of Isaiah, in naming and exposing the deep desire for, the need for, change.

I often hear people worrying about this strand of Jesus' teaching; and many scholars describe him as an end-times prophet who, frankly, failed in his proclamations because 2,000 years later we're all still here. But this worry is rooted in a too-literal and superficial reading of this kind of prophecy. Prophecy isn't prediction, it's prophecy. Prophecy upends time itself by naming and exposing truth in the present, in the light of eternity.

If this sermon of Jesus' is *parenaesis*, that is, strongly urging his hearers to do something, what is it that Jesus is urging people to do as he tells stories of fig trees and stars, moon and sun? This *parenaesis* is a way of urging us to take action without delay. And to do two related things: watch and pray.

Watch. By calling on the imagery of the skies, Jesus urges us to live our lives alert to what is happening. Learn to read the signs of the times around you. Learn how to become more and more attentive.

This might sound simple, but in today's society, perhaps even more than for Jesus' contemporaries, it's costly. There is, frankly, too much to see, too much to hear. Our senses are assaulted all day and all night by voices, perspectives, stories, images. Some of the underlying signs of the times are hidden in plain sight. It's hard, seeing and knowing; having your eyes and ears switched on to the suffering, injustice, and indeed even the glory of living. Sometimes this awareness, this alertness can be hard to bear. But we are asked to bear this cost and keep watch, not turn away.

This is linked to the next instruction, which is to pray. The burden of remaining alert is unbearable without it. Much is said about how to pray, what to do, when to do it. But it's a lot harder – and simpler – than we often think. Don't think about it, or make a plan for it, or read a book about it. Just try it. Advent invites us to set aside time every day to listen to God, to become more aware of God, attentive to the movement of the Spirit in the world and inside you, however that happens, in your day.

Let Advent be Advent. Watch and pray.

Bringing together Isaiah, Mark, Advent into the present: it matters who you are, and it matters what your context is, listening to this prophecy and apocalypse, as to how you will hear it.

If you have experienced inequality, poverty, exile, disruption, dislocation, then this powerful language for change is balm for a weary soul. Because change is what you need.

If life is good as it is and your circumstances mean that you have little incentive to want fundamental change, then this teaching can be somewhere on a spectrum between frightening through bewildering to dispiriting.

It's always important, as we often say, to read Scripture with hearts and heads. It's important to take scholarship really seriously. But in the end Isaiah the prophet doesn't belong to the academy, Isaiah belongs to the synagogue and to the church: to the lived experience of religious communities making their way in the real world.

But further too, Isaiah's prophecy belongs to any society or group that has experienced disruption, exile, distress and inequality.

In a different way, we are in a situation of dislocation and disruption; and there are powerful voices – please God more powerful still – that call for change.

We are perhaps, like the people of Israel, longing to get back to something like what we knew before. But our society is different now; different groups have experienced this pandemic, this social exile, in different ways. On the journey of return from exile, we will be, are already, fractious; our society is fragmented.

An Advent church has an important contribution to make into this moment, as we begin to see some sort of ending of this episode of suffering. However hard we work, or campaign, deep change is possible only when it's rooted in contemplation.

And from that place we have to keep building and sustaining a community that will renew itself, keep trying to tell the truth, keep returning to God who contemplates us as we are and showers us with love.

It is to live, as one brilliant collection of prayer-poems puts it, in a state of revolutionary patience.[1]

From my reading of Jesus in Mark's Gospel, I take revolutionary patience to mean living life immersed in the renewing energy of God, living life alert to the utterly beautiful presence of God in every person, on every street, in every heart. A trustful way of living, watching and praying, attentive, alert, awake. A trust too in the timeliness of things, and God's pace, God's *kairos* time, which is usually either more slow, or more quick, than our assumption.

Revolutionary patience as proclaimed by Jesus is to live life not measured by unforgiving minutes of busyness, but in moments of meaningful, just action rooted in prayer. Life becomes a series, not of relentless minutes, but of spacious moments shot through with eternity.

Revolutionary patience doesn't mean being passive or quietist or accepting injustices and inequalities as they are. On the contrary, it can be the fuel for a life of just action and righteous protest. But all the action, all the protest is rooted in contemplation of God, who is with us in the face of each person who in the cold November early morning comes to have a hot breakfast with us, in each person who is watching this service online now or later.

Revolutionary patience is a characteristic of a Christ-shaped life and a Christ-shaped community.

I pray that this Advent, infused with the prophecy of Isaiah and the *parenaesis* of Jesus, we will learn more and more deeply what that means.

Two inspirations to end with. It was William Blake's birthday yesterday. Baptized here in St James's Piccadilly, his colossal imagination was placed at the service of justice in society. He was fiercely critical of church and state, and wrote and drew his way into a truth-telling that exposed the worst and the best of London's inequalities. His advice is helpful as we might feel from time to time overwhelmed by the enormity of the challenges facing us today. 'He who would do good to another must do it in Minute Particulars: General Good is the plea of the scoundrel, hypocrite, and flatterer, for Art and Science cannot exist but in minutely organised Particulars.'[2]

Day-to-day ordinary living matters more than grand statements of intention.

And the inspirational Maya Angelou, as an African American poet and campaigner, gave – and gives still – energy, vision and hope for a new world. Her words at the Presidential inauguration in January 1993 give shape to our task today: 'History, despite its wrenching pain, cannot be unlived, but if faced with courage, need not be lived again.'[3]

As we embark on this adventure of Advent, as we embark on a new church year, as we come out of this national lockdown and emerge into a way of life that means still so much strain for so many in our city and society, may we be people of revolutionary patience. May we be a community that gathers to contemplate and be contemplated by God, a church that finds courage, in that depth of prayer from Isaiah, to call for change and to be part of that change ourselves. That, at the urging of Christ, we may commit ourselves to watch and pray, and be always ready to take action. Not hastily or thoughtlessly, or to fulfil our own need to do something, but patiently, trusting in the revolutionary power of love that will come in the vulnerability of the Christ-child and in the light and power of the sun.

Notes

1 D. Soelle, 1977, *Revolutionary Patience*, New York: Orbis Books.

2 W. Blake, 1908, *The Poetical Works of William Blake* (edited with textual notes by John Sampson), London, New York: Oxford University Press.

3 M. Angelou, 1993, *On the Pulse of Morning*, New York: Random House.

3

Christmas Day 2020

Luke 2.1–20

When I was a teenager there was a long-running quiz show on early-evening television called *Blockbusters*. With a catchy theme tune, the contestants were all young people, picking letters on lit-up hexagonal blocks to make their way across a screen to achieve a Gold Run – at which it was possible to win serious cash.

A school friend and I decided we'd like to go on this programme and so we wrote off to ITV – I have to admit the letter was written and posted at a party in the middle of the night – and much to our complete surprise we found ourselves some months later recording the programme.

We did not cover ourselves in glory.

Simply not quick enough on the buzzers, we were beaten easily by a boy called Alun from North Wales; and our humiliation was complete when we were knocked out by a question to which the answer was a musical instrument I played.

In between questions, Bob, the quizmaster, would chat with the contestants. The answers we gave under the studio lights on a wet Tuesday in 1985, answers casually given by eager-to-please teenagers, have of course become the stuff of legend now that we are old and grey and keen to remind one another, even now, of our paltry winnings: £40. Which as my friend often reminds me, we had to share.

And one of the comments I nervously made on that show has followed me around ever since. Bob learned that I was into music.

'Oh really,' he asked, 'what kind of music?'

'Oh,' I said breezily, trying to be casual, 'both: classical, jazz and pop.'

Both, I said, and then gave three answers.

With the wisdom of youth, with no thought in my head of ever wearing a dog collar or studying theology, right there I had summarized the theological paradox of Christmas: Incarnation rooted in the doctrine of the Trinity.

And perhaps more than any other festival, Christmas is a way of marking the contingent reality of human life. Whatever kind of year we have had, at the end of a calendar year that will have brought both accomplishment and disappointment, delight and regret, Christmas is still Christmas.

What is so wrenching about the celebration of Christmas is that it starts and ends with the heart. And the heart is 'both'; bodily bearing and a symbol of love.

Christmas describes both the transcendence of eternity as described by St John – 'In the beginning was the Word and the Word was with God' – and also the political realities of life recognizable today: frightened leaders, crowded outhouses, populations of night workers and the birth of children in dangerous circumstances.

So the first question might be, in a celebration of Christmas Incarnation: where do we start, from God's perspective as in John's Gospel or from the human perspective as in Luke?

Do we remember that the stories about angels and mysterious visitors are designed to point us to the deep mystery of God with us, or do we focus on the probability that Jesus of Nazareth was born in what we call October between four and six years before we thought he was born? At Christmas, should we go for mystery or history?

Both.

Christmas is a festival of the heart because in our hearts is where we know the paradoxes and complications of living.

And religion is at its best, at its most powerful and transformational, in response to a question asked or a point to be debated, when our response is not one or the other, but both.

Because focusing on one at the expense of the other not only unbalances the season but risks missing the utter beauty, the can't-take-your-eyes-off truth, that God is with us.

Christmas invites us into a different kind of knowing.

These nativity figures are a case in point.[1] They are real, they are wooden, they have been made. The catalpa tree from which they were made stood in the courtyard here for over 90 years. The baby's form is dynamic, being wrenched up from the earth itself, and Mary his mother presents him to the world, in the manner of many Orthodox ikons, in recognition that his vocation was for the world. Across the back of the little group of Joseph and the shepherds, you can see the marks of the iron cuff that was put around the trunk after it was bombed in 1940. This tree witnessed children being blessed under it, coffins being carried past it; trade and music, commerce and conversation happened under its branches. It survived the violence of war, and now the tree's life extends to us praying alongside it, crafted as it is into the likeness of Christ.

And this year, on the last Sunday we were together, on 22 March, we planted wheat seeds, as part of the art, science, theology and prayer project Daily Bread. The buried grain grew in the darkness. At Easter it was green shoots; on St James's Day in July it was harvested, threshed and winnowed by the congregation; at Lammas in August it was milled and made into bread. It was winnowed and threshed by us when we could. And now, this same wheat that has accompanied us all year, today on Christmas Day is the hay in the manger.[2]

The paradox of Christmas is that contingent reality, fleshly stuff, is revealed to have been made holy by the incarnation of God.

This theological 'both/and' has real-life consequences for a life of faith, lived in the everyday world. Yes, we will describe this as divine life becoming incarnate; theological words for trying to describe what is more often a felt truth: that the God of the universe is intimately with us.

The theological doctrine of the Incarnation means that, as a religion, Christianity can't allow itself to be primarily a philosophical approach or a list of beliefs, or even to rest on an intellectual assent that there is a God at all. Christian faith is more of a language than a list, more of a road than an arrival, a life lived before it ever developed the doctrinal scaffolding that seeks to draw boundaries and encourage believers to patrol its borders. A Christian approach to living will always insist on the importance of bodies, yours and mine; it will insist on gently caring for the bodies' cuts and bruises, the birth and death of bodies – because one of the languages that the Creator has used to connect most deeply with the creation is the body language found in the birth, life, death and resurrection of Jesus. It matters where I put my body, because it mattered where God put God's body in Jesus. Which was in a stable, on the road, on the cross, in the tomb.

Christmas is a festival of Incarnation and as such is a festival of the heart because it is a celebration of love. The feast of the Incarnation links the infant body of Jesus, needing the attentive care of other adults to survive, with the adult choice that Jesus makes to kneel and wash the feet of his friends. The love celebrated at Christmas is embodied. Love is the washing of bodies that cannot yet or can no longer wash themselves. Love is the wiping of another's saliva, and what is euphemistically called 'personal care' that involves the smell, the stickiness, the contingent fleshliness of another body.

Without this practical love, Christmas religious practice is in danger of turning the glory of the angels' song of peace into some kind of apolitical ambient noise: a 'gloria in excelsis Deo' that plays in the background, indiscriminately, inadvertently, blessing all the inequality and injustice to which it bears witness.

But similarly, without the intimations of glory, without the heavenly proclamation of love, we are in danger of believing that, if only we were more perfect, worked harder, made fewer mistakes, we could fix all this hurting world, heal ourselves, make things bend to our will. This leads to a futile pursuit of perfection that congeals our hearts rather than melting them.

Love, with us and beyond us, invites us to live with paradox, not to try to resolve everything, sort it all out; but it asks us, too, not just to leave it as an unsolvable, disinterested maths problem – 'fully divine, fully human'.

We are asked to hold, to inhabit, to 'do' both.

This is why theology is so important when it is in creative conversation with life as it's actually lived, because this 'both' transcendence and immanence isn't an imposition of a theological scheme on to life that we can't recognize. I don't know about you but I experience human life as full of paradox. Not least in the area of our complex emotions: we can be both afraid and courageous at the same time; we can be both in despair and hopeful; we can be grief-stricken at the same time as being full of love; we can be at times both confused and insightful, and so it goes on. We are full of contradictions, able somehow to hold different truths at the same time.

And so, because we know what we're talking about as contradictory, paradoxical humans, we are asked, like the shepherds in the story, just to get up and go there; to step into this nativity scene without understanding it all. Just to turn up, and look, and be looked at by God with the wordless love of a child, with innocence and compassion, with a chosen dependency that teaches us how to live.

And to find there, at the end of a year full of paradox, an utterly beautiful expression of creativity, of love: of Christ whose awesome presence lies at the heart of the cosmos and whose tiny heart beats in the hay.

'Both,' said the nervous teenager, self-conscious and keen to impress.

Holding on to 'both', as on that day, risks humiliation and misunderstanding, but also invites us into a different form of knowing that rests, not in the logical resolution of a problem, but in the lyrical acceptance that life is eternal and love is immortal. It rests in the felt knowledge that you and I are invited, in the presence of the incarnate God at Christmas, to listen to the transcendent song of the angels, who sing to us in life, as in death, songs of peace and protest and glory. Who sing, too, in the sound of nativity silence, the home of all music, the home of all words.

Notes

1 Large nativity figures, commissioned by the PCC and carved by Clinton Chaloner in 2004, are placed in the side chapel at St James's Piccadilly from Advent Sunday to Candlemas every year.

2 The Daily Bread project with accompanying original poetry by Diane Pacitti is available at www.sjp.org.uk.

4

Holy Innocents

Matthew 2.13–18

One of the features of being a central London church like St James's Piccadilly is that we host a large number of carol services and concerts during December. By doing this, as a church, we raise money for a huge number of projects: the Rays of Hope Foundation, granting wishes for terminally ill children; the Amos Trust, working for peace and justice in Bethlehem; the Chain of Hope, an organization founded by the inspirational heart surgeon Sir Magdi Yacoub, which works in developing countries helping children with heart conditions, and many others.

One of the favourite readings at these events is the comedy sketch by John Julius Norwich called 'The Twelve Days of Christmas'. It is a series of letters written by a young woman called Emily to her betrothed Edward, thanking him day after day for the gifts he has been sending her. She starts off grateful, if a little bemused, as on the first day he sends her a partridge in a pear tree. On the second day, two calling birds, on the third day, three French hens, and so on. By the seventh and eighth days she is fraught with stress because the seven swans a-swimming and six geese a-laying have played havoc with what was left of the lawn, and in the end her mother is taken away in an ambulance having suffered a collapse. This sketch always raises the roof as the audience slowly realizes what's coming each day with the increasing desperate tone of the letters, pleading for the presents to stop.

For all its silliness, the sketch reminds the audience that Christmas is a 12-day festival, culminating in the arrival of the Magi on 6 January, Epiphany. But even in church, what tends to happen is that we build up to Christmas Day and then, along with everyone else, fall into a turkey/nut-roast-induced stupor for the rest of the week, in no fit state to celebrate anything. The truth is that we *start* celebrating Christmas at Midnight Mass; and, rather than the folklore 12 days of Christmas where true love is expressed in the contents of an aviary, these 12 days are rich with symbolism and feast days, marking a variety of themes after the birth of Christ.

The first day after Christmas is St Stephen's Day – the day commemorating the first Christian martyr. Stephen was stoned to death and the coats of the mob were laid at the feet of a young man named Saul, who was later to become Paul, one of the greatest proponents of Christian faith. Then comes the feast of St John, the author of the famous prologue we read at Christmas, 'In the beginning was the Word'. And then today comes what has become known as Holy Innocents: the commemoration of the slaughter by Herod of all the boys under two, his intemperate reaction to the news that a new King had been born in Bethlehem. Tomorrow is the commemoration of Thomas Becket, the Archbishop murdered by four knights in Canterbury Cathedral in 1170, followed by that of the fourteenth-century translator of the Scriptures, John Wycliff.

Straight after the wonder and awe of the birth of Christ, we are plunged into the reality of the violence of the world, the abuse of power, and, powerfully today, the inexplicable and indefensible murder of children. It's tough stuff for these first few days when the afterglow can't yet have worn off.

And yet that is a hallmark of Christianity, which is, thank God, a messy religion – a faith that dares to suggest that God is with us, in the massacre of those days and in the barbarism and fear of the world today.

Much is speculated about the historical nature of the event we remember today: the order by King Herod that all the boys under two years old in Bethlehem should be killed. With a good deal of guesswork and historical detective work, out of an estimated population of the town of Bethlehem at the time, this may have worked out at maybe 20 children. It is an echo of the slaughter of the boys under two years old ordered by Pharaoh at the birth of Moses; and Matthew is, some scholars would say, wanting to make the point to his predominantly

Jewish audience that Jesus is the new Moses. So there are, as often in the Gospels, at least two echoing parallel stories being told at once. Other scholars point out that Herod the Great was a singularly cruel ruler and carried out casual executions and massacres more than once – so this massacre is perfectly possible as a historical reality.

If you go to the Holy Land today, one of the most extraordinary places you can visit is the winter palace of Herod the Great: a vast, sprawling complex of buildings in the middle of the desert with, importantly for a desert, an extremely impressive water management system which meant that hot baths were available all year round, even in one of the driest places on earth. As a symbol of hubristic power, conjuring up a working set of luxury baths in the middle of a desert takes some beating. A monarchical demonstration of how he had kingly control over nature itself. Such an unassailable ruler is portrayed in Matthew's Gospel as acting in a duplicitous way with the Magi and then in a violent way with the population of the small town from which it was prophesied his rival would come.

Although of course it's an interesting project to investigate the historicity or not of this terrible event, this isn't where its gospel power resides, because this very atrocity happens now. The incomprehensible murder of 132 children in Peshawar by Taliban gunmen just before Christmas is all the evidence we need to make this gospel real. It's all the evidence we need to make appalling sense of the moving quotation from Jeremiah: that Rachel weeps for her children, refusing to be consoled because they are no more (Jeremiah 31.15). The world is full of uncomforted mothers and fathers, and uncomforted children.[1] The world is full of despotic rulers and abusers of power. A mature spirituality will acknowledge before God that there are some traumas that will not mend in this life; there are some griefs that will never be comforted.

For us to be faithful disciples in the world as it is, part of our spiritual task on the day of Holy Innocents, alongside asking for the courage to face the horrendous events of a violent world, both then and now, is also to dare to get to know the uncomforted parts of ourselves: the Rachel inside you who still weeps inconsolably.

Our inconsolable selves will be so for as many reasons as there are people; but today, so soon after Christ's mysterious and miraculous birth, we are given a moment to acknowledge the losses we live with, the losses we normally suppress in a daily routine that rarely has room for this kind of time.

This might not feel like a very Christmassy message. There certainly isn't much tinsel to accompany it, but an acknowledgement of the parts of ourselves that remain unconsoled through life is an acknowledgement, too, of the incarnate God who dares to face this with us, and who will not let us go.

The 12 days of Christmas form a series of commemorations that teach us that, whatever happens, God is with us, and meets us most nearly, in those inconsolable selves that we think we should hide if we're proper grown-ups in a proper grown-up world.

It's important to take time with the enormity of the Incarnation, just as it takes time for new parents to come to terms not only with the birth they prepare for but with the life of the child they bring home afterwards.

Over these days, there is some time to come to terms with the reality of God present in the world as it is. And we have the chance, gradually, to let it sink in that, even in the sulphurous shame, fear or grief that forms what is inconsolable in us, Christ is born. Even there. Even and while we remain uncomforted, Christ is born and grows and stays, however we are doing and whatever we have done.

Note

1 The description of Rachel as an 'uncomforted mother' is taken from W. Breuggemann, 1998, *A Commentary on Jeremiah: Exile and Homecoming*, Grand Rapids, MI, Wm. B. Eerdmans Publishing Co., p. 287.

5

Epiphany 3

Preached in 2014 in the week of Holocaust Memorial Day

1 Corinthians 1.10–18
Matthew 4.12–23

As part of my ministry I am involved with a secondary school in North London. We have 1,700 students, an early years centre and a newly opened unit for students who are on the autistic spectrum.

One of the most memorable things that happens within the school year every year is that someone comes to talk to the students and staff who survived the Holocaust. It will happen again this week and is something that stands out as a horrifying yet necessary day in the education of this generation of British schoolchildren. Auschwitz was liberated 69 years ago tomorrow, and so it is not for many more years that this direct link will be possible. Today's teenagers listen to the testimony of those now in their 80s and 90s, and are often left weeping and appalled that they are meeting a person who has experienced hell.

Only 69 years later the full meaning of what happened has probably not been expressed. This industrialized killing, the attempted extermination of Jews, of Romany people, of homosexuals, of anyone the Nazi regime described as degenerate, toxifies European memory and can pervert contemporary national and religious interactions on this continent and across the world.

The hundredth anniversary of the beginning of the First World War will be marked in August this year. And the punitive ending of that 'war to end all wars' provided the seedbed, as many historians will argue, for the the election of the National

Socialist Party in Germany in 1933, whose leader Hitler had fought in the 1914 war.

Today is a day of memorial, not for political comment, but there are important philosophical and spiritual themes that emerge from our marking of Holocaust Memorial Day as a Christian church, not least a determination to remember and pledge to learn everything we can from the testimony of those who were there.

In previous sermons, I've reflected on the work of two women who were twentieth-century Jewish philosophers: Simone Weil and Hannah Arendt. Today I want to listen to the reflections of a third: Gillian Rose, who wrote much about the Holocaust as a British Jew, and the depth of whose reflections and insights have made her one of the most respected philosophical voices of the last century. She died in 1995, too soon from cancer, but her work is astonishing in its power and honesty.

Gillian Rose was appointed by the Polish government in 1990 as part of a committee looking at how the death camp at Auschwitz should be preserved and presented, after the fall of the Berlin Wall, to reinterpret it for visitors after the end of the Communist regime.

Gillian Rose reflected and wrote much about how to remember such a cataclysm, and she did not spare her readers. She was critical, for example, of films such as *Schindler's List* which, she challenged, put the viewer in the role of innocent bystander or remote judge. She challenged her readers to resist the easy characterization of ourselves as neutral observers of a horrible historical evil. This would be to recuse ourselves, she argued, excuse ourselves from what has to be, in the end, a deeper acceptance of our own complicity. She wrote this about the process of observing and involvement:

> In a nature film, we could be made to identify with the life cycle of the fly as prey of the spider, and we could be made to identify with the life cycle of the spider as prey of the rodent. We can be made to identify with the Peking Opera singer who is destroyed by the Cultural Revolution and we can equally be made to identify with the rickshaw man, for whom the Cultural Revolution was the 'beginning of para-

dise'. It is only the ultimate predator whose sympathies can be so promiscuously enlisted.[1]

Here she is making a very profound statement about human nature: human beings have the capacity to be the so-called ultimate predator, able to be drawn in to identify with every predator, every victim, depending on the level of what she identified as propaganda, the persuasion of art. She makes a distinction between sentimental predators – which we can rather cosily identify with – and the real capacity we have as ultimate predators for collusion, deception, complicity.

Gillian Rose commends the memoir of a Polish inmate of Auschwitz. He obviously has a clear ethical presupposition – that Auschwitz is an expression of evil – but he somehow represents himself both as executioner and victim. 'He makes you witness brutality in the most disturbing way, for it is not clear ... from what position, as whom, you are reading. You emerge shaking in horror at yourself with yourself in question, not in admiration for the author's Olympian serenity.'[2]

What Gillian Rose challenges us about is that it is easy to develop a solidarity between those who think, who would like to believe, that they are largely innocent of the world's wrongs. She argues not for a solidarity of the innocent but for what one interpreter has called the solidarity of the shaken.[3] A chilling phrase that captures perfectly the combination of terror and realization that comes with living, eyes and ears open to the suffering and inequality of the world. The solidarity of the shaken comes from being made acutely aware of the structural sins of the world, but also, almost unbearably, of our own personal complicity in them.

She is trying to find a way of building solidarity and community which, as she says, is free from propaganda. Her contention is that the only path that avoids 'propaganda', which she identifies as persuasive, pithy, emotional hits, is the path of prayer. In prayer we are confronted with another reality, a depth before which we are contemplative, where we are faced with the strangeness of God, the opposite of cosy. It is only this kind of religion that can ultimately dissolve the towering totalitarian certainties of fascism.

Religion plays a vital part, not so much, in this context, in the consolation of individuals as in the confrontation of evil, when its practice, both public and private, rests only on this kind of bracing honest prayer that refuses to give in to what she identifies as 'propaganda'. If church can be a gathering characterized by the solidarity of the shaken, then the practice of religion can 'shake us out of our delusions of uninvolved innocence'.[4]

This is an argument for religion, not just for what is often described as 'spirituality'. Because these truths, this complicity, cannot be faced safely alone. And they cannot be confronted effectively or changed by our own personal preferences for the quotes we have always found inspirational or the verses we have always loved.

Remembering the depravity and nihilism of the Holocaust also demands that the practice of religion remains resolute in its engagement with politics. Not in the sense of telling people how to cast their vote, but in being politically active in debating the issues of the day. Dietrich Bonhoeffer, writing in Tegel prison in 1945, wrote about what was necessary for Christians to be free, among which was not to be afraid of the 'storm of events'. The Church is given a vocation here that is bracing, challenged by Gillian Rose and Dietrich Bonhoeffer in the light of the catastrophe of the Holocaust. A vocation that demands the Church steeps itself in honest prayer and the public practice of ritual in order to give it the fuel it needs to stand up to the totalitarian tendencies found whenever human beings exercise their power.

It is only in that prayer, free from propaganda, and the courage that faces down fear, that the Church will be able to articulate a vision of a good and just society.

Here in St James's Church, Piccadilly last Friday, Rowan Williams spoke to an audience the largest component of which were teenage British Muslims. He was talking about spirituality, and one particular reflection was striking in its simplicity and relevance to this consideration of Gillian Rose's.

One of the strands of his reflection was that we have devalued spirituality to be something we want to give us warm feelings about who we are and about the world in general. When these warm feelings are not present or achievable, we are desolate and undermined. What he wanted to offer instead is the reflection that the movement of the Spirit is that which clarifies and connects.

When we see reality clearly, we identify injustice, or suffering, or joy, or community and we are newly connected to one another, to ourselves, to God. If the movement of the Spirit clarifies, uncovers or reveals the truth, and also leads to new connections, then, far from spirituality being something primarily concerned with warm feelings, it is first and foremost realistic, grounded, earthed. Awakening to our own spiritual selves, and taking our own spirituality seriously, leads us to recognize the fictions we carry about ourselves, cultivating in us the courage to reject them.

Because it is precisely those fictions and myths that are dangerous, even lethal, sometimes to ourselves and sometimes to others. These are nothing less than lies that can persist for a lifetime. For example, on a personal level, the lie that we are not worth as much as other people; or at a collective level, the fiction that we are basically right and everyone else is most certainly wrong.

Fantasies spawn appalling, totalizing ideologies, such as the deranged mysogyny that underpinned the slaughter of women as witches over three centuries in medieval Europe, or the totalizing ideology of racism that underpinned the slaughter and sale of human beings in the transatlantic slave trade.

And the racism and anti-Semitism that formed the environment for thousands of ordinary citizens to enable or collaborate in the murder of 6 million European Jews in the 1930s and 1940s.

To face these totalizing philosophies means that we must interrogate the tendency in ourselves to be aggressively protective of our own fantasies. Gillian Rose's challenge is clear. The only effective way to dissolve these fantasies and ideologies is to develop a realistic spirituality which is drenched in honest prayer.

It is to resist the tendency to want to form a solidarity of the falsely innocent, whereas in fact what is needed is to form a solidarity of the shaken – shaken to our core that this Holocaust is part of our cultural, political and, yes, religious history.

We gather around this altar to imagine together a world where all are fed, where justice and mutual liberation are possible for everyone. This sacrament is a sign of a new future, a hopeful and prophetic act that cultivates courage and wisdom, and real community. But it doesn't just happen, it requires returning again and again to the place where we know our own complicity and ask for the strength to bear it with others before God.

We gather then as church, who are simply those who know, not the solidarity of a fantasy innocence but the solidarity of the shaken. And we know that we are struck dumb by the human capacity for cruelty inasmuch as we are given a voice by the human capacity for resistance to such cruelty.

Let us pray.

Holy God, give us the grace and courage to immerse ourselves in honest prayer. Send us your Spirit that clarifies our sight and connects us to the truth you want us to see. Surround us with your Spirit that connects us to one another and to you, that we may walk more closely your path of justice and peace. Amen.

Notes

1 G. Rose, 1996, *Mourning Becomes the Law: Philosophy and Representation*, Cambridge: Cambridge University Press, p. 47.

2 A. Shanks, 2008, *Against Innocence: An Introduction to Gillian Rose*, London: SCM Press, p. 25.

3 Shanks, *Against Innocence*, p. 28.

4 Shanks, *Against Innocence*, p. 30.

6

The Feast of the Presentation of Christ in the Temple

This sermon, like that for Ash Wednesday, was preached during the renewed lockdown of 2021.

Luke 2.22–40

During these lockdowns, I've been involved in a couple of debates in one of the political magazines that tries to take a longer view than a daily newspaper. Other political magazines are available, but the one I'm talking about is called *Prospect Magazine*.

In a previous lockdown, I debated with a philosopher who said that if access to ventilators was limited and had to be rationed, then it was more important to save younger lives. I disagreed, putting forward a different definition of value, based not on length of life but on the intrinsic value of every life.

The latest debate is in this lockdown – which so many people are finding harder. It's with a writer who, while supportive of the Church's moving online, keeping projects going such as food banks and services to homeless people for instance – that is, while supportive of the Church doing community-type things that are obviously helpful and useful – is wondering why there has been no real debate about or turning to God in this situation. He has thrown down the challenge that the absence of God in the public conversation illustrates the weakness of religion and the indifference felt by most of the population. His point is that, to be frank, you would have thought that in the middle of a life-threatening pandemic God might have made more of an appearance; and that people would turn towards

God or the Church to look for answers to the questions the virus poses.

To be honest, the jury's still out on what effect this pandemic is having on faith. But it's a huge gift when someone cares enough to criticize or challenge those of us who are part of church, and this is an important challenge. If he's right or even half right, then among the many things that Covid-19 may have revealed is that the Church's place is not even as valued as its critics thought it was before. The Church has not found a sufficiently compelling way to resist some of the fiercest temptations of modern life: a kind of spiritual cosiness, privatized clubbiness, spirituality only expressed in personal preferences, what I like or what makes me feel good. And so perhaps church is not offering as distinct a way of life as it might? In a common phrase at the moment – intended to be one of encouragement – you be you. Sure, yes, absolutely – you be you – but please be you in such a way that I can be me and, most importantly, we can be us.

Human beings are not foolish – well, actually, we really are – but one of the things we care about a lot is a search for what's real, what we also call authenticity and truth. We often only really know it when we see it. In our internet conspiracy age, it's one of the most important issues of the day, and today's rather delicate and beautiful feast of Candlemas speaks directly to this contemporary dilemma.

Anna and Simeon knew authenticity when they saw it. And they wasted no time, at their great ages, in seeing that things would be different from now on, and that they would accept this new path, with trust, openness, faith and realism.

The gospel of today is the story of mature people, who know what life can do, who have experienced – well, Anna has at least – bereavement and loss, grasping a new truth, a new reality right before them. And following wherever it would lead them – in Simeon's case, understanding that his own death was close.

In the middle of a global pandemic, for those of us who are in this exploration called faith, this is not the time to be falsely soothing, or attempting to answer questions no one is asking. It is a time to listen hard to our hurting world and, in the spirit of today's gospel, to invite a deep and profound encounter with a divine presence that is as challenging as comforting, as provocative as soothing.

This is a place to invite an encounter with God, utterly holy, utterly trustworthy, utterly other from all the domesticated images or words or pictures we've been carrying around with us from the past. God who is broken-hearted at the unequal suffering being meted out to our divided populations. And in that encounter, to throw ourselves on this eternally merciful God, knowing that, even without a pandemic, we are needy. We are lonely, we are distracted, we are full of avarice – sometimes for things, sometimes for experiences; we are anxious, we are determined to get perfect so we can fix everything ourselves. It is a place to encounter this God before whom we dare to admit our worst fears and the things of which we are most ashamed. And the miracle is that we find our scars are not just tolerated or stroked – but seen and loved. And even more than that, we find that it is in the behaviour, in the events, in the moments when we are most ashamed, most grief-stricken, and feel most lost, that God meets us; as Christ was crucified outside the city wall. That's where God is to be found and that's where salvation waits for any of us who dare to go there.

We learn, at this crossroads between time and eternity, that we are both lost and loved. And that my fate is tied to yours by the umbilical cord of shared humanity; that I am not well until and unless you are well. And more than that, that we are not well if the planet is not well.

As we make our way through this global pandemic, new challenges face different populations at every stage: not least, concern about 'vaccine nationalism'. The World Health Organization has said that when the UK has vaccinated its most vulnerable groups, it should then pause its programme so that other less prosperous countries can get going on theirs. Are we going to do this? Is our vocation as Christians to argue for it? I would say yes.

We are asked by today's gospel some really profound questions. We are asked to listen to Anna and Simeon and join in their open-hearted recognition that Christ was born, is born – and that, in this birth, all created life is Christ-like, a life haunted by grief and shot through with miracles.

We are asked to apply to ourselves the image that Simeon puts before Mary. What is at stake for us today, what is at stake in this Eucharist where we are seen as people who are both lost and loved? In this pandemic, a sword has pierced our hearts in so many ways – our lives have become more acutely haunted by grief and shot through with miracles.

At the same time, we can see that humanity brought this on ourselves. It's clear from the climate scientists that we have destroyed the necessary buffers of rainforest between us and the creatures: the gap has become so narrow that even an airborne virus can jump across and start to suffocate us.

And so, even because of this alone, we approach this altar of creation crawling, hardly able to accept the gifts it offers us – gifts of radical welcome, of love like we have never known, of connection with eternity that will stop us in our tracks in time.

And I'm not talking about sensations or warm feelings or making me feel superficially better, although those things can happen. I'm talking about everyday encounter as Simeon and Anna experienced it, which leaves us rocked by the truth we see anew, but with immense hope for a new future opening up in front of us, full not just of temporary comfort but of deep and enduring consolation.

This lockdown has been so hard for so many; it's a daily struggle just to keep our equilibrium. For my part, I don't want to be part of a church that makes yet more demands for good behaviour or competitive creativity, or even a church that looks after or helps people in need. I want to be part of a church that is full of people in need themselves, full of people who are struggling, who know their need of God, people who are going through homelessness of the body or homelessness of the soul; who are seeking asylum from state or church persecution or seeking asylum from a punitive picture of a cruel God. We are us; what Simeon's message about Christ says today is that there is no 'them'. 'A light to lighten the Gentiles and the glory of thy people Israel.' At the heart of this radical statement is an inclusiveness – such an overused word – an inclusiveness on God's part of which you and I have hardly touched the surface.

A final thought about this gospel that is more directed to us as individuals.

And it's about the poignant and challenging song of Simeon, known as the Nunc Dimittis, which is sung every day at Evening Prayer.

Simeon was going about his business day to day. For him there was an epiphany: a person – in this case a baby – who opened up for him an utterly new vista; he glimpsed into the heart of God. And he was able to say in response: my God, now you can let me die – I would die in peace now if I died today. Because I've seen what I have been waiting for all my life. After all these years of showing up, being faithful, keeping going, now I can see the shape of the future; it's full of suffering, but it's shot through with miracles. And it is an inclusive future, where no one is left behind. It's a future full of light; and so I make my peace with my death, trusting that the next generation will take on what I pass on.

This sentiment of this prayer is profound, hard, hard to say. Hard to pray.

A modern-day version of this song of the Church – the Nunc Dimittis – is Dr Martin Luther King Junior's speech on 3 April 1968, the night before he died. Speaking about the just society of his dreams, he said: 'I may not get there with you, but that's all right because mine eyes have seen the glory of the coming of the Lord.' He was assassinated the next day.

In this pandemic, you will have known people who have come close to death and who may have died.

What is it that would have to happen for you to say that, today, you would be content to die? That's what Simeon says. That's what 84-year-old Anna is waiting for.

Each of us will have deeply personal answers to this question rooted in unique individual circumstances. But it takes courage even to ask the question. For some of us, the question might feel some way off. And for most of us, the answer to the question might feel some way off – and so we continue to wait with what I have before described as revolutionary patience.

The duty that Mary and Joseph are fulfilling is to present their child; God is presented to God by humanity and, in the presentation, new truth is found, deep consolation is revealed. It is this life-and-death-ness of what is at stake that might lead us to pray for our own presentation, as we are, unvarnished, acknowledging all that is just too hard right now, and throwing ourselves on the mercy and love of God who is utterly trustworthy and always there.

Let us pray.

Show me myself as I am. Help me to name the fantasies I build and the hiddenness of the truth. Show me where, like the Christ-child in the gospel, I'm wordless for now; and give me people who can give me words. Show me myself even when I resist you, when I fight myself, when I wish I were someone else. Show me myself so I know that you see me, my scars and my fragilities, that I belong here at this altar. And give me back to myself as you made me, with hunger for justice, fearless and full of love. Amen.

7

The Sermon on the Mount

1 Corinthians 3.10–23
Matthew 5

Imagine the fun in the Sermon on the Mount! It's quite possible that in this gospel Jesus is cracking jokes. It's hard to get the timing and the humour across the chasm of translation and time – but none the less ...

Jesus knows his audience. He's a consummate storyteller, full of detail and fun, as lively as some of the current superstar stand-up comedians that are packing out theatres and clubs and Saturday night TV. As Matthew tells it, he's getting the crowd to imagine that they're being sued for their clothes – a lively story. They all know in any case that it's against the law to demand a person's cloak – it says it in Deuteronomy (24.12–13) – in case that person freezes to death when they sleep at night. So the picture that Jesus paints – of a person being sued for their cloak – is in itself a bit edgy. And then he says, yes, but give them your tunic too. That would leave the disciple naked.

The writer Sara Maitland has commented that each of us has a different tolerance of our own nakedness. Some are comfortable being naked in front of others, even those they don't know very well. Others are not comfortable naked in their own room alone with the curtains drawn and the lights off. The law has quite a lot to say about nakedness too, in terms of when it is allowed and when it is not. It is possible to see this picture that Jesus conjures up as a lively and entertaining picture of how to subvert an unjust system. Just take all your clothes off. It's confronting, and, as one commentator has put it, by standing naked in front of your creditor, who has both garments in his hand, one shames and dishonours the creditor.

'Nakedness exposes, among other things, the greed and cruel effect of the creditor's action and the unjust system the creditor represents.'[1] In twelfth-century Italy, Francis of Assisi did exactly this in front of a church court, embarrassing the bishop and his own father by taking all his clothes off to demonstrate his commitment to his new life.

Another detail gives the game away that Jesus is a lively and perhaps a funny storyteller – with his second example. While Luke reports that Jesus taught his disciples similarly about being hit in the face, Matthew specifies what should happen when one is hit on the right cheek. If a man, for example, has hit another person with his right hand (for hygiene reasons the left hand is not used for eating or other activities), then in order to hit them on their right cheek he will have struck them with the back of his hand, as a slave master hits a slave. It is a demeaning blow. If, however, the disciple turns the other cheek, the aggressor will be forced to hit him with his open hand – the blow of an equal. Refusing in this way to retaliate to legally sanctioned violence but instead turning the other cheek, especially after being hit on the right, is a radical approach to the law and a strong and dignified reaction to violence.

The teaching about giving your cloak, turning the other cheek, has been mistaught as a teaching about being submissive to violent people. Outrageously, this has been said by pastors to women suffering domestic abuse; it was read publicly to slaves by their masters in eighteenth-century America; and it is still taught today sometimes as an ethic of submission. But this teaching is nothing of the kind. It is a radical and challenging ethic – but it depends who's reading it. If a slave owner is reading it, someone with power, then it can be used to force slaves who can't read Greek for themselves into submission in the face of unjust violence. If it is read by a nervous clerical elite whose congregations can't read Greek for themselves, then it can be used as an ethic of submission to maintain inappropriate power. If it is heard by a first-century Jew under occupation by Romans, or by a twenty-first-century Palestinian Christian, familiar with Middle Eastern contemporary ethics, then its meaning is quite different. It is about dignity and non-violent resistance.

In the twenty-first century it can be heard as a charter for victims. Roll over. Don't resist. It's wrong to fight back. Be a doormat, it's the holy thing to do to be walked all over.

No. It's not.

Of course it's an exercise in spiritual imagination to make this real today. There will be some for whom this has been a literal reality. To have been hit across the face is humiliating, stinging, shaming. To get up and defiantly offer your face again seems foolish and is a dangerous prospect. In the Sermon on the Mount there is a context to this, a build-up, and there are other ways to react proportionately to an aggressor. This will at times be important and life-saving.

But the principle explained here applies not only in violent confrontations but in conversation, in daily interactions with friends and strangers, and it is ultimately rooted in compassion. It requires us to dig deep into whatever resources we might have of peaceful, tenacious compassion. It is also a measure of stubbornness. The narrative goes something like this: I will not allow the violent language or action of this person or group of people to draw me into acting in a way of which I will be ashamed. The Benedictines have an ethic of doing this, which is to develop the practice of withholding interior consent. It is an aspect of living compassionately. When you witness violence, whether in mean-spirited conversation, the trashing of someone's reputation or a refusal to help another person who needs help – when we witness this violence, we withhold our consent from it. This will lead to us sometimes acting to defend another, sometimes intervening to help, sometimes, when the violence has been directed against ourselves, getting up and, even with our faces red and hot from embarrassment, acting with dignity and openness.

Let's switch this round. If it's challenging to think of living like this when we are on the receiving end, then let's for a moment inhabit the other side of this dialogue. It's easier, and lets us think better of ourselves, if we identify with the one being struck – and Matthew's telling of this story encourages us to do so. But what does it feel like to be the other one – the one who has lashed out in the first instance? At work or among friends, in our family or in a shop with a stranger, it's a daily occurrence to be quick-tempered, irritated, self-absorbed, so that the proverbial slap across the face comes from us in the first place. We put others down all the time in order to deal with our own insecurity. How on earth do we live differently? How on earth is there room or energy to live passionately and compassionately in such a demanding life? What would our reaction be if someone offered their other cheek to us? Would we carry on or would we stop?

This is why Christianity is radical in itself. This is provocative and confronting stuff. To reclaim this teaching from the misinterpretations that have been damaging is to insist that there is something profound in this teaching. It's so challenging, it's almost out of reach. When people say to me that Christianity is retro, conformist, boring, I am ashamed of what we have done to the liberating gospel – like this. Whenever people say to me that Christianity is irrelevant and old hat in a world that is too full of retaliation, I want to point to a gospel like this. This is one of the moments that confirms criticism of Christianity from the outside, like Gandhi's sharp comment: 'I like your Christ, I do not like your Christians. Your Christians are so unlike your Christ.' That's because it's very hard to live like this, and our anxiety and our self-absorption make it even harder. Truthfully, we won't live like this unless we daily turn again to God, to the source of compassion. We can't hope to live like this unless we daily reorientate ourselves towards the light, the love of God that illuminates the radically different way of living that this gospel calls us to.

A cartoon appeared not long ago in the national press showing two warring sides: one was checking with the other, 'Are we on tat or tit?' At work, at school, in church, in family, in our personal relationships – someone, some time has the opportunity to break the cycle of retaliation. There is a better way, says Jesus of Nazareth – with strength, compassion and not a little humour.

Refuse cynicism, and the small-minded expectations of yourself and others. It's much easier to live that way of course. It's safer – you will never be disappointed. But refuse to scapegoat, from a position of strength, refuse to be a victim. This gospel shouts out that you are stronger than you think. You are capable of great forgiveness, great strength; as we are told in our first reading from Corinthians, you are nothing less than a temple – a place where God is present. And by drawing on the presence of God in you, you will help to stop the cycles of verbal and actual violence with which we all live.

The key thing, as we approach Lent in the run-up to Easter, is that Jesus didn't just say all this – Jesus fulfilled his own words at his trial and in his dealings with his political and religious enemies. He did not retaliate when he was hit by his enemies and he himself was stripped of his cloak and tunic.[2] This is therefore not just empty rhetoric, but lived compassion; which is the context for the last, slightly worrying, injunction – be perfect. Again, we can't just hear this as we think of perfection, because the perfection demanded is not a sanitary, churchy perfection but a demanding, costly love. To be 'perfect' in biblical terms is in fact to be completely whole ('holy as I the Lord am holy', Leviticus 19.2).

Wholeness, not a sterile perfection, is something for which we long as we are only too aware of our own brokenness. At this Eucharist, we come knowing that we have heard really tough teaching about how we are to live. And so we come to be fed, to drink deeply of the life-giving nourishment – food for the journey – knowing that we will make mistakes today, tomorrow and every day. But we gather around this altar affirming that we will try to live in this extraordinary and challenging way and that, in doing so, we allow God to set ourselves and others around us free.

Notes

1 R. Burridge, 2007, *Imitating Jesus: An Inclusive Approach to NT Ethics*, Grand Rapids, MI: Wm. B. Eerdmans, p. 215.

2 Burridge, *Imitating Jesus*, p. 217.

8

Sunday Next Before Lent

Racial Justice Sunday

Mark 9.2–9

Reading the Bible is not always a comfortable thing.

Take Jesus, for example; in my experience, he's not so much meek and mild as more often urgent and awkward.

The liberation theologian Carlos Mesters said it was important to read the Bible not only with your eyes but with your feet. At St James's, we often say that it's important to read the Bible with your head – yes, to understand it – with your heart – to let it change you – and with your feet. That Scripture is to be lived, to be walked into; to step into the story of God and the story of God's people invites us to change the way we live now. Reading Scripture with our feet is where it starts to shape us, challenge us, change the way we live.

I read the gospel for today and I felt sick.

In so many ways this story of Jesus being transfigured is beautiful. At the top of the mountain, such profound mystery, such exhilarating encounter with God who is beyond, utterly other. This mystery of God's presence sets the disciples alight with such hope for the future; they are energized, ready to go and change the world. And it's so overwhelming that it's hard to leave. They've climbed high with Jesus – the view is amazing from up there! And Peter – it's normally Peter who jumps in with these kinds of ideas – says – this is brilliant – 'Let's stay, let's build a shelter so we never have to go back down.' The voice that really matters says, 'Listen.'

So, what's not to like? Why did I feel sick when I read it? Because Scripture is a sword that pierces the heart. And, as necessary as it is, it is not always easy to face.

Today is the last Sunday before Lent. It is also Racial Justice Sunday.

And this Gospel story joins other parts of Scripture in reinforcing whiteness as something that represents goodness, holiness, the presence of God. The appearance of Jesus' clothes is so shining white that no one on earth could possibly make them any whiter. This whiteness is a sign that God is especially present, intensively so.

Reading this gospel aloud in public in the light of Racial Justice Sunday demands public reflection on these scriptural assumptions. Racial Justice Sunday is about precisely that: racial justice. Which is a collective goal, a joint endeavour, a public value that everyone is involved in strengthening, not a private wish that other people could somehow be nicer, but all this doesn't apply to me.

The gospel that proclaims the healing and liberation offered by Christ speaks directly into situations where power is unequally distributed, where privilege is exercised either unconsciously or deliberately.

There are many who are tiring of what they are calling identity politics, not least in the Church. We are all one, they say; we're all the same human beings, part of one world; these discussions are just divisive. Others will focus on the individual: I am more than the sum of a number of identities – I am me, unique and made in God's image.

Of course these things are true. There are some ways in which I am like every person on the planet: I need water, I breathe, I am sometimes afraid to die. On this basis, I can connect with any other human being from any other place or time. There are other ways in which you are utterly unique: no one has your fingerprint or your eye colour. There is no one with your combination of desires, dreams, fears and hopes. Every one of us is unlike every other one of us.

In these two areas, it's safer to stay, and much comforting spirituality depends on staying there. But there's a middle area: the place where I am like some other people on the planet but not all, because of my skin colour or the language I speak, the fact that I am able to read or that most days I am hungry, or that I own a car or use a wheelchair. In this middle category, where I am like some other people, politics happens, justice and injustice operate, and the negotiation of power and the ordering of society get attention.

And, these days, we recognize that each person inhabits a multitude of identities, each operating with differing influence in society: a person who is white-skinned and who identifies as gay, for example, will experience both privilege and prejudice in different situations. Similarly, a Black heterosexual man or a Brown trans woman. And so on.

And it's not long down this road before people start to say again, 'But we're all human beings, a common humanity, bound together by more that we have in common than divides us.' This is absolutely true, and Christian teaching will always want to affirm this.

But going too quickly or easily to this appeal to universal experience – we're all the same – is not just disingenuous, it's dangerous. Especially for white people, it helps avoid a highly problematic history of colonization and domination of darker-skinned people; it also has the effect of smoothing out, delegitimizing, the real suffering that centuries of this prejudice – white is good, Black is bad – causes today.

As Lemn Sissay's brilliant poem 'Colour Blind' says, a white person trying to claim that they are colour blind is just not facing facts. And his challenge is that the beauty of the colours Brown and Black are missed, by denying them:

> If you can see the sepia in the sun
> Shades of grey in fading streets
> The radiating bloodshot in a child's eye ...
> Why do you say you are colour blind when you see me?[1]

If you are a white-skinned person in the majority, then it's important to reflect on this on its own terms. I'm proud to be a Governor of Queen's Theological College in Birmingham, which is the only theological college in the UK with a dedicated Centre for Black Theology, an academic discipline that stretches back to Dr James Cone in 1960s America and in the UK is being developed by Dr Dulcie Dixon McKenzie, Dr Anthony Reddie and Dr Robert Beckford among many others.

Of course whiteness is a thing. White theology is a thing. White church is a thing. White spirituality is a thing. But it claims to be universally applicable. It writes the invitation on smart card and expects everyone to say yes – and gets cross when some say no.

The search for language appropriate to describe white theology is not straightforward because many of its associations are so ugly. The resistance to thinking about whiteness as an ideology, not just a skin colour, is strong.

One theologian starts to try to describe white privilege, white access in a white-majority society or church like this:

> White theologians move through doors so easily ... The door opens, the dean, the secretary, the clerk, the banker, the broker, the boss, smiles; the entry is made ... Inside is outside; outside is in. They are the same. The air of the white room is conditioned without air conditioning. For the white person, there is no 'exterior' problem, no dilemma of the outside ... but then there is no inside either – and here is the beginning of the problem. It is all available without obstacle, without change.
>
> The problem with white theological talk is that it is almost always about race without ever mentioning race. That is its burden. It is an untaught pedagogy. A problem of the ear, failing to hear its own cadence, its walk. Whiteness is a walk without a talk, a talk unconscious of its walk, a modern meaning of 'talking head' verbosity, oblivious of its body.[2]

Just to remind us, we are all carrying multiple identities; so this isn't the experience of every person with white-coloured skin if there are other identities – class, gender, sexuality – that temper this kind of access. But whiteness as a system, as a set of assumptions, as a way of being in the world, carries with it on the one hand a thoughtlessness when in the majority, and on the other hand a defensive attempt to dominate when in the minority that is a centuries-old embedded way of operating and is evident in the Church too. 'White discovery of the meaning of whiteness will involve passing through self-horror.'[3]

Today's scripture confronts me as a white Christian, as a

white priest, with a history that I know is appalling, which this scripture and others have been harnessed to support.

The contemporary theologian Dr Anthony Reddie puts it similarly:

> So, whiteness operates on the basis of stealth, holding a pivotal central place for that which is considered normal and as it should be. It becomes central to all that is concerned to be ideal, better than and considered the epitome of supposed civilisation and acceptability.
>
> ... most White people take this so much for granted that it rarely occurs to many of them that we live in a world in which whiteness is so embedded as the norm. It is accepted as the way of seeing and organising the world to the extent that it can be likened to a fish swimming in the sea. The fish is so normalised to its existence that all it knows is that the sea represents its total existence.[4]

Jesus' transfiguration is linked to his disfiguration: this mysterious shining illuminates and interprets the wounds that will surely come, the blood and the sweat of Holy Week.

And so I ask for strength and courage for the transfigured Christ to reveal to me, through the physical whiteness I inevitably and irreducibly bear in my skin, my vocation and place in all this. I need his strength to bear the inevitable self-horror when the meaning and history of whiteness become clear; but, importantly, this gospel doesn't allow me to stay there, on the way to facing culpability and collusion, knowledge of which, without Christ's accompanying presence, might have the power to destroy me.

Christ transfigured reveals and dismantles whiteness as an ideology; he gives me back to myself in pieces, and offers to help me reconstitute a re-evolved white identity that can be part of a Christ-centred movement for change.

This feels complicated – I'm aware that I'm wanting to be precise in my language and the sentences are long. Perhaps, as Anthony Reddie comments, I'm like a fish trying to describe the sea.

The book *White Theology: Outing Supremacy in Modernity*

has been important for me since its publication in 2004. It remains one of very few spiritual and theological reflections on white Christianity by a white theologian. Why aren't there more? More must be written about this.

For Racial Justice Sunday to mean anything, it has to demand that people with light skin reflect on what an ideology of whiteness means. Begin with penitence, and pray for the courage – which after all starts and grows in the heart – to read, mark, learn and inwardly digest the scriptural injunction to repent and change.

James Perkinson offers another biblical story to describe and reveal the gospel clarion call for change. It's in Jesus' conversation with Nicodemus. Perkinson says that in really looking at the pervasive and overwhelming reality of racial injustice, a white perspective that is eager to help bring change finds recognition in Nicodemus's question. You remember that Nicodemus realizes how profound an invitation Jesus is making to live newly and differently when that mysterious phrase 'born again' is used. Literally starting a completely new life. Nicodemus's question can be framed as something like: 'But we're adults – this has gone so far – for so long – it's so many years – how can we possibly start again? How can I climb back to the beginning and emerge newly born, needing everything, knowing nothing? I can't not know what I know. It's too late, or too hard.'

How can we go back and start again? asks Nicodemus. And, suggests Perkinson, the same question is asked by a white sensibility that has realized the depth of the problem. Jesus' answer is of course the truth: we can't. That generations of human beings with black skin have lived and died under the merciless jackboots of white-skinned people is undeniable. The 'othering' that a group of us witnessed to when we visited Auschwitz and Nuremberg on the parish pilgrimage, colossal movements of people – a reverse exodus from freedom into slavery – had been organized by bureaucrats, transport operators, politicians, tradesmen and landowners in more than one system of totalitarian domination.

The path to salvation is lit up by the transfigured Christ, who will not allow us to stay in the mystery of the cloud but will require us to go back down the mountain and begin again, however many times it takes, the hard work of listening, properly listening, being willing to be born again, being part of necessary change.

To be in the presence of Christ transfigured is to be so confronted with the beauty of an alternative future that we realize that what happens now simply won't do and can't be allowed to stand. To be in the presence of Christ transfigured is to be shown how this Christ-shaped energy calls for the dismantling of deadly systems and cruel conventions.

To be with the transfigured Christ on the mountain top is to be willing, and to renew that willingness every day, to be stripped naked; and for all my assumptions to be called into question by the God whom I trust with my life – and my death. This means that, as an individual, I might not be, in the world's eyes, maximizing my own individual potential as I see it – because, in reality, I am not in full possession of the knowledge of what that potential is.

Our fundamental activity as Christ's disciples is not to get everything right all the time or be over-anxious about what to say or do. This kind of anxiety, especially for white Christians on Racial Justice Sunday, is once again displacement activity which serves to avoid the challenge that authentic discipleship brings.

Our fundamental activity in the presence of Christ transfigured is to know ourselves as human beings in the presence of God who are seen, lit up, illuminated. That, as for Peter, our attempts to take control or stay where we are are challenged by the Christ who demands that we go back down and start again the work of change.

Lent is about to begin: a chance to contemplate the presence of God in the world. A chance to read, to think, to pray. A chance to ask for the courage not to avoid or dissemble. And to know, whoever we are and whatever it is we have done, or whatever has been done in our name, that it is never, never too late to begin again.

Notes

1 Lemn Sissay, 'Colour Blind', http://blog.lemnsissay.com/2011/10/09/colour-blind-a-poem/#sthash.PzXzoQcI.dpbs, accessed 23.08.2021.

2 J. W. Perkinson, 2004, *White Theology: Outing Supremacy in Modernity*, New York: Palgrave Macmillan, p. 190.

3 Perkinson, *White Theology*, p. 188.

4 A. Reddie, 'An Introduction to Black Theology', *Theos*, https://theosthinktank.co.uk/comment/2020/08/12/black-theology-an-introduction, August 2020.

9

Ash Wednesday

John 7.53 – 8.11

There have been some exchanges on what's called 'Anglican Twitter' this week, and not only there but more broadly on social media and in the press, that go along the lines of, 'Well, this year, Lent can get lost. In the middle of all the deprivation we're already experiencing, I'm not in the mood to give something else up.'

Fair enough. That may be where you are. It's true that Lent in its traditional form is about some kind of withdrawal: from socializing, from over-indulgence. More time to read, or pray, or take stock.

Even for those who have been working full time throughout, the very significant changes in society as we have lived through this pandemic have, at the very least, helped us ask ourselves different questions. And so, even if it hasn't been this time of inward reflection or significant deprivation as it has been for so many, it still might feel in some ways that it's been Lent since last Lent.

Last year at St James's Piccadilly we studied the Gospel of John together in one of our Gospel Conversations series. We found it to be an utterly captivating Gospel full of signs and wonders, with profound meditations on the meaning of time, and a portrait of Jesus who is at once fearless in the storm of events and the mysteriously still Logos, at one with the eternal heart of God even while the inexorable pace of events quickens around him.

The story that forms today's gospel is, among all the other things it is, enraging. Even before we get to any interpretation of the conversation and Jesus' reaction, we have an almost unbearably affecting scene. It's hard to take if you're any kind of compassionate person – but it's really hard to read as a woman.

This woman has been forcibly dragged by a group of men, and because of the detail in the Gospel – that she had been found in the very act of adultery – she is probably partially dressed, certainly disorientated. She is dragged along the street amid a whole lot of tumult. She will be flinching in anticipation of the rocks that will be thrown at her to kill her – now only moments away. This is, as far as she is concerned, the last moments of her life, and the mob is about to strike.

It's hard to think of a more febrile situation or one more dangerous for this woman. The social structures demand that she is destroyed for what she – and the man absent from this story – have done, and there's no way out. Before any personal apprehension of this story or exploration of its spiritual meaning, it's important to pause here and say that there is a gospel teaching here for anyone who finds themselves, like this woman, at the mercy of an unjust system. This is a gospel where it's clear Christ pays attention to your unjust treatment and fundamentally challenges the system that put you there.

This is a gospel that is traditionally read right at the start of Lent. It sets a tone. Lent is a controversial season for many – and with good reason. Bad religious over-emphasis on our sinfulness can leave us feeling defeated by our tendency to sin, even if the teaching is tempered by the good news of forgiveness. Bad teaching about sin can let loose in us, who are vulnerable people, a self-alienation that can be hard to shift, a persistent, perhaps indelible, sense of shame. And it's not done us any good either as individuals or as a Church.

Because it's even easier in Lent than it is at other times for the Church to start talking to itself, making it really clear what kinds of sins are sins and making sure everyone understands the differences. It's easy for talk of sin to alienate people or leave them with an impression that church people are rather obsessed by it.

But the reality is more complicated. Part of becoming mature adults, alive and flourishing in the world, is the sometimes life-long task of accepting ourselves as we are – what we might call life in all its fullness. We learn to do this because God does this. As we are.

We also know that we live in a way that is separated from, not connected to, the utter generosity of God: sometimes inadvertently, sometimes wilfully we do things we know to be selfish and hurtful to other people. And we spend a lot of time justifying this to ourselves.

Both self-acceptance and self-knowledge in the light of God's presence are our goals in Lent, but each has its dangers.

A skewed attitude towards self-acceptance can at the extreme turn into a rigidity of spirit that meets every challenge to our behaviour with a jaw-jutting 'That's who I am – get used to it.'

A skewed attitude towards the opposite – awareness of what we do wrong – can turn into a terrible hating and rejecting of ourselves, captured by the arresting phrase of the priest and poet John Donne: Selfe murder.[1]

Neither of these extremes bears the meaning of repentance – literally turning round and changing direction – which is what Lent is all about. Repentance isn't about improving our personality or making ourselves into a better version of ourselves. It is about turning back towards the person we always were: beloved of Christ, made in the image of God.

And this Gospel story, distressing as it is, contains an astonishing invitation to live the good news by confronting us with questions. Let the gospel read you. Let the gospel read your life.

Which part of you runs with the crowd and secretly is quite relieved when someone else is in trouble for something they've done? Which part of you, despite your best efforts, is judgemental and is energized by outrage at the antics of someone else who has been caught in the very act ...?

Or, even more potently, which part of you would you be horrified to have dragged, half dressed, from the bedroom for all to see? Which part of you is waiting even now for the first rock to strike your head, waiting to be found out, frozen, sometimes for years, in front of the judgemental voices you conjure up in your head or hear in the media, which you dare not confront even in your whispered prayers?

Immersed in this gospel, we are seen by Christ. Even when

we are naked or ashamed, choking with fear, or baying with blame, Christ sees us, and gently bends down to write in the dust.

Because the final place in the story can also be taken by you.

At the very moment of your shame or your chilling judgement of others, at the moment of this blame, what would you draw on the ground?

What would you draw?

Some years ago I was part of an art workshop – I was sceptical as I just can't draw. But the person leading it asked us to draw anger.

I thought I was going to get a purple pen and make a huge chaotic mess. But I didn't. I chose a colour I liked, and drew a strong structure whose shape I have never forgotten. I learned in that drawing that anger did not destroy me; it was a fuel that helped me work for a better world.

We are living in tough times. We are lonely, we are living with a higher level of distress than we have known, we may be busy at the same time as being unmotivated, we're putting one foot in front of the other.

And now it's Lent.

Don't feel that you have to give something up for the sake of it. Don't deprive yourself because you think you should. But, in the spirit of this gospel, if you and I can make some choices that involve finding compassion for the part of ourselves that is most ashamed, or if you and I can find a way of praying together through blame, then Lent will be doing its work.

Because in this service, shortly, we will be taking a moment together to draw. Not in the dust but on your skin.

On your head, that brittle, bony vessel for that brilliant and troublesome organ – your brain which whirs away, sometimes busy without purpose, hammering away, worrying away.

We invite you in this service, separated as we are physically, to pause, and to draw.

By drawing a cross on ourselves, we draw close to the mystery of Jesus' exchange with this woman, who speaks from her experience and tells him the truth.

'Has no one condemned you?'

She said, 'No one, sir.'

And Jesus said, 'Neither do I condemn you. Go your way, and from now on do not sin again.'

A statement of hope, and trust in this woman, in you as you draw the shape of the cross – as you draw the shape of grace with ash if you have some, or with oil if you have some, or simply with your own hand. Pause and draw the shape of grace into your skin, and know that we come from the earth and will return to it again one day.

And that God is with us in life, in death, in life beyond.

Note

1 J. Donne, 'The Flea'.

10

Lent 2

John 3.1–21

The Gospel of John is full of conversations. Some of them are one-offs, lasting just a few minutes. Some of them are not so much one-offs as on-and-off longer conversations that last for some years. Friendship is formed by the to and fro of years-long conversations. If you are fortunate to have longstanding friendships or relationships, or family that have known you over years, then you'll know that sometimes a conversation can last a lifetime.

The Gospel conversations are mostly between Jesus and all sorts of people, and although there is a long chapter in John's Gospel where Jesus is absent altogether (chapter 9), mostly the conversations are with him. There's the rather lively, even flirtatious conversation he has with the woman at the well, the same well where Jacob fell in love with Rachel all those years ago. There's the rather irritated conversation he has with his mother when they are both at a wedding and the wine runs out. There's the conversation he has with his friend Peter that turns more into a shouting match, and then there's this conversation from John's Gospel between two teachers of religion, teachers of the law.

Perhaps much later, Nicodemus would remember this conversation as he risked his reputation, maybe even his life, to tend to the body of Jesus after it was taken down from the cross. The revolutionary power of some conversation is revealed when we realize that something happened to Nicodemus in this exchange that meant that, when Jesus died, he couldn't leave him alone.

Who is Nicodemus who visits Jesus by night? He's learned, scholarly, a teacher of the law.

This conversation wouldn't pass what's known as the Bechdel test, a test for films – named after the cartoonist Alison Bechdel, which challenges movie makers to make sure there are some conversations in their film that are between two female characters who are not talking about a man. On International Women's Day today, it's worth noting how many films, plays, church events and religious texts fail this test. Including this gospel. But that's another sermon I'll be glad to preach another time. For now, let's take a look at this conversation on its own terms.

Nicodemus is sure of himself. He knows things. He's a leader, protected to some degree by his scholarship and learning. Maybe he's one of those people who assumes he's chairing the meeting, or is used to being the most powerful person in the room.

Nicodemus knows protocol, is used to being one of the most important people in most situations he might find himself in. On this occasion, he knows how to approach Jesus and does so with respect. 'Rabbi,' he says, 'Teacher.'

In John's Gospel, daylight and night-time are a regular motif indicating, among other things, knowledge and ignorance. John mentions that Nicodemus comes 'by night'. We are therefore prepared for the exchange in which Nicodemus is shown not to know all he thinks he knows, alongside the more prosaic detail that Nicodemus wants to visit Jesus secretly.

Whatever the reason, once he's there, the man of knowledge and influence is led into a different kind of knowing. His questions are answered by questions. Jesus is asked questions in the prose of a scholar, but he answers them in the poetry of a saviour.

And for us listening in, Jesus teaches us in this conversation to listen, really closely to listen.

If we're honest, most of us don't do that very much. Like Nicodemus, in most conversations we might have day to day, we're not really listening but working out what we're going to say next. We might also be working out how to impress the person in front of us or let them know how much we know. We are often competitive creatures, instinctively shoring up our own ego, even when we might not mean to, by imagining there's some kind of victory to be won in a conversation.

Sometimes this can be born of pain. We keep talking and don't dare to stop in case someone asks us how we are, and in case we tell them. But learning to listen, not just to another's words but to their heart, is a beautiful habit of the spirit that can lead to both new insights and new faith.

Jesus really listens, not just to Nicodemus's words but to his heart. Instead of asking only 'What does he mean?' there are deeper questions that frame this conversation. 'Why has he come? What does he need? What does he desire?' Jesus listens underneath the question and hears a desire to know more deeply what Jesus means. Nicodemus listens intently too.

They are discussing something that Nicodemus has heard Jesus say: that we must be 'born again' of water and the Spirit.

It's ridiculous, says Nicodemus, impractical and clearly impossible. Using an academic's classic technique, he employs ridicule as a weapon in the argument. 'Are you actually saying that a person can climb back into the womb and get born all over again? Because if you are then it's patently nonsense.'

I know that for many this phrase 'born again' is a burden, if you have come from a particular church tradition that has placed expectations on you that made you feel distressed and damaged. And so I will be gentle with this phrase, but explore it nonetheless as it is such a key part of Jesus' teaching.

With Nicodemus, let's ask: what can it mean to be 'born again'?

The Jewish philosopher Hannah Arendt offered the startling idea that we humans really mis-describe ourselves. We call ourselves mortals, that is, people defined by the end of our life – our death.

What effect would it have on the way we live if we called ourselves, not mortals, defined by our death, but natals, defined by our birth? Our beginning is where our energy is and where our purpose comes from.

What would it be like to live our lives not so much focused on fear of our death, but fuelled by the energy of our birth?

If we are natals, then we live, reminding ourselves that we are propelled into the future, curious, adventurous, wide-eyed. We suspect always that our future is greater than our past and our best days are yet to come.

Can you recognize yourself as a natal? Do you recognize the desire mentioned in this scripture to be 'born again'? Please try hard to take that phrase away from all the religious jargon and baggage that we've attached to it.

Being 'born again' might mean that sometimes we want to go back to where we started, with all our hopes intact and our dreams ahead of us. As adults, do we yearn sometimes to unravel some of our worse decisions and dubious choices? I'm not talking about regret so much as a sort of yearning to have another go, and have everything before us.

Do we sometimes want to leave behind old hurts, or habits we have formed that now seem to shape us as adults in ways we'd like them not to?

Being born again will mean, like a baby, our skin becoming thin again. We will know afresh our dependence, not our autonomy. We will cry freely, learn to answer to our name. We will be able to scream without losing our voice.

As grown-ups, we often want certainty. We want to be sure of where we are, what we're doing, what tomorrow will bring. We make plans and take responsibilities, and it's not long before we realize that we have somehow fixed the parameters of our life. We find ways to describe ourselves to others, often based on our job or what we used to do for work, partly to reassure ourselves and partly to let others know that things are in place and we are as we are.

Jesus' quality of listening, and his refusal to enter into the competitive academic to-and-fro posited by Nicodemus, reveal God both to him and to us in familiar words but in a new way. And that is our prayer for today. The difficult history of the pressure that some have felt to be 'born again' is redeemable in the gospel, which will always bring new insight to the old ways. In solidarity with Nicodemus, and reflecting on the conversation, let us approach God in order to deepen our trust in the uncertainty and delight of being born again, not approach God to be reassured of how much we know.

Some of you have been part of this community for many years. You are in a long conversation with God. A long conversation with the Church. A long conversation with one another. Some of you are just getting started. Whatever our time frame, the opening line, the approach both to God and to one another, is something to take from this gospel.

This conversation made Nicodemus, years later, braver than he thought possible when Jesus died. This path is open to us too: we can rehearse our courage by trusting that our questions to Christ will mostly be answered by another, deeper, more searching, more kind question. Our prosaic attempts to let others know how much we know can be met in Christ with a profound acceptance of our insecurities, within which we learn to trust the Spirit which blows where it will.

We are offered here in this liturgy, in these prayers, in this community, a chance to say what it is that we have to say, from our own experience of life, and to practise a deepening trust in God who hears all our words and especially our silences. So that when we come to Christ, whether it is by day or by night, may we come with open hands to be fed. It is here we are heard, and it is here that we will hear a truth and know a love that will even now set us free.

11

Lent 3

John 4

John's Gospel is a work of art, and John, who wrote it, an artist. Every story is told with evocative symbols, layers of meaning, with little details that really get you into the scene. John's Gospel is different from the others, less basic, more elaborate: Jesus is a little less the rabble-rouser rebel of Mark's Gospel, and more the mystical, poetic, elusive teacher.

And in John's Gospel, conversation is revolutionary. Conversation changes people's lives, conversation sets people on a different path. Last week it was the elite religious leader Nicodemus. Today it's a woman, from the despised ethnic group called Samaritans. Conversation changes everything.

For the meaning of this story to be given all its layers, it's important to note right at the beginning that this woman is not anyone Jesus should be seen with. Jews and Samaritans hate each other. They 'do not share vessels in common', they keep out of each other's way. It's not so much live and let live as stay out of each other's way; Samaritans are untouchable.

Jesus meets this woman at what's called Jacob's well. This is the very well where Jacob met the love of his life, Rachel. Rachel was taking her sheep to find water – she was a shepherd. So the well – and this well in particular – is steeped in Hebrew meaning and history. It's a place of meeting, of conversation, of community. And of love.

Although it's not in the Gospels, the Orthodox tradition holds that Mary was at the well when the angel Gabriel came to visit her, and so a well is symbolically also a place of announcements, a place of new promises, a place of holy encounter. It's not a temple or a church: it's a place of work, a place of daily chores, a place where women gather – and it's there that God is especially present in Scripture. If you work in an office or a school, talking at a well is like the conversations by the water cooler or in the staff kitchen: gossip, catching up, ordinary chat.

A well is not anything that we are familiar with today. We are, as in so many aspects of urban life, totally disconnected from the source of our water. As Londoners, we know that the water we drink from the tap is excellent – but in its excellence it has also been through I don't know how many other people before us. We argue about putting fluoride in it, we fend off waiters trying to get us to have bottles of water with our meal. We might look at the River Thames or the River Lea, or we might remember the countless underground rivers that flow under our city, like the Walbrook or the Fleet, but we don't go at evening to draw water from the earth; we don't often feel its natural abundance; and we've taught ourselves to think that we probably shouldn't go out in the rain.

We are out of touch with the water we need to survive – physically and often spiritually too. You might say that many of us lead lives that in more ways than one are slightly dehydrated.

Jesus the itinerant healer and preacher is travelling home – back up north to Galilee – because the Pharisee group were becoming critical of him down south. And this woman is, curiously, drawing water in the middle of the day – the hottest part of the day – possibly indicating that she was ostracized even from her own community, made to do her chores alone, not with the other women in the evening.

John's storytelling is wonderful. After a lively, flirtatious conversation with the woman, Jesus says to her, 'What you have said is true.' What you have said is true. There is no explanation or comment on her personal circumstances, although anyone hearing the story might disapprove of her in some way. Jesus simply says, 'What you have said is true.' This truth-telling about her life sets them off on a different path: after that, they discuss God – and this woman is set alight by the conversation to such an extent that she becomes an evangelist. She is energized, articulate, generous – 'Come and see someone who told me everything I ever did.' No one is tired any more.

She is known, she is recognized. Her story is told, as it is, unvarnished, without any hubris or embellishment – with all its mixture of shame and fun, hope and playfulness, loneliness, hard work, family complexities, complicated sexual identity. She says to her friends, 'Come and see someone who told me everything I ever did.' Word of mouth. 'He's not what you think. Honestly; come and see.'

This clear-sightedness of the woman, and the truth-telling of Jesus, are expressed by the artist Sara Mark in a work entitled *Sea Well*. She describes it as 'an exhortation to clear-sightedness, holding in balance the metaphors of fresh life-giving water and healing salt water'. They are contained in glass chemical reagent bottles to suggest that they might be active substances in a process of transformation. This is a piece that Sara imagined when she was walking the Camino – the pilgrims' route, the Way of St James – through northern Spain. And she went to Finisterre – the end of the earth – to find this water.

The title *Sea Well* – s-e-a – is a playful way to express the meaning of the gospel today. Words are amplified by water itself; the gospel good news is amplified both by the water in the well where Jesus met his match and by the living water he wanted to speak of that can irrigate a dehydrated life. This living water is a way of talking about a state of spiritual awakening, awareness, drenched in life, drenched in grace.

I recognize this woman – and sometimes I can hear her voice in conversations I have today. Conversations with practical people trying to hold down a job, deal with a teenager or two, fighting their fears, their worries, hoping they're doing enough to get by.

When faced with the prospect of religious belief or conversations about God, it's easy for people to say, as this woman does, 'You're so heavenly minded you're of no earthly use. Honestly, you're speaking in riddles – stop it. Talk straight. It's all very well for you, in all your religious get-up with your religious jargon, but I'm trying to live in the real world. I'm worried about my daughter, I'm still paying off a loan, I've forgotten what it's like to go on a date. I'm getting by.'

I heard this woman in a conversation I had this week with a woman who said it took her two years to be able to say in conversation, 'My husband's in prison.' And even now that he's out, she searches the face of the person she says it to, hunting for their reaction, for their revulsion, for their rejection.

If being a Samaritan means being ostracized and isolated, then our job as a Christian community is to transgress that isolation, and challenge that taboo. Yesterday here at St James's I was thinking about this experience of being shunned, turned away from – in two ways. We hosted our breakfast, which we have here on Saturday mornings for people with no recourse to public funds. These are people seeking asylum, many whose claims have been initially rejected, who are working on an appeal or a fresh claim. As I was standing outside welcoming guests from Nigeria, Ghana, Iraq, Iran, I was in a long conversation with a British guy, who thought it was disgusting that we were inviting this particular group into the church, and not, on this occasion, including British people. It is a tough call on some levels, but he – himself homeless – was hostile to the very thought of this group being welcomed into what he kept saying was a Church of England – with the emphasis on the *England* – church.

And later in the day, we hosted a service for FACT, an organization for falsely accused carers and teachers. In the proper and necessary uncovering of the catastrophic consequences of abuse for survivors, there is a small group of people who have been caught in the crossfire of false accusation; and for the first time in their 20-year history, they came to church yesterday. It occurred to me, from their own stories afterwards, that they themselves experience the kind of ostracization, isolation and catastrophic misunderstanding that comes with what one of them called the thoroughly human, but also toxic phrase, there's no smoke without fire.

For those who are living through the consequences of having been abused, I have heard many stories of terrible shame and taboo. It seemed to me that this group yesterday, unjustly accused, also endure appalling isolation, and that the church must be a place where their stories can be told too.

From this gospel, we're asked to seek out the taboos of our own society and break them. We're asked to have conversations in the light – when the sun is high, at noon – and not allow them to be held in the dark. We're asked, tenderly as Jesus does for the woman, to contemplate the shame that we carry, and know that it is known, acknowledged, held by God; and we're asked to believe that even when the shame is venomous, silencing, there is always, in conversation with God, the possibility of transformation and peace.

Thank God for this gospel; may we pray for the women and men whose stories are not yet heard. And offer to God those parts of ourselves that we yearn to be healed, that we yearn to see well.

12

Lent 3

John 2.13–22

Jesus of Nazareth is one of the most famous characters in world history. But it's hard to get to what kind of personality he had, not least because of the way we often read the Bible, or the way his name is packed around with liturgical prayers or repetitions. Lent, if you are a regular church person, is an opportunity to de-familiarize ourselves with some of the regularity. By spending 40 days in the wilderness, we have the chance to make the stories strange again, to hear them as if for the first time. So let's try to listen to this story as if for the first time; because if there is a story in the Gospels that reveals something of the personality or the character of Jesus of Nazareth, then perhaps this is it.

First, there's a kind of comic-book version of his character that's in a way easier to absorb. But then there is what I want to call a more grown-up version which is much, much more challenging.

The comic-book version is that Jesus, meek and mild, kind teacher, turns up to church one day, and to his surprise and irritation finds people inside selling things. He gets angry very quickly, and things take a bad turn. He becomes violent – if only to furniture rather than people – and starts throwing the tables around, letting the livestock out of their cages and knocking over the float. 'You can't sell stuff in church,' he says. 'Church is pure. Don't dirty it with murky money.'

This comic-book version touches a deep nerve that has produced many arguments in church congregations ever since. Can we sell Christmas cards inside the church? What about Traidcraft? Should we put a cloth over any of the produce while the service is going on so that the prayers stay pure?

And more seriously, if a church building has an outside space – a courtyard even, like we have here at St James's in central London – what about having a coffee truck there, or a stall selling food or souvenirs? Churches and cathedrals across Europe often have independent small businesses next to them on their ground. Good questions can get asked even from this comic-book version of the story: What is the right relationship between church life and commerce?

But for me, this has always felt like a false opposition and a set-up argument. Because a closer reading of the Gospel story reveals something different from the comic-book version. The point Jesus is making is much stronger, much more challenging than saying you shouldn't sell stuff in or near a church.

If we put it in context, read it more closely, listen harder, what is this gospel saying?

Jesus of Nazareth has been to the Temple in Jerusalem many times. We know he was there for three days when he was 12, for instance, and he will have been many times since. He's not surprised. He knows the layers of courtyards that are there. He knows full well what happens there day after day. This is a whole economic system he's observed over years. He chooses to go there on this particular day and make his case with a vivid, unforgettable, high-stakes, eye-catching action.

What are those people doing there? They are not just selling stuff; they're changing money. Changing Greek and Roman money into Jewish or Tyrian coins to pay the Temple tax. And they're selling doves and livestock specifically for sacrifices required by religion.

The words used to describe Jesus' actions are incredibly energetic. They're not at all polite, but are bursting with energy, like a sportsperson accelerating down the pitch. Emotionally, perhaps physically too, Jesus is sprinting.

- ἐξέβαλεν exebalen – he threw out or drove out the sheep and oxen
- ἐξέχεεν execheen – he poured out all the coins
- ἀνέτρεψεν anetrepsen – he turned over (carrying the meaning of this being highly energetic). This verb can also mean to destroy.

And his friends see something in him they recognize: zeal. Tireless, focused energy, passion, clarity.

Zeal.

And it's the quote from the Psalms that the disciples remember as they watch him: 'It is zeal for your house that has consumed me' (Psalm 69.9). Zeal is an old-fashioned word, not an everyday one. And in today's society it gets a bad press, often for good reason. If you or I have any part of us that gets zealous, we can learn to unleash it for the good, but we have to learn to moderate it when its merciless energy gets misdirected, as it can so often, towards ourselves or others in an unfettered judgemental focus on what we think is wrong.

The people Jesus drove out were money changers. Contemporary witnesses speak of the exploitation that this changing of money often carried, with unfair rates of exchange that exploited those who were poorer as they tried to buy doves for the sacrifices they were required to make, after childbirth for example.

Other contemporary sources cite the arguments that were happening within the religious establishment and the confrontations that took place when injustices were uncovered.

Jesus knew full well the economic injustices meted out in the Temple as in society. He was familiar with the inequity and the burden that was carried by those who were least resilient. He chose his moment, and he deliberately took provocative symbolic action that would cause headlines and would challenge the religious establishment as strongly as he had challenged the political establishment by riding into Jerusalem on a donkey, not a horse. Jesus of Nazareth knew the power of symbolic action.

I want to suggest that, as an internal argument within the religion Jesus is part of, it's not the trade itself that he is objecting to. It's the exploitation practices, the unfair exchange rates, the insistence on buying animals for sacrifice even when the poor could not afford it. This is an eruption of energy that is challenging, overturning the unfairness and exploitation of the economic system that was being supported by the religious establishment of the day.

Jesus of Nazareth is a genius storyteller and playwright, and makes brilliant use of symbolic action. Riding into town on a

71

donkey, grabbing a mustard seed from a nearby tree, writing in the sand as a mob bays for the blood of a woman in front of him, and here overturning tables of money changers exploiting the poor, Jesus knew the power of symbols as much as he understood the influence of parables. Like Mahatma Gandhi and the salt marches, like Rosa Parkes who sat down, like Pope Francis who prayed at the Western Wall in Jerusalem but also at the Security Wall in Bethlehem, with all who have ever taken the knee or lifted their hands in prayer, or waved a rainbow flag or offered a flower to a solider, symbolic action matters.

The power of action taken physically, to point to a deeper spiritual truth, runs through the whole imaginative, vivifying ministry of Jesus, poetic teacher, elusive preacher, energetic prophet. The Jesus of the Gospels has never struck me as Jesus meek and mild. Here, as elsewhere, this is Jesus urgent and awkward.

The power of symbolic action, if it is imaginative action placed at the service of hope and justice, is clear. It is emotive, provocative, disruptive, good.

But a symbolic action can also be a place to hide from real change – and this is its danger.

We have a real example happening right now as we are emerging from the pandemic. The symbolic action has been to clap our appreciation for key workers in the NHS. But we seem incapable as a society to make the step change that is necessary for the work of cleaners, care workers and nurses, to be valued as highly as, for example, people who work in financial services. I'm not talking so much about the political debate over NHS pay, but about a fundamental shift in whose work is valued by all of us, culturally as well as financially.

Tomorrow is International Women's Day. Women have suffered disproportionately from the pandemic, in this and other countries across the world, because of pre-existing inequalities and vulnerabilities: in terms of economics, job security, domestic violence, or peace and security.

Symbolic imaginative actions such as clapping or drawing rainbows in our windows are good, but are not enough. In the Magnificat it's clear. Mary teaches us that God 'scatters the proud in the imagination of their hearts'. Imagination is not enough in itself. It has to be placed at the service of the hope and justice that Christ proclaims. Only then does it become advocacy and witness.

I have often wondered what happened the day after Jesus turned over the tables. Did the transactors and changers come back? I think they may have done. I think they certainly went back after he died.

The integrity that Christ calls us to means that symbolic action that provokes debate and highlights injustice is matched by the change-making that we find harder to sustain. Christ followed through: he went to the cross, and so his provocative imaginative action, like this table turning, is always seen with the shadow of the cross falling over it, pointing to a deeper truth and an enduring vision of a more just future.

In his imaginative, provocative action, Jesus reminds us that if we are not upside down, we are not the right way up.

And I want to say a little about church as a community for a moment. In common with many churches, St James's talks together about our vision, a mission action plan, income generation as part of this. And as we are making our way through this pandemic, it is a challenge before us to keep interrogating our practices so that we more closely align our income generation and expenditure with our vision, mission and values. For this physical and now digital space to be a welcoming, prophetic, sustained and sustainable presence in the city, it's not enough to be involved in provocative imaginative action like this. As with the rest of society, we have to pay attention to the infrastructure, the spreadsheets and the payroll, the legislation to which we are accountable, the challenges of being a good employer.

This takes commitment – including financial commitment – from everyone who cares about church, what it stands for, what it could be, how it must change. We are trying together to be wise. But as Paul says in one of his most inspiring letters, we preach Christ crucified, the power of God and the wisdom of God (1 Corinthians 1.18–25). Which is foolishness to a culture that will, like the money changers, like any of us who are working, saving, spending in the world, operate within exploitative parameters.

One thing I have learned, am still learning in this Covid time is that my heart becomes more resilient and faithful if I am practising foolishness, and I've noticed it in others too. I don't mean by that an irresponsibility, or, given that our church employs people and has tenants, a thoughtless risk-taking with someone else's future – but foolishness. The practice of foolishness deepens trust, because it means you are admitting that it's not altogether clear what you should do next. Trust is all we have when what we relied on before has gone. For us, this has taken the form of resisting the temptation to preserve for its own sake, loosening our grip on what we thought was important before, holding a huge consultation exercise about our values and taking ourselves into new areas of work and mission, praying for a spirit of faithful adventure, of trustful foolishness. And at the same time taking the spreadsheets as seriously as anyone has to who runs their own business or is economically active in the world.

And so as we listen to this gospel today, it's not enough for us to harness our imaginations and be gleeful about Jesus' rampage, and then use it in the service of what we already think about money or society or church.

We are asked not just to follow through the Temple courtyard with Jesus as he energetically turns over the tables of other people's exploitative practices. We have to let this gospel challenge us personally. And ask ourselves as individuals and as a church: What tables are you sitting at that Jesus would overturn if he could?

You may be at boardroom tables, canteen tables, at desks or counters or gathering places. You may be gathered in your work, in your social life, in your family, in your church, at tables – not so much physical as places you draw people into conversation or places where money is exchanged.

The tables of the money changers were used to count money exploited from the poorest in society. Their tables were used to provide a barrier between customer and exchange, were used to place the cages full of doves and pigeons sold at too high a price to people who had been taught to buy them to fulfil their religious obligations.

In the Church, we talk about the altar, the table, being a place of welcome for all.

What if this table is one that Jesus would overturn if he could?

How can the Church witness to this foolish zeal for justice in a world and society that seems so immutably addicted to exploitation – of the earth, of one another, of anyone who has less power or voice than we think we have?

As soon as we take a close look at the exploitative systems we are all part of, we realize we are lost. Because, if we're honest, we're part of exploitative practices at every turn. All of us.

But at this table, at this altar, if we listen to this gospel, we will be willing always for it to be overturned, for our assumptions and addictions to be challenged. If we are willing to be upended, the Church can witness, point away from itself, point towards a just and beautiful future which is fuelled by the holy rage of Christ.

That's why the energy of the gospel has the potential to save us even today from the dangers we constantly fall into: when we reduce spirituality to a collection of warm feelings, or when we allow the institutional drag of money and buildings to suffocate our energy, vocation and mission.

In these pandemic and divided days, if there is anywhere a place to talk about sickness, death, fear and injustice in a way that bears witness to the possibility of healing then it can be in the public, sacred space of the church, around a table always at the point of being turned upside down.

What tables do you sit at that Jesus would turn over if he could?

If you know them, maybe it's time to walk away.

If you don't know yet, then we can pray together at this altar to become more foolish this season of Lent. Because true foolishness requires trust in God. And for us, while it may seem alarming in some ways, it is not clear what will happen next. It's not an easy place to be, but it's a creative and faithful place to be.

The gospel isn't in itself counter-cultural for the sake of it. But if we spend time really getting under the skin of a story like Jesus turning over the tables in the Temple, if we ask for the willingness to be upended ourselves, or to challenge the injustice and exploitation we see, then we will let go of the comic-book figure who won't let us buy or sell stuff in church.

Instead, we will find a redeemed rage within us that is much, much more challenging to the way we live.

Let us pray.

Holy God, help us to know how to rage with you. Give us energy and grace as we begin to emerge from the pandemic days we have known. Help us to see the tables we sit at: which ones to invite others to and which ones you will want to overturn. And help us accept the invitation to be foolish for your sake. Amen.

13

Lent 4

Mothering Sunday

Exodus 2.1–10

As we make our way through Lent each year, this fourth Sunday
is also Mothering Sunday. And we celebrate it this year in a
week that has been a bleak one for many women. The celebration just a week ago of International Women's Day has been
subsumed by frenetic and forensic examination of the role of
the first mixed-race woman to be a senior member of the royal
family, with all the attendant sound and fury on social media,
not to mention breakfast television. But if only that were the
main reflection on gender to have come out of the events of
this week. Last night's vigils in memory of Sarah Everard,
murdered in this city as she walked home alone, were can-
celled, but the pictures today of women held down by police on
Clapham Common have led to the first female Commissioner
of the Metropolitan Police to face calls to explain herself. The
terrible crime committed against Sarah Everard has sparked
a conversation, not just about the random attacks on women
by strangers, because in fact there are more random attacks
on men by other men, but about the everyday harassment and
violence experienced by women because they are women.

Ever since I was a teenager I have walked in the middle of
the road with keys between my fingers. And if a recent UN
report is right, then at least 7 out of 10 women have been
sexually harassed in public in the UK.[1]

And just as the most recent iteration of the Black Lives
Matter movement has emphasized the role of white institutions,
groups and individuals as obviously the problem, so the public
conversations this week have also emphasized the role of men,

all men, in challenging the behaviour of other men, rather than leaving it to women. One prominent media outlet was criticized for describing the news item as 'women's safety concerns' and was challenged to change it to 'male violence concerns'. The Bishops of London and Gloucester have been part of sponsoring amendments to the Domestic Violence Bill going through Parliament to ensure that women trapped in situations of domestic violence, which we know have reached epidemic proportions in lockdowns, will still be able to access help even when they have no control over their own money.

A serious consideration of public festivals, rituals and conversations about and by women, and a serious reflection on gender, will include Mothering Sunday, not least because Christianity has form in being part of the problem for women.

Until womanist and feminist perspectives, and now gender-fluid or trans perspectives, began to bring life and creativity to the consideration of gender and religion, Scripture telling the stories of girls and women has been preached from a male perspective only, which is why it is so important that women are public figures and leaders in religious spaces.

And so Mothering Sunday takes its place in this public reflection; and it has the potential to be a deep and fruitful moment, not a shallow, commercial reinforcement of unhelpful stereotypes.

I hope that most actual mothers have a really good day today despite the restrictions. I hope that there are deliveries of flowers and cards; maybe some socially distanced walks in a park for exercise. I hope that there is some fun, some Zooming or Facetime, some chances to acknowledge across the generations that becoming a mother is one of the most demanding, challenging, heartbreaking, anxiety-provoking, joyful jobs in the world. I hope that many mothers today feel thanked and appreciated, I hope they feel seen.

There are two biblical women in the readings today. One of them doesn't have a name, although later in the book of Numbers her name is revealed as Jochebed. This woman's astonishingly brave actions save the life of her baby. She is living as part of an enslaved people, the Israelites in Egypt. In the previous chapter of Exodus, the Pharaoh has issued an instruction to the midwives who attend Israelite women that, in order to control the enslaved population, boy babies should be killed, while girl babies can be spared.

Thus, in common terminology, you could say that the baby boy here is in danger of both gender-based and racially motivated violence. So his mother hides him for three months and, when she can't hide him any more, makes a water-tight basket and floats him in a thickly covered part of the river. She stations her other, older child – Miriam – to watch and make sure that he doesn't fall in, hoping perhaps that someone might come and rescue him.

This is mothering in a highly precarious situation; mothering that many mothers in the UK will recognize as they try to teach their sons how to survive in a situation where as young men, especially young Black men, they are more likely to suffer discrimination and violence. This is mothering in a highly precarious situation; which will be recognized by many mothers in the UK today who in this pandemic have visited foodbanks for the first time, asked elder siblings to look after younger children while they hold down two jobs, tried to find ways, even to the point of giving their children away, of ensuring a better life for them in a precarious financial and social situation. The choices that Jochebed makes are recognizable to women across the world, and to many women in the UK.

Moses her son grows up to be the figurehead for a movement of liberation that leads the people into the desert, away from slavery. He doesn't get to the promised land himself, but he knows that the people will get there. And he owes his own life to the actions of a mother and daughter in a shockingly dangerous occupied land.

Being a mother when there is little money, systemic violence, state-sponsored discrimination is something that women across the world know today. Mothering Sunday doesn't have to be a saccharine celebration of an ideal that women, mothers or not, simply can't live up to – although it can feel that way. Mothering Sunday is about discovering the agency of these biblical women who were determined to act bravely and wisely even when the societies they lived in told them they had little power.

The Gospel figure of Mary is sometimes even more difficult

to reach, dressed as she is in centuries of artistic representation in lapis lazuli, rather wan, rather passive.

But the biblical Mary is nothing of the sort. In this gospel, short as it is, there's so much there under the surface. Mary is in the Temple as a new mother. She's first of all simply amazed at the reaction her new child provokes, as new parents often are; second, she's on the receiving end of some very unwelcome truth; and third, she's identified as a woman who will suffer – and here the language is violent in itself, a 'sword through your very life', which modern translations often describe as her 'soul'.

 - The figure of a mother is indelibly marked into every human life. Either because of the presence of your biological mother or because of her absence. Or because of the mothering you have received from another person, whatever gender they may be.

That we have all been born, somehow, means that the relationship is an irreducible one whatever twists and turns life takes.

So this day is complicated. For some it is just straightforward, but I'd like to suggest that's not really true for many. Maybe you are missing your mother today, or conversely really glad she's around. You may have been afraid of your mother, or you may have never known her. Maybe you are grieving the loss of her. Maybe you were desperate to be a mother yourself and in the event you struggled with it, or else you never were. Maybe you never wanted it and felt judged by a society that thought you weren't a proper woman unless you did.

But alongside focusing on actual mothers, there is something about Mothering Sunday – for all its complexities and tensions – that goes very deep, it seems to me. I don't *only* mean the recognition that there are people beyond your immediate family whose nurture commitment has been a kind of 'mothering'. I mean something wider again: 'mothering' as a kind of giving over of yourself to something or someone; mothering as that which draws out resources you didn't know you had.

Today's biblical women invite us and challenge us. Biological mother or not, after the example of Jochebed, what is it that you will fight to save, even when you are in a situation that seems hopeless and you think you have no power? For whom will you stick your neck out, take action to protect? For whom or what will you challenge the system? Be creative in getting round the rules?

And in the spirit of Mary, we might ask ourselves: who or what is it that unlocks our heart? Even to the extent that our lives can be pierced through, by the consequences and demands of the same love that first stormed its defences and threw wide the doors? The poet Mary Oliver wrote in her poem 'Lead' about her desire to break hearts, but only so that they would 'break open, and never close again/ to the rest of the world.'[2]

What *is* that, for you? What does that to you? What do you love? What do you want to protect, and see grow, and set free? It might be your work, your children, a cause, another person, a project, some form of artistic expression, something or someone you teach ... What breaks your heart – by breaking it open so that it never closes again to the rest of the world?

To love like that is to give expression to something of the fierce, utterly self-given, utterly available, patient, creative love that's holding the stars apart and the universe in being, and that became incarnate and visible in Christ, and Christ crucified – the fullness and utterness of divine love, whose fingerprint is on every soul. Perhaps that's something of what we mean when we speak of being made in the image of God.

And the miracle is that it's on you too. All the fullness of that compassionate, creative, divine love is focused and poured, not on some impossible ideal of anything, but on you as you are – all the time, endlessly, inexhaustibly. And it's focused and poured in equal and inexhaustible measure on the person in front of you at any given moment. It's when we begin to see ourselves and one another as objects of that endlessly creative and compassionate love – as we are, not as we or anyone else thinks we should be – that the kindness and patience and forgiveness that Paul talks about as the marks of the new community in Christ which we call the Church can begin to grow and develop.

And so our prayer today might be that, both as individuals and collectively in our hurting society, we might pray honestly and daringly for change in our society, which must begin with us. That we, whatever our gender, might more deeply discover our capacity for mothering, and dare to pray: God, as I live in your world and go through my life, break my heart ... may it be broken open so that it never closes again to the rest of the world. Amen.

Note

1 www.unwomenuk.org/site/wp-content/uploads/2021/03/APPG-UN-Women_Sexual-Harassment-Report_2021.pdf
2 M. Oliver, 2007, *New and Selected Poems*, vol. 2, Boston, MA: Beacon Press.

14

Lent 5

Preached on the second Sunday of the first Covid-19 lockdown, at a service livestreamed to worshippers confined to their own households.

Ezekiel 37.1–14
John 11.1–45

One of the key things that happens in church services is the telling of stories, ancient and new. Sometimes they are mysterious stories, with vivid characters or strange happenings, but also, quite often, they are very ordinary stories about human beings making their way through life. These individual stories are told within the broader story of humanity living in the light of the story of God – which is our Scripture.

And today's stories are both humdingers.

The story of the raising of Lazarus is very famous.

The action is quite simple, if dramatic.

Jesus hears of the sickness of a good friend called Lazarus. Instead of going to see him, he stays where he is for two days, during which time Lazarus dies. Lazarus's two sisters – Martha and Mary – react in different ways, but both are grieving. Martha doesn't wait for Jesus to arrive in the village for the funeral – she goes out to meet him and challenges him, saying, quite confrontationally, 'If you'd been here, my brother wouldn't have died.' Fabulously direct, Martha is straight-talking, an emotionally intelligent and brave woman.

At the tomb, Jesus acts very dramatically. He is incredibly distressed, and he demands that the stone be taken away from the entrance to the tomb. Again Martha speaks up. 'No,' she says, 'you can't possibly open up a grave because the body will be stinking. It's been in there for four days.'

Jesus insists, and shouts – the Greek word really means that he yells – Lazarus's name. To the astonishment of the crowd, Lazarus emerges, still wrapped in the grave clothes.

It's a dramatic story, full of vivid characters, highly emotional. And the meaning of the story, the deep layers of meaning, take a lifetime to unpeel.

Like some of you perhaps I've heard this story many times. And as I've pondered on it over the years I've asked my rather obvious questions: could that really have happened? Why is John's Gospel the only one to tell this story? If it was so important, why don't the others tell it too? I find too in Martha a role model of faith, not just for women but for men, for anyone, in her energy and honesty. And as I've heard this story over the years, one detail has always eluded me. It's near the beginning. Jesus obviously loves Lazarus and the family – but when he hears he's gravely ill, he stays where he is for another two days.

The classic theological interpretation of this is that Jesus has a plan, that he doesn't come too soon, because the point of the story is to show the glory (*doxa* in Greek) of God – a recurring theme of John's Gospel. The human cost of that timing is the grief that Mary and Martha feel, and the fact that Lazarus has to die.

Theologically that has a certain logic: it reinforces an interpretation of this particular Gospel that Jesus is perhaps more other-worldly – transcendent – than in the other Gospels, and these themes of timeliness, of the revelation of God's glory, and of the singular vocation of Jesus make sense.

But while the academic theology is an important tool in our own interpretation of the meaning of Christ's teaching and life, it's also important for us as a living Christian community not simply to nod and accept these kinds of interpretation as the whole truth, because there are many different ways of knowing what we know and believing what we believe. And, for anyone who lives in the real world of life and faith, chaos and fluidity accompany a sudden death like this a lot more closely than a theological interpretation can convey.

What's more, the quite extraordinary way that Jesus' behaviour is described doesn't sound decisive or aloof at all, focusing on the timeliness of God's glory. In fact, at the graveside, our English translation says that Jesus is 'greatly disturbed'. But actually, the Greek word used for this is really quite extreme. It's the same word used to describe a horse pawing the ground, snorting. Jesus is crying. The picture painted of him by John is of a man simply beside himself with emotion. And at the point of raising Lazarus, the word used for Jesus calling Lazarus's name is the same word used to describe the crowd baying for Barabbas a few days later. It isn't a polite 'calling'. It's shouting. Jesus screams.

It's a story that is dusty, messy, full of grief and shocking change.

Remember Ezekiel's valley of dry bones from the first lesson?

This too is a vivid story that is dusty, messy, full of grief and shocking change.

As I was reading these passages in preparation for today, I felt my heart racing – but to be honest, perhaps like yours, it's been racing for a while. This gospel spoke straight into the sudden change in our circumstances at the onset of the Covid-19 pandemic, the realization of what is at stake, the prospect of illness for ourselves or people we love. The unusual nearness of thoughts about death.

This story of Lazarus is so vivid, so arresting, that there's an infinite amount to say about it.

But today, it's that detail of Jesus staying where he is for two more days that has new meaning. I've not ever really understood it, as I mentioned, despite the logical theological explanations offered for it.

But now I can see something in this that I have never seen before.

That sometimes – and now is one of those times – it's important to stay away from the people you love to show your love for them.

Much of what is happening now is counter-intuitive. I have heard many people speaking about this as a war, and that might be helpful in some ways but not in others.

Because, in a war, our instinct is to get together, to comfort each other, to strengthen our resolve by being together.

What we're being asked to do now is not that. It is to stay

away from one another physically. As in this gospel, even when we know someone is ill, we need to stay where we are and find other ways to connect and communicate.

This isn't true for everyone of course – the regular evening applause for NHS workers and carers has brought many to tears in the street.

But for most of us, in forcing us to act in ways we find extremely difficult, this 'social distancing' is uncompromisingly requiring us to act in one another's best interests, not our own. And because it is such an uncompromising requirement, it seems to me that's why it's taken a while for it to sink in.

At every level of behaviour, every day, this situation challenges us to ask ourselves: by my choice today, whose needs are being met? Mine – because I want to be the one who defied the rules to continue to help others? Or the needs of another person whose well-being, even life expectancy, may depend on my decision to stay where I am for a while longer?

We're in the fifth week of a six-week season – Lent. The 40 days before Easter are sometimes called the 'sad springtime of the Church'. It is an achingly beautiful season, full of longing, in tune with the creation of which we are part, surrounded as we are with intimations of new life everywhere, but not quite yet, not quite there. Lent is a season of energy confined, of new life, for now curled up in a bud, buttoned up in a seed, wrapped up in a blossom that heralds the fruit not yet here.

Stay where you are. Wherever that is. Even while your Lazarus is sick and even if your Lazarus dies, stay where you are. For there, mysteriously, without warning or explanation, God is with you.

And even for those who are still moving, still going out, still walking towards situations the rest of us are asked to stay away from, this odd and mysterious detail in the story can hold cavernous meaning. Because in a crisis such as this we are being divided into two kinds of people: those who become extremely busy, with government and other programmes to devise and administer; with ventilators to design and manufacture; with care homes, hospitals, hospices and mortuaries to run to capacity; with children to home-school, with drugs to administer, with deliveries to organize.

Others, however, become strangely still, with nothing, absolutely nothing to do except worry about the sudden loss of income, circumstances and prospects.

And still others, whose life before was one of confinement, find it now more perilous than before. For some the 'Stay at home' message is a horrifying one. It's perilous to stay at home if home is not safe because it's a place of violence and abuse. Anyone in that situation is urged to seek help. Today.

And practising social distancing is confusing if your mind has been 'fractured by life',[1] if you have dementia or serious mental health problems and are living in an institution. 'Stay at home' sounds like a bad joke for the men and women whose home is the streets. I spoke with several yesterday in central London who are feeling hopeless and distressed now that all the public spaces where they usually find some respite – public libraries, some coffee shops, church buildings – are shut to them. 'It's never been like this,' said one man we know well here at St James's who had slept fitfully on a night bus.

Buried deep within the Christian tradition is a profound spiritual teaching that asks the same of us as is being asked in these days. It was practised by the fourth-century desert mothers and fathers in the Egyptian desert, whose most famous saying has come to us down the centuries as a teaching from Abba Moses: 'Your cell will teach you everything.'

That spiritual teaching is also described as an encouragement to stay where you are. This is not so much a physical staying – although it can be linked with that – but a spiritual staying where you are.

This has always been a challenge but is perhaps in today's society especially so. Staying where you are is a counter-intuitive message in a world and a society where progress is best when it is fast, where 'moving forward' and 'going forward' have become clichés, not just of business leaders, but for all of us.

Staying where you are, as Jesus stayed where he was, for the good of another, for the good of the whole, is something that has been taught for the whole of Christian history.

While our society is, to use the colloquial phrase, 'on lockdown', and movement is restricted, our society looks as if it has become still. But far from it. The restriction of our physical movement can cause something of an emotional and spiritual explosion; we are permanently – inside anyway – in a state of flight or fight. Because the situation is so challenging, we will do anything – anything – to distract ourselves from it. We become less mobile physically, but our minds, if not tended to, become places of vacuous over-activity, morbid thoughts, fears and perilous anxiety. It is this perpetual rumination, what the Greeks called *logoismoi*, that the monastic spiritual teaching to stay seeks to address.

This fourth-century wisdom challenges us to stay where we are but not allow that to be stagnation. It is a stillness that enables us to sink down, deep into the heart of who we are, expecting to find God, the spark of the divine, in the depths.

It takes huge courage to 'stay'. What we normally want to do is flee the deepest parts of ourselves. We deliberately create a hectic, distracted society outside ourselves – either physically or online – in order precisely to stop us facing the reality that we are a messy mixture of valour and selfishness, of hubris and stunning generosity, of violence towards ourselves or others, and at the same time capable of the most imaginative acts of peace-making.

Stay where you are.

This means face yourself. You and I are asked to inhabit our own lives as they are, knowing that we are held and loved, forgiven and freer than we can possibly imagine, even while our physical movement is confined.

As you are.

Not as you wish you were, or as that person over there.

Stay where you are for the good of the whole.

This means spiritually as well as physically.

Because if we want to develop a spiritual practice that will better serve the world, it will be rooted in what might have to be quite a bracing acceptance of the unfinished creature that we are, the human being God has made and is remaking. A real practical acceptance, not a flight into a fantasy version of yourself that you thought you should be by now.

I will be more able to love my neighbour as myself when I stop trying to flee into the empty distractions I surround myself with. They will be different for all of us but can include over-busyness, competitiveness, anxious comparisons, self-administered anaesthetics of all kinds – distractions that look as if they will make me happy but which in the end find me, like Ezekiel, sitting in the valley of the dry bones of my life, begging them to remember how to dance.

The life, death and resurrection of Jesus is what you might call God's body language; and so in this gospel, so near to the end of his own life, Jesus stayed where he was for the good of the whole world.

It cost him dearly; he wept and yelled and, in the end, by God's grace, new life emerged from the grave blinking into the light.

Please God, for us too, let it be so.

Amen.

Note

1 R. S. Thomas, 'The Kingdom'.

15

Good Friday

A large wooden cross was placed in the church as a focus for devotion.

I was visiting someone in hospital recently and I saw at the end of the ward, a few beds along, a young woman. She was wearing the familiar hospital gown, her hair was gone, and the sign saying 'chemotherapy' happened to be by her bed. But unlike the other patients, she wasn't in the bed. She was sitting on the floor almost underneath it, her back leaning against the wall, eyes closed, clearly feeling extremely unwell. She was almost transparent. I thought that if I'd reached out to touch her, my hand would go straight through her. I was struck by the attentive looks of the nursing staff, who simply left her to do what she felt was necessary; there was no forcing her to move, to conform, to get back to where she was supposed to be. If I'd met her in a supermarket or in an office or at a party, I would have seen a different her. Maybe she would have been laughing or irritated; I might have seen her run or dance; I might have marvelled at her leadership skills or her capacity for public speaking. But this was the her I saw; a young woman sitting on a lino floor, leaning against a wall; sick, quiet, somehow just getting through this endless afternoon.

An endless afternoon is sometimes how Good Friday feels; time is suspended, the story has its own momentum, its own rhythm, and it moves inexorably towards its conclusion.

We are in the third hour. Soon we will hear the rest of the story; and before long, we will start to feel the relief of the cool linen cloths, we will remember that this body will be washed and covered, and spices brought. This balm is not far away – but it might as well be, as for that young woman in the cancer ward.

Because in this mystery of Jesus' death, we can see again the reality of our own lived experience, and the lived experience of those we share this life with.

And we know from our own experience of life that it is given to some people to suffer. There's no reason, no justification, no background logic. Sometimes we are witness, either in our own lives or someone else's, to the reality of howlingly unfair suffering.

We see it in Yemen. Children too young to understand why their stomachs bend with the pain of hunger.

We see it in Syria. Sleeping families poisoned by vicious chemicals dropped on them in the night.

For them, suffering comes unannounced, unasked for; exactly as a bomb falls from the sky, life turns in an instant.

By contrast, we have chosen to be here, chosen to draw nearer to this suffering which reminds us of our own. This liturgy weaves its way into the lived experience of our own lives and gives us a way of contemplating real life with God.

Whether we face this cross head on, or sit in front of it, or, more likely, sidle up to it, look at it out of the corner of our eye, that we have chosen to come and be here means that we have somehow, deep down, understood that it is, even in all its horror, an invitation to live differently.

While all our instincts in the modern world are to be competitive, to negotiate a better position for ourselves, and while we receive daily, hourly invitations to collaborate with unjust systems, Jesus' signposting of what God's life demands is deeply shocking.

This cross says: live by other rules. And when we try to live by other rules, we learn again that if we love, we will suffer. That grief is the price we pay for love; and the more deeply we love, the more deeply vulnerable we become. It is the paradox of a Christian life: we are asked to live as undefended as we can manage, knowing that in this undefended life, God's life is undefeated.

This undefended life is very nearly impossible for us human beings.

One of the reasons is that, as we listen to the story today, we hear that Jesus is put to death by occupying forces, a toxic combination of frightened politicians and threatened religious leaders. So it's easy to fall into self-righteousness about this – to externalize the bad people who do bad things, the collaborators, the ones who cooperate with the enemy treacherously and traitorously, the ones who betray us and let us down.

But we will have our own occupying forces that have settled and stagnated our souls. In our own lives, we can realize with a start that we are expending energy every day manning our own checkpoints, maintaining vigilance over all the interactions we might have, busily controlling and marshalling the landscape of our own hearts. A spiritual discipline is to ask yourself, by what have you been over-run? By fear or pride or need for approval or desire for oblivion? What are the occupying forces in my life? When this question becomes live for us, in the presence of the cross, we discover that we are all of the people in this story: the gambling soldiers 'just obeying orders', the collaborators with the occupying forces, the sincere, confused disciples hoping for a better world, and also the ones practising beautiful, peaceful resistance.

We know that very often our own pain isolates and numbs us; we live under occupation.

We may have had experiences like the young woman I saw this week; you may be there today – when all you want to do is sit on the floor and lean against the wall.

Part of the mystery of today is that we realize that God's pain is not isolating or numbing but a means of connection with us. And we are invited not to live under occupation but to live freely, spaciously, prophetically. God's pain is shared with my pain; and so I am safe to bring all of me, even and especially the parts of me that are inconsolable, to this cross. Where I see Love, undefended but undefeated.

16

Good Friday Three Hours

Preached at St Martin-in-the-Fields during the Three Hours devotion.

Talk 1: God made strange

> So they took Jesus; and carrying the cross by himself, he went out to what is called The Place of the Skull, which in Hebrew is called Golgotha. There they crucified him, and with him two others, one on either side, with Jesus between them. Pilate also had an inscription written and put on the cross. It read, 'Jesus of Nazareth, the King of the Jews.' Many of the Jews read this inscription, because the place where Jesus was crucified was near the city; and it was written in Hebrew, in Latin, and in Greek. Then the chief priests of the Jews said to Pilate, 'Do not write, "The King of the Jews," but, "This man said, I am King of the Jews."' Pilate answered, 'What I have written I have written.'
> (John 19.16b–22)

The temptation, of course, is to try to be eloquent: to be elegant, to find rich words, heightened language, ringing sentences. Because Good Friday is the solemn day, the catastrophic day that God died. And so the temptation is to find ways to be eloquent about it – not only from the pulpit but in the deeper recesses of our hearts. To talk to ourselves about it; to summon up the emotion we think we should feel; to go backwards and forwards with snatches of poetry, flashes of theology; to speak, to interpret, to understand, to codify. And, with Pilate, at the end of it all to be able to say to ourselves, 'What I have written,

I have written': the final sentence completing our own take on it all, our understanding of this day of days, this death of deaths. In the elegant surroundings of this church, we experience now both the beauty and horror of life in the world and the death of God. The chaos and dirt of the cross catapult themselves into our imaginations this April afternoon; perhaps then it really is, as T. S. Eliot would have us believe, the cruellest month. And perhaps counter-intuitively, those of us who habitually go to church are in the greatest danger of not being able to connect with this cross. As one commentator has put it:

> To know Christ sacramentally only in terms of bread and wine is to know him only partially, in the dining room as host and guest. (It is a valid enough knowledge, but its ultimate weakness when isolated is that it is perhaps too civil) … it begins in the soil, in the barnyard, and in the slaughterhouse – amidst strangled cries, congealing blood, and spitting fat in the pan. Table manners depend upon something's having been grabbed by the throat. A knowledge ignorant of these dark and murderous 'gestures charged with soul' is sterile rather than elegant, science rather than wisdom, artifice rather than art. It is love without passion, the Church without a cross, a house with dining room but no kitchen, a feast of frozen dinners, a heartless life.[1]

This cross then, with all its chaos and shouting, is essential for a living faith.

Or as Rowan Williams has simply put it: 'Jesus Christ, the one human being who is completely in tune with God – with what God wants and what God is doing … has let himself be betrayed and rejected, executed in a humiliating and agonising way, and yet has not turned his back on us.'[2]

The title I have given to this set of reflections is 'God Made Strange'. I hope to explore, in the presence of the cross, some aspects of this.

It may seem at first a contradiction: isn't the whole point of Jesus to *connect* us with God in a new covenanted relationship? Isn't this cross therefore about connection and, frankly, isn't the point of Jesus' coming to make God less strange; that is, in the life of Jesus, God becomes recognizable to us, one of us: Emmanuel, God with us?

Yes, of course. But in this cross, in these days, God is revealed to be utterly different from the inevitably anthropormorphized picture of God we carry around with us. I suppose one of the things that occurs to me at the foot of this cross is that what we do with Jesus' life, teaching and death is sometimes to the detriment, not the benefit, of our deeper understanding and covenanted relationship with God. But more of this later.

We begin with something more familiar: a sign written by a bureaucrat, a public notice describing a crime. 'The King of the Jews', writes Pilate, and hangs the sign on the cross.

A while ago, I spent some time with members of St James's congregation in the public gallery of the Central Criminal Court, the Old Bailey. Unless you are a barrister, a judge, a witness, on a jury or the accused, it is unlikely that you would spend time in a Crown Court, where the most serious cases are heard. What was striking, apart from the slow and deliberate pace of the criminal justice system, painstakingly going through phone records or statements about timelines, was the way in which chaotic events, violent, confused, midnight events, were described as calm, practical, logical – one thing after another. Blood and knives and burning and shouting were faint echoes in the mumbled words of the witnesses and the logic of the lawyer's questions. Did you? I did. Were you? I wasn't. Are you lying? I am not, Sir.

The charge against Jesus was the crime of blasphemy, acknowledged by the Roman authorities, whose description, John is eager to tell us, was argued over. The disagreement was ended by Pilate's famous statement, 'What I have written, I have written.'

This kind of discussion, this kind of service even, with all its words, can, if we're not careful, leave us with the impression that we have the power to name, to describe, to codify what is happening on this cross. That is the trick of this cross: an event in history, a measurable act in time, generates the illusion that we can somehow measure God in this event. We have the description of the offence, we have the Gospel writers' papyrus etchings – bound now, thanks be to God, in our own language.

And we have the words of Jesus himself, spoken from the cross, words we will hear later. And so we believe that we have the capacity to say what this is. We have formed sentences ourselves over the years: God so loved the world that he gave his only Son. Or, as St Paul had it, 'For the message of the cross is foolishness to those who are perishing, but to us who are being saved it is the power of God.' And between ourselves, we have the same discussions today as Pilate had with the religious authorities: what did he say about himself? What is it that he said? Or can we dare to define him for ourselves?

We come quickly to the realization that, for all our love of Scripture, for all our need of good theology and evocative prayers, words are completely useless at the same time as being utterly indispensable. In the book of Genesis, we humans are the ones who give things their names; we can't help ourselves, it's one of our glories and also our gilded prison. We ourselves build the walls and bars of our best and favourite sentences, those we learned from childhood or read in the latest theological publication, and we think, 'That's it.' And we're relieved and maybe a little excited: we've got it! And just when we think we've got it, we have understood our capacity for misunderstanding and the cross moves away, resolutely free from our desires and attempts to reify, reduce or explain.

I was struck by the fact that the third most Googled question of 2014 was 'What is love?' It came just above 'What is fracking?' and behind 'What is Ebola?' and 'What is Isis?' 'What is love?' is apparently the question asked by millions of people alone at their computers, maybe with some time on their hands, surfing the net. 'What is love?'

The Christian answer is: this – this is love. Churches at their best are places where the things we can't measure, the things we can't describe, are experienced, celebrated, shared. And where every person – *every person* – can be made welcome, whatever you've done, whatever mess you've got yourself into, whoever you are and whatever your questions. Because we ourselves are a mixture of the ones who go out to ask the question 'What is love?', who are focused not so much on religious practice as on the practice of compassion and love in our everyday work and home. We are the ones, too, who collude with systems that hurt rather than free, and there may be parts of ourselves that we hate, the parts of ourselves that collaborate. We know from the gospel that these are the parts given special attention and taken seriously. Our confusion is held and addressed, and the strange hope of change offered freely and without condition or coercion.

And so before this cross, like Prospero at the end of Shakespeare's *The Tempest*, we know that our powers are exposed and gone, we are rendered speechless.

Job knew this as a result of his own suffering:

Then Job answered the LORD:
   'I know that you can do all things,
and that no purpose of yours can be thwarted.
"Who is this that hides counsel without knowledge?"
Therefore I have uttered what I did not understand,
   things too wonderful for me, which I did not know.
"Hear, and I will speak;
   I will question you, and you declare to me."
I had heard of you by the hearing of the ear,
   but now my eye sees you;
therefore I despise myself,
   and repent in dust and ashes.'

Job, like Jacob wrestling, has met God; knowledge has moved from his head to his guts. Job knows God in his feet, in his travelling, in the pit of his stomach. And the path to this kind of knowledge of God is paved with the vital futility of words.

And so at the beginning, our prayer has to be, with Job, one of repentance.

With the medieval mystic Meister Eckhart, I ask God to rid me of God. This is my prayer throughout my life: *I ask God to rid me of God* in order that I will remain unaccustomed to the comfort of knowing that I know what this is. Such power to define is not mine or yours. But we will always try, because God uttered in creation, and Jesus uttered on this cross; we who are made in God's image will always want to speak at the same time as praying for all our words to be taken away.

I end with a poem written by a tortured prisoner in the Public Jail of Santiago, Chile, in July 1974:

Right there
Where the light of the sun
Lost itself
More than a century ago,
Where all gaiety is impossible
And any smile
Is a grimace of irony,
Where the stone stench of darkness
Inhabits those corners
Even the spiders have abandoned as inhospitable,
And where human pain eludes that which can be called
    human, and enters the category of the unprintable –
There I am writing.[3]

Talk 2: Let us not tear it

> When the soldiers had crucified Jesus, they took his clothes and divided them into four parts, one for each soldier. They also took his tunic; now the tunic was seamless, woven in one piece from the top. So they said to one another, 'Let us not tear it, but cast lots for it to see who will get it.' This was to fulfil what the scripture says, 'They divided my clothes among themselves, and for my clothing they cast lots.' And that is what the soldiers did. (John 19.23–25)

Jesus lived under occupation, in a militarized society. Soldiers and their demands were part of everyday life, and much of his teaching in context is directed at a people whose property could be requisitioned at a moment's notice.

Under occupation, a population has a choice to collaborate, to resist, or to ignore the situation insofar as that's possible.

Jesus demonstrated shocking compassion towards individuals caught up in the occupation. He healed the centurion's servant and he dealt too leniently, according to some of his disciples, with the hated tax collectors – Matthew and Zaccheus, for example, collaborators with the occupiers. He also had, as part of his inner circle, Judas Iscariot and Simon the Zealot – both more than likely to argue for strong if not armed resistance to their oppressors. His closest friends represented all shades of political opinion when it came to Rome.

So the soldiers administered Roman justice; and this routine execution – one crucifixion among hundreds – caused them to look for an advantage, gambling for the clothes of the condemned man.

So far, so ordinary.

Jesus, like many of his fellow countrymen, had come up against the full force of the occupation. He was arrested, handed over, and after a sham trial now hangs here, dying as much a political death as a cosmic one.

The reality of being arrested is described powerfully by the Russian writer Aleksandr Solzhenitsyn, himself arrested and imprisoned many times:

> At what point, then, should one resist? When one's belt is taken away? When one is ordered to face into a corner? When one crosses the threshold of one's home? An arrest consists of a series of incidental irrelevancies, of a multitude of things that do not matter, and there seems no point in arguing about one of them individually ... and yet all these incidental irrelevancies taken together implacably constitute the arrest.[4]

He describes the incremental ordinariness of this encounter: a series of incidental irrelevancies. There seems no point in arguing about one of them individually, he says, but in the end you find that you are bound and at the mercy of others.

Last year, I found myself in conversation with a former Head of MI5 (not, I have to say, a situatation I have often found myself in!). I was expressing sympathy, or so I thought, with the demands placed on our security services, the ones who 'stand on the wall' that we don't have to stand on, who do things in order to defend our freedom that I don't have to do, who live at the boundary of what is morally justifiable and right. He chided me for this rather too separated view of what security services are required to do on our behalf. Quoting Robert Peel, the nineteenth-century founder of the police in Britain, he insisted that the public are the security services and the security services are the public; and so we civilians simply can't absolve ourselves from the choices – about rendition, imprisonment without trial, the extent of surveillance – that are made by our elected representatives or by those whose job it is to protect us. It's not good enough for us to give even tacit permission to others to cross moral boundaries we ourselves would not want to cross. He was asking from me, a citizen, both more accountability and more support. As one character says in Wallace Shawn's play, *Aunt Dan and Lemon*:

> And if those who protect us need to hit people in the face with the butts of their rifles, or if they need perhaps even to turn around and shoot, they have our permission ... The perfectly decent person who follows a certain chain of reasoning, ever so slightly and subtly incorrect, becomes a perfect monster at the end of the chain.[5]

The 'soldiers' are not a breed apart; they are versions of us.

While all our instincts are to be competitive, to react, perhaps to negotiate or collaborate, Jesus' signposting of what God's life demands in this situation is deeply shocking: live by other rules. And when you live by other rules, you will know the truth of Psalm 22: 'I am poured out like water, and all my bones are out of joint; my heart is like wax; it is melted within my breast; my mouth is dried up like a potsherd, and my tongue sticks to my jaws; you lay me in the dust of death ... I can count all my bones.'

Who do you think are the collaborators, the despised ones, the ones like the soldiers colluding with or shoring up a system that is being exposed as oppressive? I met a woman who came to pray in our church last week. She didn't want to tell me that she worked in a hedge fund. She didn't think she would be welcome in the church. I told her she was. Just in this corner of London, what about men who go to the brothels a stone's throw from this church and don't ask whether the men or women they find there are trafficked? What about the ones who are trafficking men, women and children, with the false promise of a better life? What about the tax avoiders – the ones who seem to breathe the rarefied air above democracy or accountability? Every community has its despised ones, the ones some consider to be collaborating with the enemy.

It's so easy to be self-righteous about this – to externalize the bad people who do bad things: the collaborators, the ones who cooperate with the enemy treacherously and traitorously, the ones who betray us and let us down.

But we will have our own occupying forces that have settled and stagnated our souls. We will be manning our own check-points, vigilant over the parts of ourselves that want to be free. A spiritual discipline is to ask yourself, by what have you been over-run? By fear or pride or need for approval or desire for oblivion? What are the occupying forces in your life? If this question is addressed honestly, we discover that we are all of these people: the gambling soldiers, the collaborators with the occupying forces, the sincere confused disciples hoping for a better world, and also the ones practising beautiful resistance.

This strange God teaches playful, joyful resistance to the forces of occupation: it's what brought him to this cross, giving us the potential for setting ourselves and others free.

Talk 3: Standing near

> Meanwhile, standing near the cross of Jesus were his mother, and his mother's sister, Mary the wife of Clopas and Mary Magdalene. When Jesus saw his mother and the disciple whom he loved standing beside her, he said to his mother, 'Woman, here is your son.' Then he said to the disciple, 'Here is your mother.' And from that hour the disciple took her into his own home. (John 19.25b–27)

It's long been recognized and discussed on Good Fridays over the years that Mary and Mary Magdalene stay standing near. This is in stark contrast to the male disciples who run away: Peter denies him, Judas betrays him, all the others are either locked in a room out of fear or heading off on the journey to other places like Emmaus. The women are the ones who stay, along with John whom Jesus loved; and they are the ones who, along with Nicodemus, in a few hours will take the body down.

The actor Fiona Shaw came to our church during her recent run at the Barbican of Colm Tóibín's play *The Testament of Mary*. She performed extracts from the play and discussed the implications of Tóibín's imaginative and vivid descriptions of Mary's reaction to her 'son who could have done anything' with his 'misfit friends'. It was funny, provocative, moving; and Mary herself came alive for me in a new way, especially at the very beginning of the play when Fiona Shaw, dressed in lapis lazuli blue, was seated in a glass box on stage, there to be photographed, murmured over, stared at, less venerated than eaten alive. I found this dynamic between actor and audience disturbing and alarming – which set the tone for everything that followed. She came out of her glass box, and revealed herself to be a lively, angry, articulate woman whose son had been to her at least as much curse as blessing. She disapproved of the raising of Lazarus, was being held prisoner by unnamed apostles, but perhaps the most confronting detail of this imaginative exploration of Mary was that, in Colm Tóibín's monologue, Mary revealed that she didn't stay to the end. She stayed at the foot of the cross for some of the time, but, at some point before he died, she had to leave.

We discussed this in front of an audience and it proved a rich seam of reflection. Many of the mothers in the audience, especially some whose grown-up children had died, could relate to and understand this Mary more closely than the perhaps perfected vision of motherhood that is often found in paintings of the deposition. Could they stay to watch their child die? Some thought they could, others knew they hadn't. Tóibín's imagination may seem like an unnecessarily provocative poke at a traditional Christian interpretation of Mary and her son, but what I discovered was that it released the mothers in our audience to be bracingly truthful about the centuries-old teaching that Mary stayed, steadfast and silent; and that this teaching in itself was, alongside being an inspiration, also a crushing expectation that made many of them feel condemned. That it is possible to imagine Mary leaving before the end was, to them, compassion from a religious tradition that seemed to ask of them too much.

Standing near to this cross brings with it dangers as well as inspiration.

Because standing too near means that we can get mawkishly focused on the appalling human details of this story, and we then anthromorphize God, and domesticate God for our own often unacknowledged purposes. One writer who has been hugely influential in this area was the Jesuit priest and writer Gerry Hughes, whose recent death revived interest in his insights into Christian spirituality.

He was convinced that the picture we carry around of God affects how we believe, but also how we pray – whether we *want* to pray – and how faith 'feels', intuitively, which in turn affects the way we live. He produced a kind of 'identikit' picture of God called 'good old Uncle George', based on how, in his experience, God had been communicated to people who *had* given up on Christianity and walked away.

God was a family relative, much admired by Mum and Dad, who described him as very loving, a great friend of the family, very powerful and interested in all of us. Eventually we are taken to visit 'good old Uncle George'. He lives in a formidable mansion, is bearded, gruff, and threatening. We cannot share our parents' admiration for him. At the end of the visit, Uncle George turns to address us. 'Now listen, dear,' he begins, looking very severe, 'I want to see you here once a week, and if you fail to come, let me just show you what will happen to you.' He then leads us down to the mansion's basement. It is dark, becomes hotter and hotter as we descend, and we begin to hear unearthly screams. In the basement there are steel doors. Uncle George opens one. 'Now look in there, dear,' he says. We see a nightmare vision, an array of blazing furnaces with little demons in attendance, who hurl into the blaze those men, women, and children who failed to visit Uncle George or to act in a way he approved. 'And if you don't visit me, dear, that is where you will most certainly go,' says Uncle George. He then takes us upstairs again to meet Mum and Dad.

As we go home, tightly clutching Dad with one hand and Mum with the other, Mum leans over us and says, 'And now don't you love Uncle George with all your heart and soul, mind and strength?' And we say, 'Yes, I do,' because to say anything else would be to join the queue at the furnace. At a tender age, deep conflict has set in and we keep telling Uncle George how much we love him and how good he is and that we want to do only what pleases him. We observe what we are told are his wishes and dare not admit, even to ourselves, that we loathe him.[6]

Uncle George is a caricature, but a caricature of a truth, the truth that we often construct a God who is in fact an image of our tyrannical selves. Hellfire sermons are out of fashion at the moment, but they were in fashion a few decades ago, they're in fashion in many places in the world, and they may well come in here again. Such sermons have a great appeal to certain unhealthy types of mind, but they cause havoc with the more healthy and sensitive. The Uncle George kind of God I began with is the kind of God that many have seen in this story; the wrathful, vengeful God who needs to be appeased by a blood sacrifice to atone for all the sins of the people.

I suppose my own starting point is to be curious about this, rather than immediately dismissive. The world we live in is a world of wonder and delight, adventure and abundance. It is also the world of Auschwitz, Kigali, Nagasaki, Columbine, Passchendaele and Mount Sinjar. In the face of this depravity, the spiritual tensions are almost impossible to hold: judgement with mercy; wrath with forgiveness.

Uncle George comes from our inability – when we read Scripture, when we pray, when we think about God at all – to do anything but anthropomorphize God. Standing near to the cross, despite our best efforts, we probably imagine that, when we're dealing with God, we're dealing with someone essentially like us, only bigger. *We* know about wrath: anger, fury, violence, jealousy, the alarming and scary feelings that we have. And we imagine therefore that *God's* wrath is like that, only bigger – which makes it even more violent and more frightening.

And we end up with something like Uncle George.

But crucially, one of the most important things Christian theology wants to say about God is that God emphatically *isn't* like us only bigger. God is *unlike*: is other, free – disconcertingly so – utterly holy, completely undefended, the Creator completely given over to relationship with creation.[7]

In the story of Good Friday, the God we encounter in Jesus is God so utterly given over to the risks and vulnerability of relationship that we can hardly contemplate it, let alone understand it. And you and I know, because we're human, that this is *not* what I'm like. For us, in relationship, there's always something held back, something competitive, something defended and suspicious and afraid, which comes between me and my Maker, and me and my neighbour. From the intimacies of lovers to the geopolitics of nations, our resistance to relationship, self-givenness and vulnerability produces small and vast indifferences and multiple cruelties.

But in the light of what we know we're like, to speak of God's action in Christ as some kind of feeling that God entertains towards us is to mistake it completely. I want to suggest that Good Friday reveals something like *unimaginably deep divine dis-content* with who or what we have made ourselves. Was this sacrifice necessary? How does this express the salvation of the world? Any attempts to describe a God who demands sacrifice, even the sacrifice of what is most precious, is an attempt at language to express divine dis-ease, divine dissonance, agony, fury even, at the profligate waste and widening injustices of a violent, risk-averse and small-minded humanity which bury its gifts in the sand to hide them and keep them safe.

Our problem is that we have so often formulated God's relationship to us in the language of Uncle George that we have jettisoned the notion altogether of a God who is utterly other or resolutely strange. This leaves us much poorer spiritually; and, I want to suggest too, it leaves us with an equally damaging sort of faith – just as damaging as the Uncle George fantasy – which is what you might call a Great Aunt Oprah kind of God: an 'I'm OK, you're OK' kind of a God. This kind of God can do no more for me than stroke the bruised parts of my ego, can't help me with the damage I do to myself and others. This

God, disastrously, simply leaves me as I am – and us as we are, and it as it is …

This kind of God is just as damaging a fantasy, because this domesticated God does nothing to challenge our preference for safety over trust, for illusion over truth, and is a God we can recruit to our own programmes and prejudices instead of the God who sets us free.[8]

And so, some years, especially if we've been doing this a long time, perhaps we can, with Mary, stand near, but not so near that we mistake this for a recognizable death, and, with her, quietly slip away when it's too hard, knowing that the distance will remind us that God remains free from our need to be thought of as holy.

One last thing: the artist Mark Cazalet, when commissioned by a convent here in London to paint a set of Stations of the Cross, imagined together with the Mother Superior what Mary would have done on the evening of Good Friday. They imagined together that she would have gone to visit Judas's mother. Two women, sitting together at the end of a terrible day, remembering their sons, both dead in the service of salvation.

Talk 4: Full of sour wine

After this, when Jesus knew that all was now finished, he said (in order to fulfill the scripture), 'I am thirsty.' A jar full of sour wine was standing there. So they put a sponge full of the wine on a branch of hyssop and held it to his mouth. When Jesus had received the wine, he said, 'It is finished.' Then he bowed his head and gave up his spirit.
(John 19.28–30)

In contrast to what I said in the last address, there are of course aspects of this death that have to be the same as all deaths in order for the defeat of death to be real for us. Because I thought I should, not really because I wanted to, I went to see Mel Gibson's *The Passion of The Christ* when it came out in the cinema. It was by far the most violent film I have ever sat through, and I was sickened as many were. But actually, as a Christian, my overwhelming reaction wasn't so much that Jesus endured all that suffering for me, but rather that this is happening now in corners of the world, under oppressive regimes and unjust systems, where everything is inverted, where the collective fantasy of a society has deemed good evil and evil good.

A danger we should surely avoid on this day is, by way of dealing with our own squeamishness, to make it so special to Jesus, or something that happens 'over there' or 'long ago', that we forget to look at today's atrocities. Torture like this flogging and crucifixion is part of the apparatus of modern societies as much as it was of medieval ones. And the practice of such violence and torture is framed by a fundamental set of assumptions about how we live together, to whom we belong, what kind of society we imagine, and where we find our own place in it.

There are characteristics in this story of Jesus that are recognizable across centuries of abusive political behaviour from the world of Hilary Mantel's *Wolf Hall* onwards. There is an urgency and tempo involved in the questioning and answering demanded of the victim. A manufactured energy; where women and men are dragged around cells by their hair; where electric wires are attached to feet, to head, to genitals; where confessions are forced under threat of the murder, not of the victims themselves but of their children or mothers or fathers. Torturers combine a sense of urgency with an unhurried assurance that this could go on for ever. We saw this paradoxical and torturous use of time in the false deadlines set by ISIS: deadlines for the execution of hostages. Manufactured urgency combined with a horrifying assertion that they have all the time in the world. This pain will never, ever end.

A powerful book by the theologian William Cavanaugh draws a contrast between the human practice of torture and the Church's liturgical life. In *Torture and Eucharist*[9] he sets out the vocation of the Church as a body of people who can resist not only torture itself but all the depravity and abuse it represents, by contemplating Christ on the cross, as we do on this day.

Torture is an 'anti-liturgy'.[10] It is often ritualistic, repetitive, timed. It is a liturgy of fear and hatred, of dehumanizing another. It is a complete fantasy of omnipotence on the part of the state in question, which both takes and gives life; the walls of the torture chamber, both physical and mental, are built and maintained by the torturer. Control is complete. The alpha and omega of pain. A world is created where torture seems almost reasonable, justifiable, understandable in the face of the threat. William Cavanaugh explains:

> Here the torturer stands in as the vicar of the state, the pre-sider at the manifestation of the state's awesome power. Torture is an efficacious sign by which the state enacts its power over its subjects' bodies in purest form.[11]

Pain is the great isolator: in mental or physical or spiritual pain, we are in a crevasse of grief, numb, dulled. Sheila Cassidy, the English doctor who was tortured in Chile, writes of her time: 'It was as though I was suspended over a pit; the past had no relevance, and I could see no future. I lived only for the minute that was, and in the fear of further pain.'[12] She goes on to say elsewhere that in this torture and death of Jesus, as with other people she has known, there is 'a terrible agony in watching someone hollowed out with a knife even if the end result is a an instrument on which is played the music of the universe'.[13]

The meaning of this death, this execution, this crucifixion will always be a mystery to those of us who draw near to it. We can have theories and theologies, suspicions and scepticisms, but in the end we have a body, a story of gentleness betrayed by fear, of love given over to destruction. And we see the fire of love and forgiveness, the iron will of peace-making, destroyed by the forces of fear and death. Today, God dies with a cry of abandonment and no hint of Easter promise; there is sicken-ing violence and hopelessness. This is the real experience of people today. If torture is an anti-liturgy, a sick ritual, then the Eucharist is a liturgy that acknowledges and confronts this sickness and subverts it. 'The cup of blessing that we bless, is it not a sharing of the blood of Christ; the bread which we break, is it not a sharing of the body of Christ?' asks St Paul.

The persistence of contemporary injustice is confronted head-on in the Eucharist where all are fed, where the cup of suffering is acknowledged and shared, and where all, *all* are welcomed and celebrated as part of the precious creation made good by God. So, contrary to the isolation that torturers wish to inflict on their victims, the Christian economy of pain makes the bizarre claim that it can be shared;[14] that we, in this cross, share in the pain of the world now, and that in the Eucharist, which we will not celebrate again until Easter Day, we share in the new future that this death brings.

This makes visible the suffering of people made in God's image – all people, now, today, in cells and torture chambers around the world. And it defies the claim of any human state to define what is right or wrong, what is true or false, what is beautiful or ugly.

But it doesn't have to be the pain of torture that is somehow contained in this cross. Old griefs, losses as yet unnamed, incalculable sadnesses we carry or bury – all of our human experience of loss can be brought here, and sat with, and honoured and inhabited. One Good Friday I found myself listening to a preacher who asked us all to think about the cross we wore around our neck, if we had one. What was its story, how long had we worn it? As I remembered the story of the cross I wear, I found myself suddenly inconsolable: I was taken back to the jewellers' shop and the laughing we did as I bought the cross for a young man for his twenty-first birthday, and then the incomprehensibility of having it removed from his body after he was killed in a climbing accident just 18 months later. What is the story of the cross you wear? It will have a story, a history, a meaning that is, at one level, impossible to share.

So part of our spiritual tasks on Good Friday, alongside asking for the courage to face the horrendous events of a violent world, both then and now, is also to dare to get to know the uncomforted parts of ourselves: Jeremiah's Rachel inside you who still weeps inconsolably. Our inconsolable selves will be so for as many reasons as there are people; but, today, we are given a moment to acknowledge the losses we live with, the losses we normally suppress in a daily routine that rarely has room for this kind of time.

This crucifixion pain of God's is, unfathomably, capable of being shared with us. The strangeness of this is plain in a life where we know, deep within ourselves, that our pain isolates and numbs us. God's pain is opposite to this. It is shared; and it somehow becomes eternally present in the inconsolable self I bring to this cross.

Talk 5: A new tomb

> After these things, Joseph of Arimathea, who was a disciple of Jesus, though a secret one because of his fear of the Jews, asked Pilate to let him take away the body of Jesus. Pilate gave him permission; so he came and removed his body. Nicodemus, who had at first come to Jesus by night, also came, bringing a mixture of myrrh and aloes, weighing about a hundred pounds. They took the body of Jesus and wrapped it with the spices in linen cloths, according to the burial custom of the Jews. Now there was a garden in the place where he was crucified, and in the garden there was a new tomb in which no one had ever been laid. And so, because it was the Jewish day of Preparation, and the tomb was nearby, they laid Jesus there. (John 19.38–42)

A woman visits the grave of a young man the day after the funeral. The ground hasn't quite settled; the headstone, although the quotations have been hastily chosen in the days since he died, is not yet carved and up – and so a makeshift wooden cross has been put in the ground to mark where his head is.

Where his head is is deep underground now. She can't believe that this has happened and can't bear to think of his body, the body she knew well, under the ground, so far down – so far down she wants to dig it up and hold it. She can still feel the fleshy part of the base of his thumb as he held her hand. But now she looks at the earth, muddy in the September chill, and involuntarily falls forward, putting her hands out to save her-self, planting them in the mud. This is the closest she will be to him for ever now, for however long she lives. Only a matter of feet, but solid mud, through which she can no longer make her-self heard. She drowns every night in that mud in the dreams that won't let her rest. She is with him, hammering to get out of the coffin lid that is resolutely and irrevocably closed. How did this happen, this curiosity called death, the sudden stilling of limbs that ran so fast, that hugged so tight. The mud is cold and strangely comforting in its inert sludge. From the choking heat of her head, from her hot tears, the blank, dull, cold mud is a relief, even a balm, even a moment of rest. A new tomb.

Although it may feel ordinary to those who are familiar with it, what we are doing in church here today is unusual, and more unusual in contemporary society than arguably it has ever been. We have been here together in silence. Together, alone. We have had things to look at if we keep our eyes open; the light from the windows, the building itself, the confronting cross; we have things to read on the order of service, but a good part of our time together is silent. We trust one another not to break it or disrupt it: we guard it for one another; it is a gift we can give to our neighbour, to help create the space for whatever is going on in there to be free.

Silence is these days counter-cultural. We fill the gaps, worried what will happen if we stop talking. We put the radio on in the car, in the kitchen; we put the TV on, choose the music to the soundtrack of our lives. Because silence is dangerous. Not least because deep down inside it evokes in us our fear of the final complete silence: the silence of our own death.

There are different kinds of silence. There are anxious, awkward, bemused silences, and there is the silence of grief, when all you want to hear is the voice of the one who is gone. Silence can be a weapon, a disaster, a withholding of your consent.

But there is a silence that holds us, that we guard, the silence that is the home of words and the home of music. A silence inside that's expressed by physical silence and is a relief.

This silence, if we can find time to seek it in a busy life, guards the fire inside us. The painter Vincent Van Gogh wrote beautifully about this: 'There may be a great fire in our soul, yet no one ever comes to warm themselves at it, and the passers-by only see a wisp of smoke coming through the chimney, and go along their way.'[15]

He puts it so well: there is a great fire in our soul, but most people see a wisp of smoke coming out of the chimney.

Silence guards the fire.

Of course words are important, not least for the reasons I mentioned earlier: they are ways in which we can name injustices, express love or anger, make connections with others, try to say what we mean. But the power of silence is deeper than these words; and silence after words is different from silence after music; qualities of silence are sometimes so palpable we can touch them.

Spending time in silence is like learning to live in a different element: learning to breathe under water. Somehow we dive down to touch the bottom of the ocean that is made of our experience, our tears, our memory.

At the end of it all, Jesus is laid in a new tomb. A tomb unlike any before or since. A tomb that, yes, confines, but is ultimately not stony enough to contain the exuberant bursting out that is surely coming if we wait long enough.

That's another paradox of this story, of this silent cross: even while he is pinned, disabled physically by the method of execution, any encounter with the Gospels finds in Jesus, even in this person conquered, a God who is free. Even on this cross, Jesus is free; and the physical horror of the spectacle almost means that it is not possible to degrade him any more than this. People have died before and since in greater pain than this and in more horrible ways than this – but the point of this death is that it is this life, a life lived freely, a life made up of the energy and delight of God, bringing peace and forgiveness to a violent world, that is ended in this way. This is what God does in the world today. God dies with those who are slaughtered, weeps with those who weep. God is shamed with those who are shamed; God is destroyed with those who are destroyed.

And in this, we know that when isolation and shame are at their most profound, that is the very moment when God is close with you in the mess. At the moment when you have no idea what to say, what to pray – even whether you want to have anything to do with such a God – God is not elsewhere. God is here.

It's not easy to stay. It's easier to leave. Although when you've left, walking down the road, glad to have got out, you might feel like you really wanted to stay.

But 'staying' sounds as though all the effort is with us; it sounds exhausting. We might feel that concentration is the thing; we want to concentrate, but then we feel bad or worried when our attention wanders. But that's not the kind of staying that this is; or at least, I want to suggest, it's not what it should be.

This 'staying' here with the cross is not a concentration marathon for us, making such an effort to look at it; it is for us *to allow ourselves to be contemplated by the cross itself.*

We don't sit here contemplating the cross, although we think that's what we've been doing.

The cross contemplates us.

The movement of God from free-spirited rampager through the universe, the brooding, whirling, utterly generative Spirit of God, capable in our imagination of spraying atoms and planets, roaring through dark matter – this awesome presence underpinning the universe – has been confined, reduced, captured, nailed. The confinement of this overwhelming, vivid God to these nails, to this stuck, pinned, futile place, makes no sense at all.

It is unalterably strange to us. And it is scandalous to any right-thinking person.

It makes no sense if ... I like my religion neat, affirming all that I already think or do or am. It makes no sense if I want a God in control of all the events in my and everyone else's life.

It makes no sense if I want a God who is non-threatening and nice, which I would never admit that I do, but is absolutely the case. Or a God who is easy to believe in when I want to.

If I want faith to be essentially a mechanism to shore up what I already think or feel about life, then this faith is not for me. This cross is not for me if I want a spirituality I've chosen, with all the bits I like from a variety of traditions which becomes unchallengeable in my head because it is self-referential and self-absorbed. If that's what I want, then this cross is not for me. If what I am looking for is a set of beliefs and values that will make me feel that I'm basically right, then what I should do now is walk away into Trafalgar Square, take a breath of fresh air and be relieved that I've left it all behind.

This cross makes no sense if what I'm really looking for is a spirituality that offers a series of fantasies, laced with avoidance.

But it makes all kinds of sense if you are a human being living in the real world, if you are a human being who knows that bodies will fail today in hospitals before their relatives can get there to comfort them; who knows that 150 young Kenyans were slaughtered yesterday over a terrifying 13-hour siege in a place where they were learning to teach; in a world where hundreds of Muslims are given shelter by a priest in the Central African Republic under threat from machete-wielding so-called Christian militia; in a world where that same priest refuses to leave even when he is threatened with being burned alive.

This cross only makes any kind of sense if our spirituality is realistic, if we resist the formation of our best fantasies about ourselves and others; it makes sense in our recognition that our own cruelty is ours, that sometimes we are merciless, to ourselves, to people we love, or to the ones we might (despite our best efforts) secretly despise.

This cross *contemplates us* with God's evident and irreducible refusal to dominate or force, with the saving – yes, saving – presence of God choosing to be destroyed by the forces of death, risking the completeness of that destruction. This emptying of God's self into the world is an act of finishedness. An intervention in time of eternity.

And the cross asks us questions when we are open to its contemplative fire. Being contemplated by this cross is deeply confronting – and one of our responses is to throw up our hands and say something like, 'Well, I don't want to be made to feel bad about myself. I'm not responsible for all the sadness in the world. If Jesus died for me, I didn't ask him to.'

If we have all these perfectly understandable thoughts jumbled up in response to this cross, the cross simply remains silently contemplating us, inviting us to stop talking, admit our need, accept our confusion and let go of our desire to explain what's happening.

We're not asked to decide or define. But we are asked to stay, and be seen, and be forgiven, and be drenched with grace and love. So if we are to stay, and be willing to have all our assumptions about life and faith overturned, we might hear something in the words of Rowan Williams:

It is the intractable strangeness of the ground of belief that must constantly be allowed to challenge the fixed assumptions of religiosity; it is a given whose question to each succeeding age is fundamentally one and the same. And the greatness of the great Christian saints lies in their readiness to be questioned, judged, stripped naked and left speechless by that which lies at the centre of faith.[16]

And so we have been together in front of this intractably strange cross, daring to ask to be contemplated by it, daring to stay and listen, and daring to ask to be changed.

I end with a poem written by Eric Fried:

It is madness
Says reason

It is what it is
Says love

It is unhappiness
Says caution

It is nothing but pain
Says fear

It has no future
Says insight

It is what it is
Says love

It is ridiculous
Says pride
It is foolish
Says caution
It is impossible
Says experience

It is what it is
Says love.[17]

Notes

1 A. Kavanagh, 1978, *The Shape of Baptism: The Rite of Christian Initiation*, New York: Pueblo.

2 http://rowanwilliams.archbishopofcanterbury.org/pages/chris tianity.html.

3 Quoted in S. Cassidy, 1991, *Good Friday People*, London: Dartton, Longman and Todd.

4 A. Solzhenitsyn, 1974, *The Gulag Archipelago 1918–1956*, New York: HarperCollins.

5 W. Shawn, 1994, *Aunt Dan and Lemon*, New York: Grove Press.

6 G. Hughes, 1985, *God of Surprises*, London: Darton, Longman and Todd.

7 I am grateful to the Revd Dr Carole Irwin for discussion of the ideas in this talk.

8 Again I would like to acknowledge the helpful contribution of the Revd Dr Carole Irwin, especially a sermon she preached at Easter 2016.

9 W. T. Cavanaugh, 1988, *Torture and Eucharist*, Oxford: Blackwell.

10 Cavanaugh, *Torture and Eucharist*, p. 30.

11 Cavanaugh, *Torture and Eucharist*, p. 34.

12 S. Cassidy, 1977, *Audacity to Believe*, London: Darton, Longman and Todd, p. 198.

13 Cassidy, p. 5.

14 Cavanaugh, *Torture and Eucharist*, pp. 280ff.

15 Letter from Vincent Van Gogh to Theo Van Gogh held in the Vincent Van Gogh museum, Amsterdam, category number Letter 155.

16 R. Williams, 1990, *The Wound of Knowledge*, London: Darton, Longman and Todd, p. 1.

17 E. Fried, *Love Poems*, new revised edition 2011. A bilingual edition of a selection of poems from *Liebesgedichte* (1979) and *Es ist was es ist* (1983), translated by Stuart Hood, London: Alma Classics Ltd.

17

Easter Day

Preached, unusually, from the pulpit of St James's Piccadilly, rather than the lectern.

John 20.1–18

Today I'm speaking from the pulpit – not so much to be up high – although the preacher being seen and heard was a key aim of the architect of this church, Christopher Wren. Regular attenders at St James's will know preachers normally speak from the lectern.

I'm here because pulpits don't only exist in churches. A pulpit on a boat is the space right at the front from which you lean out as far as you can in order to drop the anchor more deeply.

As we wonder together about the astonishing mystery of the resurrection, perhaps I can offer some words while we together lean out as far as we can into the ocean of faith in order to try to help ourselves drop an anchor more deeply into the mystery of this day. And while we know, too, that as we proclaim Christ risen from the dead there is terrible news of our fellow Christians being killed as they gathered for Easter in Sri Lanka. We pray for them today as we know we are bound to them by our baptism. Because, however you believe it or express it, this Holy Week, culminating in today, is at the very heart of what it means to be a Christian. We say today in time what is eternally true. That Christ lives, that the stretching, tense, violent days of this week are followed by this new day, new life, new joy, new peace.

So where to begin?

Perhaps a good place to begin is a very ordinary story from yesterday.

Yesterday I took my spaniel for a walk around central

London. Because of the Extinction Rebellion camps at Marble Arch and Oxford Circus, we were able to walk through Hyde Park, down the middle of Oxford Street and Regent Street, and home again. No traffic. Empty roads.

Our church supports Extinction Rebellion: although we can't expect everyone to agree with the methods of the movement, the issue itself is one that all commentators accept as urgent and vital.

But it's not that specific issue that I want to offer as a reflection on resurrection; it was simply the experience of walking around the same streets, the same environment, with the same buildings as I have done hundreds of times before, but the experience being utterly different. A familiar landscape completely transformed.

The infrastructure and street furniture was all still there. Traffic lights moved from green to amber to red still; the red and green figures still told me when to cross the road even though there were no cars. On the pavement, instructions remained: Look Left, Look Right, Look Both Ways. All redundant.

The air was fresher, the atmosphere quieter.

I noticed different things. With no double-decker buses on the street, I had a clear view of the Barbara Hepworth sculpture on the outside of the John Lewis store on Oxford Street. I listened differently too: the loud R'n'B music from fashion stores was no longer competing with the noise of traffic and so seemed a constant accompaniment, blasting its beat out into the quiet street. Even with all the crowds still shopping down Oxford Street, I could hear one cyclist whistling.

What's the link with resurrection? Well, it's to try to resist the obvious and often easier way of thinking about resurrection as a happy ending to a sad story. Resurrection is not a happily-ever-after ending to a story full of woe.

Resurrection performs a fundamental reordering of all our assumptions about what life is, what death is, and what living in the world is like.

The point I'm making is that living in the light of the resurrection is like having your whole inner spiritual environment reordered, like being able to walk down the middle of Regent Street on an ordinary working day. Familiar landmarks of life are bathed in a different light; signposts for living, old instructions and rules are no longer needed.

Living in the light of resurrection means continuing the journey of living in such a way that I become at peace with my own death. I am invited to pray every day that I might live in the light of eternity, which invites me to live a less self-serving life, less focused on my own preservation.

Living in the light of resurrection means I see all other living things in the perspective of eternal oneness, and I start to behave accordingly.

Living in the light of resurrection, I am asked to accept, deeply and profoundly, in the manner of Peter, Judas, Mary, Thomas, and other disciples whose encounter with the risen Christ was transformative, that there are some things that will not be mended this side of eternity, but that eternity is the context for that mending.

None of this should make us complacent. None of this should make us superficially happy. But it will call me to a deeply truthful and connected life, acutely aware of all my recurring and depressingly repetitive shortcomings and damaging tendencies, but equally aware that I live in a resurrection cycle of repentance and forgiveness and starting again.

Living in the light of resurrection means I am invited in my everyday life to listen more closely as Mary Magdalene did for the calling of my own name, to become free as she did; not to cling so closely to the old heroes or ideas I thought would save me, but instead to be freed to speak out good news to whoever might listen. And love without ceasing all those who won't.

The resurrection gospel is that women came to the garden where Jesus was buried to anoint his body. They were expecting to tend to the body of a martyr. They came looking for their dead hero so they could mourn and commemorate. And they found they were looking for salvation in the wrong place, the place of the dead. Because he was not there.

And the intimate conversation in a garden in the early morning, with an exhausted Mary Magdalene not at all clear who she is speaking to, isn't a kind of Narnia fairy-story faith, accessible only out the back of some kind of Christian-only wardrobe full of Christian-only clothes.

This gospel is profound revelation about all life and all death. It is at once mysterious, disturbing, a bit frightening and, after the example of the disciples, not necessarily initially welcome. But nonetheless a deep revelation of the eternal unity which is at the heart of all creation.

The risen cosmic Christ isn't just re-appearing as his old self to carry on because there was more to do. The presence of the risen cosmic Christ in creation, then as now, transforms the entire human story that precedes it.

Resurrection is deeply confronting. I am confronted with the question: can I now see the depth of my resistance to the truth of living like this? To the truth of God? Can I see now the depth of my resistance to astonishing indestructible life? Can I see how far I took it?

Like walking through empty streets built for traffic, I see suddenly more clearly the infrastructure needed to make that traffic move.

Resurrection energy clears the streets of our inner landscape and we become painfully aware of how deeply we have convinced ourselves of the necessity of, for example, retribution; how complete the brittle spiritual scaffolding and infrastructure which gives me temporary reassurance that I'm right and you're wrong and it's clear that injustice is, well, inevitable.

Resurrection life is a strange disruptive energy. It's what there is the other side of nothing. All this has nothing whatever to do with how we're feeling or what our particular circumstances are or what our insides are doing at the time. Saying 'Christ is risen' is not about making us feel better, or making us worry if we don't.

Inasmuch as it's hard to look at the cross, and we may walk round it, give it sidelong glances, bring ourselves eventually to take a look at that instrument of torture, it's often equally hard to look into the tomb and find it empty. We shouldn't kid ourselves it's always easy. We get all the clues from Mary Magdalene and the other disciples: resurrection is disruptive, energizing, alarming; it confronts us with deep challenges about how we are to live in the light of it.

Do we construct our own tomb-like lives, safe, a bit gloomy, under par, not really daring to live from the joy of being alive in the world? Of course we do. We like the stone that's rolled over the entrance; it's strong, we can lean up against it, it means that not too much will be asked of us. It means that we can always say we didn't hear properly, we couldn't get up and do that, we had to stay put.

Resurrection is a disrupter in spiritual life, for an individual and for a community. As resurrection people we're asked to live together, to build our relationships with one another as people who lean not against the stone that helps us feel safe but into the much less safe mystery of resurrection.

The ways that we believe in the resurrection are a bit like the variety of ways in which we can join in singing the Hallelujah Chorus, as the whole congregation is invited to do at the end of this service. For some, theological doctrine is a detailed matter, like understanding every note and musical direction on the score of the Hallelujah Chorus. But not knowing how to read that music shouldn't stop anyone else from joining in. Even if you're not sure, or think you can't sing in tune, of course you can. Lean in and raise your beautiful voice. Just join the song. Or of course, if you wish, listen, and enjoy the sound and harmony of resurrection music all around you.

Like the different ways in which we will join in this music at the end of the service, so we circle around the melody and miracle of resurrection. A beautiful melody we're invited to sing in a fractious, violent and dissonant world.

And so I end with an interpretation of the famous saying by the fourteenth-century mystic Julian of Norwich: 'All shall be well and all shall be well and all manner of thing shall be well.'

This is good advice, but it can sound too trite if things are simply not well with you today, if you are going through a tough time. So let's take Julian of Norwich's assurance on further in the light of resurrection life, which will always reorder our priorities from the perspective of eternity.

The joy of Easter Day tells us, yes, all shall be well in the end.

But it also tells us today that, if with you it is really not well, then what that means is that it is not yet the end.

18

Easter 5

Preached in 2021 when the gradual lifting of Covid-19 restrictions was being cautiously envisaged.

Acts 8.26–40

The questions our society is facing now are complex. The phrase we're hearing a lot on the news at the moment is that society is 'opening up' again. In the UK, this is generally being used to mean that we can move about again more freely, we could share a meal with friends in a house, we could meet for a coffee inside a café and not on the street.

Meanwhile the catastrophe unfolds in India, reaching 400,000 new infections of the virus in 24 hours, the highest in the world.

Yet again, the uneven impact of this truly global pandemic exposes the endemic injustices and inequalities between peoples and nations. It's easy to feel helpless in the face of these enormous, appalling world problems.

Last night I took part in the Liberal Judaism UK national conference on an interfaith panel addressing the question, 'What is religion in a post-Covid world?' Together with Muslim, Sikh and Jewish contributors we spoke about the mental health challenges, the polarization of religious and political views, and how we all passionately wanted to challenge this polarization every day in everything we did; and the greater cooperation needed between religions, going beyond dialogue to speak together about the importance of religious practice in a world where inequality is so stark and so many suffer as a result.

On the same day, our asylum and refugee support worker sent me a fantastic picture of a member of our PCC (our church council), herself someone who has recently been granted asylum here in the UK. She is pictured in a powerful image raising her voice on a protest for the rights of people seeking asylum with a rainbow flag beside her and the placard 'No Sister is Illegal'. This picture was accompanying an online article outlining, among other things, the ways in which the UK, its self-described hostile environment and immigration policies, are de-humanizing human beings who endure the presumption on arrival in the UK that they will not be believed.

And I had a lively conversation this week with one man who has been sleeping on London's streets for many years. Frustrated with outreach workers who he says promise much but are never quite able to help in the way he wants, he told me a story of a well-meaning worker approaching his tent one evening as he was bedding down for the night. He pretended to be asleep but the person persisted.

'What's your name?' she asked.

'What's yours first?' he replied.

'What's your name?' she repeated. 'For our records.'

'OK,' he said 'my name is Dweller.'

Dweller, she wrote down. 'Is that your first name or your second name?'

'My second name,' he said. 'My first name is Tent. Now go away.'

Our conversation ended with an incredibly thoughtful question from him directly to me as a priest. We've just celebrated Easter, he reminded me. Assuming that Jesus and Judas were both necessary for the salvation of humankind, what did I think of this: Jesus suffered on the cross for a short time and is now worshipped in all eternity. Judas received a small amount of money which he didn't have time to spend, and is now damned for all eternity. In the service of salvation, who has made the greater sacrifice?

This question isn't the purpose of this sermon, although it will certainly be the purpose of another one ... But I'm telling this story as a way of describing the curiosity and energy, the agency to retain power and humour in the face of a seemingly faceless state bureaucracy, and the lively curiosity about faith, that this man showed. It has stayed with me since we spoke.

Our bureaucracies, local and national government have all

become more prominent and powerful in terms of addressing the challenges of the pandemic, taking to themselves powers that are usually only taken in wartime. The restrictions on our freedom of movement, our behaviour, our ability to connect even with our closest family have been legally enforced, not just voluntary. In democratic systems, governments of all political persuasions have found themselves more intrusive, more prominent as this virus took hold.

And now, we are starting to think about what life might be like again without that intrusion, without that restriction.

What is religion in a post-Covid world?

Into this question comes the scripture for today.

The most powerful figure in today's first reading is travelling from Jerusalem back to Ethiopia, a journey of some 1,500 miles. A bureaucrat with great power, in charge of the treasury of the Candace – not a name in itself but the title of a female monarch governing alone – this Ethiopian official carries great authority. Riding in a carriage large enough for him to read scrolls of Scripture himself, and then to admit Philip the deacon and for them to study them together, wealthy enough to employ a driver for the carriage, we can assume this is someone of high status and influence in the kingdom known as Kush. This is someone who operates from the centre of power, from the city of Meroe, known as a place of great influence and great wealth. This Ethiopian leader doesn't know that the seemingly unassailable power of this kingdom doesn't last for ever. In another 300 years it will have declined, and at about the same time, less than 400 years after Christ, Ethiopia will become Christian. For now, though, this Ethiopian is at the top of the governmental tree.

The Greek word used to describe this Ethiopian is *eunouchos*, translated into the English word eunuch. But *eunouchos* embraces a number of different sexual identities that would now be described as Queer. And documented contemporary accounts list the ways in which a *eunouchos*, whatever political or economic power they would have held, would have experienced discrimination and rejection, especially within a religious context – something well known and recognized by people who today identify as lesbian, gay, trans, bisexual, intersex, queer.

This encounter between Philip – not the Philip who was a disciple of Jesus but another Philip who was appointed a deacon of the early Christian community – is often preached in such a way that it puts Philip in charge of events, albeit prompted by the Spirit. In this interpretation it is Philip who actively converts the Ethiopian, which in itself has been used as an image of colonization rather than inclusion. And some artistic depictions of this scene are simply racist, portraying the one baptized with exaggerated features or as a child.

But a close reading of the biblical story shows something quite different.

The initiative is, at all times, with the treasury official who is already reading the Scriptures when we meet him. It is he who decides to admit Philip when Philip, prompted by the Holy Spirit, runs up to the carriage and runs alongside. Once he is inside, the Scriptures are discussed between the two of them.

We're told that it is the prophet Isaiah that is the text in question. I wonder if, as part of the discussion, Philip explains not only the importance of Jesus who has just died and risen from the dead, but a further chapter in Isaiah, a little later on from the chapter under discussion, which reads:

For thus says the LORD:
To the eunuchs who keep my sabbaths,
    who choose the things that please me
    and hold fast my covenant,
I will give, in my house and within my walls,
    a monument and a name
    better than sons and daughters ...
(Isaiah 56.4–5)

Before any contemporary church gets smug about its commitment to inclusion, the Hebrew Scriptures are often there before us.

It's not Philip who suggests baptism. The Ethiopian asks a question still asked today by many who feel the Church is not interested in them: 'Look, here is water! What is to prevent me from being baptised?' (Acts 8.36). The carriage is stopped at the Ethiopian's order and they both get out. Unlike some of his contemporaries, Philip shows no interest in enforcing any exclusion of this person on the grounds of his sexual identity or ethnicity; we never find out if the Ethiopian is Jewish or Gentile, but baptized he is and he takes a step into his new future.

In the Ethiopian church, this official is named as Quinaquis. And in contemporary theology he is often celebrated as a trans saint, a visible Queer presence in the Bible as one with authority, sent out to preach the good news to others.

The promise of Isaiah comes to fruition in the memory of Quinaquis's story, a monument and a name, in Isaiah's words, for this authoritative, energetic and curious person who read and discussed the Scriptures and took life-changing action as a result.

Jesus' words in John's Gospel are equally vivid: they rest in the invitation to you and me to abide. Not just to turn up or to stay around or to hang about, but to abide. To connect with the divine presence here and now: to know ourselves, root and branch, immersed in God in whom we live and move and have our being.

I love this word 'abide'. It can also be translated as 'dwell'. Somehow it's much more than to exist or even to live. It is an invitation to deep connection, to rest, to return to the source, to know ourselves never alone.

In these days, there is so much to be concerned about, there is so much distraction and fretful planning going on amid great uncertainty for the reopening of society and the re-establishment of movement and activity.

At this very moment, we are given the gift of this energized and active Quinaquis from Ethiopia as our example and guide.

And we are invited ourselves into the centring, purpose-filled existence infused by love that we call abiding in Christ.

Know yourselves to be part of all that is, to be part of a much bigger story that holds you and deepens your spirit.

What is religion in a post-Covid world? For Christianity's part, may we be a community eager to study the Scriptures and discuss their meaning, from the wealthiest business person or court official to the poorest person who sleeps on the street. And a community of people who know ourselves to be connected deeply with one another, abiding ultimately in God.

And may we see each other, in Rowan Williams's phrase, as someone from whom God cannot bear to be parted.

May we strive to be such a community as we emerge, blinking in not a little confusion as to what should happen next, bruised from the isolation and separation that has saved lives, not sure of the balance between going back to what was before with relief or making necessary change for a world changed for ever.

May I invite you to know yourselves as ones who abide in Christ, to find rest there in these fractious days, and to know that you, as you are, are utterly known by God. And that with Quinaquis you are given a monument and a name as a precious human being grafted into the story and presence of God. A presence that holds us, nourishes us and asks us to grow.

19

Easter 6

John 15.1–15

As a way into this sermon, please, if you can, I'd like you now to think of someone you love.

Think of their face. Their voice. What are they like? What kind of personality do they have? What kind of things do they say?

For some of you that might have been pretty straightforward. You thought of the person that you thought you should have thought of. All clear. All fine. That's the person. The obvious person. And if I asked you to say who it was out loud, you wouldn't mind other people knowing.

For others of you, you may not have been able to think of anyone. Followed by a crashing sense of anxiety that you weren't able to think of anyone.

For some of you, you thought of someone you have lost – and it's made you so sad you can't really concentrate on what I'm saying right now. For others of you, you thought of someone who doesn't know you love them – someone you think you probably shouldn't love – but who you know, if you're honest, that actually you do.

For some of you, you thought of one of your children. Then the others. Or your grandchildren. For others of you, you didn't think of your children. Any of these might have caused you a bit of a stir.

Love is a word that's said a lot in church. And it's part of our regular vocabulary quite a lot of the rest of the week too.

Love.

It's something we think we agree on. We know what it is, and we're supposed to be something of an expert if we say we are Christian, because it's the thing that Jesus talked a lot about. As he did in today's gospel.

'Love one another,' he said.

The easiest sermon in the world to preach would be one where I explore the love that Jesus is talking about, then list all the ways in which you and I don't live up to it; I would talk especially about the shortcomings of the Church, and then say, with a bit of a liturgical shrug – well it's all very difficult … but … come on folks – let's do our best. Let's not give ourselves a hard time about this. Love is hard – and, you know, who knows what it is anyway.

This would be the easiest sermon to preach. I could illustrate it with stories of how hard it is to love, and how we angst about it, and remind us of the stories in the Bible about loving and how God loves us but how hard it is for us to love properly, and how none of the disciples really got it.

But I don't feel like preaching that sermon. I feel that if I preached that sermon, I would, even more than in other topics, be really searching for a way to avoid talking about real life.

Because in talking about love, the biggest danger is falling into draining clichés. I'm really going to try not to avoid telling some truth about love.

It's a commonplace to say that the ways in which our contemporary society talks about love are pretty narrow. We have narrowed love to mean a set of feelings that are most evident in a short period of romantic sentiment, which gets reduced, especially in film and TV, to a formulaic exchange. It builds up to one individual saying to another individual, 'I love you.' And an expectation of the reply, 'I love you too.' It's a modern liturgy – perhaps like saying, 'The Lord be with you' – 'And also with you'. 'I love you' – 'I love you too'.

This exchange is, of course, when it's meant, absolutely beautiful.

But, given the ubiquitous and complex ways of loving, it's important to acknowledge too that it's a restricted definition of love and what love is. Therefore, for the purposes of this sermon, I want to acknowledge its beauty and set it aside.

If Jesus had carried a banner around with him, or had been someone with a catchphrase, it would arguably have said 'Love one another'. He told people to do it; he seemed to be living it. And yet, as far as we know, he didn't go in for that one-to-one romantic exchange, 'I love you' – 'I love you too'.

In contemporary conversations about love, there is often much discussion of the agency of an individual. It's often said that we have a right to love. It's a key aspect, for example, of LGBTQ+ campaigning. You can't help who you fall in love with. Of course this is true. Love is love, whoever you fall for. And we in the Church should get behind this if love is, as we say, important to us.

But the love that is characteristic of Christian faith isn't quite so much focused on choosing and claiming this right to love, however that might be helpful when times have been hard. Human beings are very often not, despite the yearning of the poets, masters of our own destiny and captains of our fate. We are subject to the immensely complex dynamics and desires of others, their exercise of power, their own ability to love. And we are subject to the vagaries of our own bodies and their desires, strengths, vulnerabilities and obsessions. We are often, too, at the mercy of uninvited dreams and thoughts of the night. So much of our life is frankly 'unchosen', and so, rather than focusing on our rights to love, I want to try to talk about learning to love in the middle of what we have not chosen, because it seems to me that it's that love that is at the heart of the gospel. We love because God loved us first.

If it is loving in day-to-day life that Jesus embodied, then it is loving amid the unchosenness of life – when you wanted love but couldn't find it, when you mistook lust for love, when you didn't recognize love when it was there, when you've made some choices which mean that you live now in loveless relationships or when you are losing, helplessly, one that you love.

How to love in those circumstances?

The love Jesus talks about has a strong element of sacrifice; there is no greater love, he says, than to lay down my life for my friend.

This raises a question for us as disciples: am I willing? And if I'm not, or if I find this idea very hard, how does that sit alongside my faith?

The possibility of love is held out to us as a defining characteristic of Christian faith. And so the question arises when we try to live this out, setting aside the romantic love I mentioned at the beginning: what does this love look like? How is it that I am asked to make a connection between my life and yours – what does that really mean? Is the church a distinctive kind of community as far as love is concerned? Are we at the frontline of loving, and if not, why not?

If, as St Paul says in his amazing poem about love (1 Corinthians 13), that love is itself patient and kind, then I want to add a word to that about what I find in the way that Christ loves. Love is not just patient in a quietist way, sitting back and waiting to see what happens, because the love that Christ embodied, and that we are asked to take part in, is nothing less than revolutionary.

So this love is revolutionary kindness. And I have mentioned before the theologian Dorothee Soelle's powerful reflection on an aspect of Christian spirituality that she calls revolutionary patience.[1]

This idea is helpful to us in different contexts, but I want to suggest that it is helpful here when considering love, and particularly the commandment to love that Christ left us.

The root of the word patience carries the meaning of suffering, allowing, giving way to. And the way, it seems to me, that Jesus loved was to exercise this revolutionary patience. Living now, but according to another timetable, another set of priorities. Jesus stayed beside people as they worked things out for themselves. He answered anxious questions, usually with another, patient question. He taught the timeliness of healing, and the timeliness of dying. And what theologians call 'the Christ event' – the whole event of Christ's living, dying, rising – is marked by revolutionary patience, which I am suggesting is love in the context of sacrifice. It understands in a profound way the unchosenness of much of life, not mistaking our human agency for a god-like autonomy, free from anyone or anything else, but instead showing a real and profound recognition of our interdependence with all created things.

Jesus' words are embarrassingly clear. Love one another.

I guess that Dorothee Soelle's reflections are on my mind

because I believe I have witnessed such revolutionary patience very recently.

I have just come back from a trip to Syria. I was there for a week, travelling around, meeting Christians in Damascus, Homs, Aleppo and some places in between. The tragedy of that country and the trauma of its people are almost unspeakable.

But for now, I want to say that the themes of love, fear, forgiveness, cruelty and bitterness, and the toxic abuse of power, were key features of my experience there. One story I will tell you now, which has given rise to this sermon about love. A monk is living in a monastery in the Syrian desert. He is there now. As Syria is two hours ahead, I guess he's been to Mass this morning and said his prayers. He was kidnapped by ISIS and held for 118 days in 2015. I met him, a man whose long beard and quiet eyes made him seem older than he was. I would guess that he is actually in his 30s. In 2015, he had been visiting the monastery, trying to decide whether he felt a call to become a monk or not. It was while he was visiting that he was mistaken for a monk and kidnapped. He was held in a cell with four other people, and he guessed that in the whole building where he was held, there were maybe 200 people. He was held with Muslims and Christians together. He was tortured. And during his time in captivity, his kidnappers held a knife to his throat three times, in mock executions. He told his story in a low voice, a gentle voice. One of the journalists with our group wanted to know details. And so he revisited his experience – an incredibly generous thing to do for a group of visitors.

And then a journalist with us said: 'Do you forgive them?'

In the room there was a silence, but actually the monk himself smiled, as if it were a rather foolish question. 'Of course,' he said.

'Did they allow you to pray?' asked the journalist, a bit too quickly.

'Yes,' he said. 'I prayed for the members of ISIS. We'd been praying for them anyway, before I was taken, so I continued. All the time, I prayed for them.' It seemed totally obvious to him – not something that required any discussion or elaboration.

It's easy to idolize this monk for his attitude. He is certainly incredibly impressive as a person, because he is living in a country that has been almost destroyed by the violence of its government, which continues to bomb relentlessly areas of its own cities. Other parts of the country are at the mercy of terrorist groups, yes, but also now at the mercy of world powers fighting a proxy war.

I suppose what I want to say is that it might seem that there would be more moral clarity in an extreme situation like the Syrian war. Good and evil are cast clearly. So we can, from over here in the UK, make a clear assessment about what is right and wrong in that context, and pronounce accordingly. But that wasn't my experience. It is far too easy from this distance to judge good and evil from far away.

The uncomfortable truth is that many Christians I met expressed a different attitude from the one held by the monk. They were distraught, angry, furious with indecisive and contradictory Western foreign policy and media, and supportive of the government. And, it seemed, many didn't want to know the extent of the government's bombing or the torturing in the prisons undertaken by the government in their name. All they wanted was for the 'Islamist terrorists' to be destroyed and to get on with something resembling a normal life. And the brutality of ISIS or Jabhat al-Nusra or any number of groups active in the region lent weight to this choice.

The man I met is an individual monk. He is not a politician, making choices about the deployment of military force – or a freedom fighter, fighting for democracy instead of dictatorship. But, in the most extreme of circumstances, he was somehow able personally to combat the toxic, traumatizing sickness that has overtaken much of the society. And he embodied, for me at least, a revolutionary patience that lives according to another timetable, that has committed itself to love without borders, that will be fierce in love's defence, fearless in somehow finding the strength to forgive. And most especially this struck me because the entire society – its media, its feared secret police, its compliant members of Parliament, set in its war-torn landscape – is telling him to live another way.

In a society not at war, it's important not to convince ourselves that these choices are somehow clearer in a war: they often aren't. And the pilgrimage our parish is about to take to

Berlin, Nuremberg and Auschwitz will reveal this in our own continent. The complicity of millions of ordinary people, the now shocking film footage of Lutheran bishops standing with Adolf Hitler, highlight all the more the unusual raised voice of Dietrich Bonhoeffer, living by another set of rules. Another kind of love.

This kind of love is lived with a courage that is only evident when it's tried. It is not afraid to get things wrong; it is a love that will risk saying the wrong thing, will risk overstepping the mark. Love risks its own reputation in the service of another way.

The way that Dietrich Bonhoeffer was able to speak up only three days after Hitler was elected and, against the prevailing view of most of his fellow Christians, challenge the rhetoric of their new elected leader was because he was rooted in his own spiritual practice, in his theology of God and in the love that is at the heart of the gospel. He was able to make a radio broadcast so soon after Hitler came to power because his life was rooted in another, more fundamental reality. His radio broadcast was entitled '*Gott is mein Führer*': God is my leader. The charge he laid against Hitler so early on was that of idolatry. Regular prayer, creative theology, ancient liturgies, a commitment together to an ethical and spiritual practice rooted in forgiveness – these are powerful tools at our disposal as we try to commit ourselves to love, whether in a time of peace or a time of war.

The love at the heart of the gospel is not individualistic sentiment, or a collection of inviting feelings that dissipate as soon as the winds of political complexity start to blow it about.

This love is a commitment to a patience that is at once resilient and revolutionary; a refusal to be made bitter or mean, judgemental or even verbally violent. A deep and prayerful recognition that I am complicit not only in my own violence but in the violence of another, because we are fundamentally interdependent, connected by our creation to one another and to all that lives.

The Eucharist is a broken-hearted celebration of the love that is embodied in the life, death and resurrection of Christ. In that life, we learn that love can't be separated from grief. Our own broken-heartedness finds a place at this table, where we too find the joy that in turn gives us the strength to love.

Note

1 D. Soelle, 1977, *Revolutionary Patience*, New York: Orbis Books.

20

Ascension Day

Acts 1.1–11

Today's service is shaped throughout by words and images from a strand of spirituality called mysticism. Mysticism is a strand of most religious practice and, in Christianity, our traditions are enriched by centuries of women and men whose words and music we treasure today: Hildegard of Bingen from the twelfth century, Julian of Norwich and Walter Hilton from the fourteenth century, Thea Bowman, Evelyn Underhill and Thomas Merton from the twentieth century, and the musical mystic Olivier Messiaen whose meditation on the Ascension we heard at the beginning of the service and will hear again at the end. Astonishing music responding, as Messiaen himself said, to birdsong and the ancient rhythms of the earth.

Why use these rich words, images and music today? Because it's Ascension Day: the ritualized movement of God from 'here' … to 'there and here', the biblical witness to God's disappearance from view having been unignorably present in the person Jesus. The fleshly, contingent dust and fury of the three years that Jesus spent teaching, healing, provoking and challenging are over. The 'in-your-face' confrontations between Jesus and the religious and political authorities of the day are done, for us to take up instead.

Today, as the gospel tells us, Jesus moves through time 'back' (although of course he never left) to eternity. And because of this movement, Christianity plunges into the mysterious, often wordless connection of God with humanity in the mystery of eternity.

Ascension Day, far from being a kind of comic vision of feet sticking out from a cloud, is a defining movement of God that pulls us through a portal, that calls us into a deeper spiritual connection with the divine presence we cannot see.

And the mystics show us the way. The paradox is right there in the gospel: stay in the city, says Christ. Stay in the city, with all the injustices and complex society you find there. Stay there but know that you are clothed with spiritual power.

The mystics help us see that 'God is present in everything. In the universe, in creation, in me and all that happens to me, in my brothers and sisters, in the church, and in the Eucharist – everywhere.'[1]

These are the words of the twentieth-century Roman Catholic Sister and mystic Thea Bowman, who in her life obeyed that command to 'stay in the city' at the same time as remaining deeply contemplative, rooted in personal connected prayer.

Thea Bowman was an African American civil rights campaigner and religious, who died in 1990 from cancer aged only 52. Just weeks before her death she addressed the Catholic Bishops conference. It's a striking film (you can find it on Youtube): a Black woman preaching to a room full of white dog-collared men. And her energy and incisive challenge, issued from her wheelchair, is both joyful and sharp, often a combination characterizing the mystics. Advocating for change, proclaiming the truth of the matter, she is rooted in a love of the Eucharist and the Church that doesn't prevent her calling out all that's wrong.

In the spirit of Jesus' words in the gospel, her lived experience is of the visible complexities of the city, at the same time as her joy in being alive is rooted in the love of God invisible.

Thea Bowman, like Julian of Norwich, like Evelyn Underhill, like Walter Hilton, brings together the contemplative and the active that is expressed in our gospel today. That we are to stay in the city, remain involved in human affairs, but at the same time have a mystic's perspective on living.

And what is this 'mystic's perspective?'

It's a perspective that insists that now is important. Because now, in reality, is all we have. By which I mean that all that matters is God now, and everything else falls into place around that priority. That grand plans mean very little, and personal interaction and connection mean a lot.

It can be our Ascension Day pledge to give some room to discovering our inner mystic. There is a mystic inside each one of us – wherever you are passionate about life and living, wherever you become impatient with the structures, strictures of institutional Church, wherever you find that tears are not far away, wherever you feel, however fleetingly, that actually things are pretty simple after all. Wherever you know yourself connected to all that is, seen and unseen, on a cliff top or looking at the night sky.

Wherever you know, even fleetingly, that you're not waiting for life to start, but that real life is now, with the people God has given you to love. That's it.

For some, this will be expressed in a direct and emotional connection to Jesus, risen, ascended, closer than a breath. This personal devotion is an expression of mysticism.

For some this will mean a sense of connection to all that lives in creation, a oneness with the world often described by mystics from other religions – in Sufi or Buddhist meditations, for example.

For some this will mean an inexplicable but irreducible desire to pray. People often say to me something like: I want to pray – I don't understand it fully and I'm worried I don't know how to do it – but I want to pray. To go somehow to the centre of things, where I know what matters and what is true.

Wherever you befriend your own desires and longings for the peace the world cannot give, there you are a mystic.

In all these places and experiences our mystical spirituality finds a home.

When I was trying to discern my path in my 20s, and I'd become quite convinced, before women could be priests, that a priest was what I was going to be, I carried a book around with me called *Praying with the English Mystics*.[2] On the bus going to gigs as a singer, working in bars and hotels, I carried this book of mystics. It seemed that, for them, life was simple. Or at least they had their priorities straight. Now I'm older I know that of course Julian of Norwich lived through at least two wars and a pandemic and she endured very poor health herself, so of course life wasn't any simpler for her than it was for me. It wasn't at all simple for Thea Bowman or Thomas Merton either. But in their allowing the mystery of God to be what God was, not in a disinterested or passive way, but in a passionate way, connected to their longing and desire, I found a language that, although intensely personal to each one of them, was a language I could learn for myself and know that I wasn't alone.

In today's gospel, Jesus 'led them out as far as Bethany ... While he was blessing them, he withdrew from them ... And they returned to Jerusalem with great joy.'

This spiritual experience brings both clarity and joy; it is a priority-straightening day when all that matters is plunging those spiritual depths of oneness with God and with all that lives. All our fretful planning and jostling finds its fractiousness calmed in these deep mystical waters.

The mystics find a way to become more and more deeply fearless. Freed from endless anxiety about what other people think, freed from the judgements or assessments of others, we too can join the mystics in giving space to our sometimes deeply buried desire, but desire all the same, to live profoundly present in our lives: present to God, to others, to ourselves. Fearless and free.

And the paradox is that such connection deepens at the moment that in this gospel God seems to move away. We come closest to this kind of 'connected parting' in facing eternity ourselves.

Thea Bowman was diagnosed with breast cancer aged 46. Weakened by chemotherapy she continued to preach and sing and advocate for change. With the simplicity and fearlessness of a mystic, when she was asked how she made sense of suffering, she answered, 'I don't make sense of suffering. I try to make sense of life ... I try each day to see God's will ...'[3]

As Sister Thea contemplated her own movement from life through death, she was asked by her priest and dear friend Father John Ford ST what she wanted him to say at her funeral.

Sister Thea responded with reference to another clear-eyed and fearless woman, the freed slave Sojourner Truth, whose strength pulls me – and I pray pulls you too – through to believe the good news of the Ascension gospel for today. Sister Thea said to her friend:

Tell them what Sojourner Truth said about her eventual death,
'I'm not going to die.
I'm going home like a shooting star.'[4]

Notes

1 T. Bowman, interview given to US Catholic website, www.uscath olic.org, 15 March 1990.

2 J. Robertson, ed., 1997, *Praying with the English Mystics*, London: SPCK.

3 Bowman, US Catholic interview.

4 Sermon preached by Father John Ford at the funeral mass of Thea Bowman, Holy Child Jesus Church, Canton MS, 3 April 1990.

21

Pentecost

Acts 2.1–21
John 14.8–27

Sometimes this feast of Pentecost is called the birthday of the
Church. Sometimes in children's activities and sermons there
are balloons and 'Happy Birthday' is sung.

In the rhythm of the year in the life of church, actually we're
at the end of something today. We're at the end of something
that began in December last year: Advent, the waiting season;
then nativity – Christ is born; then Epiphany, the season of
miracles; then Lent, Holy Week and Easter, the story and
meaning of Jesus' life, death and resurrection; then the Easter
celebration season itself including Ascension, the beginning of
Christian mysticism – when Christ disappears; and now – and
now, and now, the mysterious and energizing story of Pentecost when the story of the community, the group, the gathering
of people who were fired up by this new vision of living got
going.

If there is any story that gives us our foundation story as a
church, then it is this one. A group of people gathered together
for whom collective spiritual experience became their defining
character.

We call them the Early Church.

And although here we are 2,000 years later in what soci-
ologists call late modernity in a mature capitalist society, I
think we are still in the Early Church. Because our perspective
is from and towards eternity. And humanity hasn't been at it
for very long.

Today in Trafalgar Square there will be a crowd and church
leaders with music and prayers celebrating Pentecost. Like
the Eid celebrations in recent weeks, the Diwali celebrations

in recent months, Trafalgar Square will be the place where a large crowd can gather to celebrate their own religious festival as part of this diverse city.

With thousands of people there, it will look as if the Church is full of celebration. And so it will be. But on this day of Pentecost, when we mark the sharpening, revealing presence of the Holy Spirit, it seems more appropriate to reflect on the challenge of Pentecost, not simply a straightforward celebration of who we are.

We are celebrating Pentecost in this city society, the one where people work and live all through the week. And so with the perspective of eternity, while at the same time rooted in reality, what have we got to say?

At Pentecost, the Church reflects on its own nature and its relationship to the society it serves. I very often talk to people who don't have any contact with church, and their reviews from what they see are often not great. The appalling revelations of the habitual abuse of power, especially sexual abuse, especially by clergy, have made many people sceptical to the point of revulsion. Or they express the expectation that church is somewhere between boring and judgey, or is an uncomfortable building full of self-righteous people who form what look like unjoinable communities meeting behind closed doors.

But after these initial sharp criticisms, often other yearnings begin to emerge. That church could be a unique space in society that they might value. A place not only to find some peace, but to be given a different perspective on life, and life together. A space to reflect on the deeper questions that life throws up: What am I for? How should I live? And beyond those individual questions, a place to keep trying to form community, like no other in society today, where music and prayer form publicly accessible rituals, and an expectation that we will together face the cruelty and violence that all of us indulge in and work for a better world, that the ambiguity of this can be held and offered, and forgiven by God in eternity. Church sounds a bit more exciting and challenging when it's put like that.

The story in Acts is an evocative description of an ecstatic experience a long time ago. And these collective experiences were viewed by many, then as now, with not a little suspicion.

We heard Peter trying to explain: they're not drunk, he says, honestly, this is something else.

The Spirit that we learn about in the story of Pentecost drew people out of themselves towards each other, and changed them. It was a collective experience and the very words that they spoke were transformed.

This week, we held a funeral service for our friend I, who was for decades incredibly active in our church as an advocate for refugees, perhaps in part as a response to her having fled Nazi Germany as a Jewish teenager, arriving in the UK on the Kindertransport. We heard in the funeral service about her going back many years later to her family home in Berlin that had been confiscated by the Nazi regime, and simply knocking on the door to tell the people who lived there now who she was. It was incredibly moving to hear how she befriended the occupants of her former house, and forgave them for benefiting from the stolen house. She forgave them to the extent that she would go and stay there, and sleep in her old room as a guest.

I's practice of forgiveness was forged in the crucible of the suffering she and her family endured. And so part of her legacy to us is to encourage us not to over-spiritualize festivals like Pentecost when the real-life consequences of its transformative energy can be enacted in the Church today.

As she was dying of cancer, close to the end of her life, the Jewish philosopher Gillian Rose issued a similar challenge when she identified what she thought was the obligatory sickly-sweet serenity identified with well-being, which was often encouraged by Christian spiritual teaching, even in the midst of disease or shame or accusation. She described this overly comforting niceness in Christianity as, in fact, 'the counsel of despair which would keep the mind out of hell'.[1]

She preferred a bracing recognition that there is hell on earth and that naming and facing this reality is more truthful than pretending or wishing it away. She goes on, 'The tradition is far kinder in its understanding that to live, to love, is to be failed, to forgive, to fail, to be forgiven, forever and ever.'[2]

The Pentecost story is vital in helping the Church define its character and purpose in society. It is an enlivening story, of empowerment, of mutual accountability, of communal experience and shared vision.

The Pentecost scripture tells us several things about ourselves in relation to God. The Spirit did not come to one lone disciple asking him or her to bear the weight of it all by themselves; the Spirit was poured out on to the community. From the dramatic change in the behaviour of the people who experienced this, we discover our own mandate and pattern for how to be church together.

The Spirit dignifies and ennobles us, especially the most marginalized among us. The Spirit inhabits us, stretches and draws us out.

This story of Pentecost is linked to the Hebrew story of the Tower of Babel in the book of Genesis (11.1–9). And this contrast gives us our way in to what it is to be church. The people in Genesis were building a tower and a city 'so that they could make a name for themselves'. Tower of Babel energy is drawing everything to itself, people, possessions, capital, all in the service of making a good reputation for the ones who built it. A narcissistic statement of self-reliant power.

This biblical story was used by white theologians in the Dutch Reformed Church of 1960s South Africa to justify the system of apartheid, arguing that theologically it was God's will to separate races. They argued that God had separated out the people into languages and continents, and that separation must be in the natural order of things.

The trajectory of the building of Babel is a centralizing one: the accumulation of power, the hubristic building of a huge tower, and the justification of the separation of human beings from one another as a consequence.

By contrast, the dynamic of Pentecost is centrifugal. From an intense centre, people are sent out and are connected, able to hear each other, and understand across differences; they are sent to share the spiritual energy that has galvanized them. Perhaps it's one way of framing a choice that has to be repeated time and again by churches who can teeter between these two: a Babel kind of church, keen to draw everyone to ourselves, or a Pentecost church, servant of the outsiders, pouring out welcome and energy to those who don't belong, striving to understand across different languages and cultures. Most church communities are a combination of both. But the biblical trajectory is clear.

The call to be a Pentecost church has been such a powerful influence over Christianity and Christian practice, but it's important to notice how slender an account it is. There isn't really much detail at all. It's only four verses. And it is really very circumspect. The sound heard by the disciples is compared to a rushing wind and the tongues that appear are compared to fire.

In the way he sets out this amazing story, Luke is letting us know that the point of it is not what we might call the pyrotechnics of theophany (an appearance of God) but spiritual transformation.

Isn't the point Luke is making that the real 'event' of Pentecost is the empowerment of the disciples and the widening of the mission to include people from the whole world? That would explain the detailed description of the nations listening to Peter, in contrast to the short description of the strange behaviour of the disciples.

In the light of the use of theology to try to justify the wicked ideology of apartheid, we can listen to the theology of Pentecost to combat the theology of Babel. There are resources to help lead us here. One theologian has reflected on what he identifies as white theology in response to the systematic separation of peoples in racist ideologies.

Theologically, he says – and I want to suggest that this is helpful for us in direct response to the contrast between Pentecost and Babel – the task of changing that faces white people who inhabit and benefit from a long legacy of privilege is big, but necessary for salvation.

> The conundrum of race is such that there is no salvation for whites as white, and there is no solidarity with others except as white. Neither exemption from the history nor captivity to the identity can be tolerated. Learning to confess guilt in responsibility and simultaneously embrace the teachings of uncertainty are both requisite. The demand is double and damnable.[3]

The contrast between Babel and Pentecost is such that a white-majority church is led by the Spirit to the demand that is 'double and damnable'. The speech we heard Peter give in the Acts story charts a path through. He uses Psalm 15 and Psalm 109, but ultimately asserts that Jesus risen from the dead is the cause and source of this gift of the Holy Spirit. Peter's challenge to all who will listen is that we must, first, change our perception of Jesus and his followers; second, share in the meaning of the conviction that Jesus is the one who was to come; and, third, take part in the experience of the prophetic Spirit being poured out.

A major theme that runs through the Acts of the Apostles is introduced in this ecstatic experience right at the beginning of the book: that humans are challenged to respond, to join in, to notice and then get involved with God's activity in their midst. To this end, the Spirit teaches us an obliged freedom; she teaches us an absolutely unfettered liberty that is at once bound in the service of others. At Pentecost, the Spirit is poured out into the life of old and young men, women and children. As Isaiah reminds us, this is the Spirit who, when upon us, will send us to bring good news to those who are oppressed, release to the captives, recovery of sight to the blind, and comfort to all who mourn.

The Spirit teaches us a dynamic picture of who we are in relation to others, dependent on the belief that God created each person. The Spirit teaches us that we are to be a church that celebrates the empathy, connection, clarification that was revealed at Pentecost. This in contrast to Babel is a vision of life where people understand one another in new ways, make new and deeper connections and hear each other in ways they have never heard each other before. The Spirit teaches us that when we approach another human being, any other human being, when we approach creation itself, we act justly not only in order to receive justice ourselves, but in the knowledge that we are approaching that which the Spirit hovered over at the beginning: we approach holy ground.

Pentecost is an account freighted with meaning and energy for us today whenever we are in danger of being narcissistic, focused on me and mine, tempted to build a Tower of Babel either in our own lives or together with others, and not prepared to look beyond what we are comfortable with ourselves.

One of the challenges of Pentecost is to problematize our settled complacency; in the old phrase, the Spirit is there to comfort the disturbed, yes, but also to disturb the comfortable.

For example, to be a part of changing a Babel perspective into a Pentecost vision of unity in diversity, an important step for white-majority spaces and churches is to problematize whiteness itself. As a first step, the first of many.

Pentecost will constantly challenge the Church to be a place where our own capacity for cruelty, violence, hypocrisy and abuse will be acknowledged, faced and held within the cycle of confession, forgiveness and absolution. It is never easy work; the Spirit will lead us towards a love of God and of our neighbour that we never even realized was possible. And we pray and act for this new vision beginning with the collective experience of the agitation of the Spirit at Pentecost, who irrigates our life together as church.

Notes

1 G. Rose, 2011, *Love's Work*, New York: New York Review Books Classics, p. 98.

2 Rose, *Love's Work*, p. 98.

3 J. W. Perkinson, 2004, *White Theology: Outing Supremacy in Modernity*, New York: Palgrave McMillan, p. 227.

22

Trinity 3

Pride Sunday

Galatians 6.1–10

'Let us not grow weary in doing what is right.'

The sight of what estimates say was a million and a half people out on the streets of London yesterday at the Pride March supporting 30,000 people marching was amazing: colourful, noisy, musical, exuberant. It is an annual sight that is by turns inspiring, hugely encouraging and, well, just fun. So many people. So many different people. And good humour. Possibly my favourite banner was one that declared 'If you're reading this, you're gay'.

And I find it incredibly moving to be part of such a sea of humanity, flowing through the streets like volcano lava, erupting in a determination to say we are all human beings, deeply connected to one another. Maybe Bob Marley had it right? One Love.

Some will be regretting the commercialization of Pride: rainbow coffee cups, Barclay's Bank being one of the main sponsors, the so-called pink pound taking its place in the economy as spending power exercised by people identifying as LGBTQ+ just grows stronger with prosperity.

Others will see this commercialization as a sort of acceptance, hard won and long yearned for. Never in my lifetime, for example, would I have thought that Tesco would be so full of rainbows.

This year is the fiftieth anniversary of the raid on the Stonewall club in New York City at the end of June 1969. After a police raid, what then followed was called either the Stonewall riots or the Stonewall uprising or rebellion – depending on what side you were on.

Fifty years later, in New York City and in London and all over the world, a march – an uprising – a rebellion – hopefully these days not a riot except of colour – has become an annual expression of ... well what? Discussion continues about Pride: should it be a carnival or a protest? How mainstream should it be? Who should sponsor it? and so on.

The term 'pride' is attributed to one of the people who were there 50 years ago at the Stonewall club when it was raided: a remarkable trans woman called Sylvia Rivera who made a speech that night in Christopher Street in Manhattan village. As one of her interpreters said when she died in 2002, 'She may have been the prototypical Angry Queen. Unbowed, unbought, and virtually indigestible by a gay movement she helped birth.'[1]

Sylvia Rivera's presence in that first generation of Stonewall activists was, to say the least, bracing. As a trans woman, she challenged again and again the inclusivity of the gay activists. She wanted gender identity to be front and centre alongside sexual orientation. In one of her obituaries, the story was told:

> Sylvia Rivera went out as she lived: struggling to get gender issues on the map. She was hooked up to monitors, IVs, and a morphine pump last Sunday when local gay activists stopped by the intensive care unit to ask her advice. Mortally ill, she held back the night long enough to give them hell one last time for not being inclusive enough. She died only hours later, at just 50 years old: a unique lady for a unique time.[2]

There is a prophetic essence, a commitment to truth-telling, an explosive and uncompromising inclusiveness in the spirit of Sylvia Rivera that echoes the spirit of what I find in the radical message of the gospel. The heart of the gospel is love. Simple. Made complex by us complicated human beings who need so much reassurance and mercy from one another, let alone from God.

But collective Christianity – especially in the form of institutional Church – has been woeful in recognizing and remembering that the heart of the gospel is love. It has for centuries been part of the violent infrastructure that sought to punish and destroy people, human beings like Sylvia. It's so important still to name this on a day like today. To say we got it so wrong. Get it so wrong. Because Christians, like all human beings, are not immune to fear.

It's not always easy to be a public representative of a church that many people in this country – even in this city where many churches fly rainbow flags – believe is universally homophobic and discriminatory. Many church people have said that it's easier to come out at your workplace as gay than as Christian. It's important to name that right up front. And to name the Church's shame in its theological shoring up of a fear-based discrimination of anyone who is different from us.

And again, it's so important to say that much of the distress caused by the Church to people who are lesbian or trans, genderqueer, gay or non-binary is because of how we read the Bible. And so for churches like ours it is not good enough to put a rainbow flag on the altar, and leave scriptural interpretation to those who want to say that a literal reading condemns any sexual or gender identity other than a heteronormative one. And so I want to offer a reading of St Paul that I believe is faithful to its own identity as the word of God – and is also faithful to the radical heart of the gospel, which is fundamentally and irreducibly love.

I guess there are three things to take from St Paul's letter to the Galatians, which incidentally is probably the oldest book in the New Testament, written before the Gospels.

First, that from the manner of Paul's teaching, in which he is incredibly open about his own struggles, we should expect that struggle itself is a normal, even essential part of faith. Struggling with faith, and how to live with it, within it, inspired by it, is completely normal. Not just that, but as disciples of Christ we should expect it. And I don't just mean a cosmetic 'Well I'm not sure about everything I hear in church', I mean a heartbroken struggle, sometimes furious, sometimes raging, sometimes despairing, where it can feel as if our very life is in peril. Christ sweated drops of blood, such was the force of his breaking heart. Jacob wrestled with the angel all night, and by daybreak was exhausted and limping. Mary the mother of Jesus found that a sword pierced her heart; Martha struggled with Jesus, 'If you'd been here, my brother wouldn't have died.' If we are disciples of Christ, if we are close to the heart of God in any real-life sense, then we expect to become familiar with our own tears. The Psalms are full of this: 'How long O Lord, how long?' Our vengeful tendencies are, thank God, also given expression in the Psalms – as we might feel that we want to wreak havoc on the people who have told us that we are not acceptable to God or that God stands apart from us. Our resentment, our fury will be real. But when Jacob struggled all night he was hurt by the struggle, but he prayed a prayer that I have often prayed to God, and offer to you to pray too: 'I will not let you go until you bless me.' Struggle itself is part of what it means to believe.

Second, when Paul was writing his letters – including his letter to the Galatians from which this reading comes – he didn't know he was writing the Bible. He was writing a letter. This doesn't make it any less Scripture for us, but it challenges us to read it intelligently. And remember the radical change Paul had to make. Like many of us, Paul had to leave behind much of what he had been taught from his childhood religion. He embraced, accepted, eventually shouted loud about the new perspectives and insights that he had found in Christ. He had to reassess what he had been taught about God as a child. You can hear it in this letter as he debates with his readers the issue of circumcision and whether for Christians it is still necessary. One of the spiritual insights of a weekend like Pride is that we are asked to let go of much of what we were taught as a child about God. It's not easy, because there is a loop tape playing in our heads: a kind of spiritual merry-go-round that we don't seem to be able to get off. This is especially true if you've been brought up to believe that being gay is somehow wrong, or else that even if it was possibly OK to be gay, it wasn't OK to try to find someone to love. The astonishing strength of Paul's position is that he has allowed his faith to develop, to change, to grow into new perspectives and new insights. In this very letter to the Galatians, he writes a highly creative interpretation of the identity of Abraham and the descendants of Sarah and

Hagar – a creative interpretation from which in his later letter
to the Romans he kind of backs off. He insists that this is 'what
Scripture says' even though his interpretation would be highly
controversial for his readers. Paul is much more interested, as
he states in this letter, in how we live, which gives us guidance
in interpreting Scripture. He argues that the freedom the Spirit
brings to us as human beings translates into service of others,
and that service for others is, for Paul, essential context for
the wise interpretation of Scripture. Living a life of love and
service is, for Paul, essential to our capacity to understand
what Scripture is saying.

This teaching of Paul leads me to the third point I want
to make on this day. Paul says we are to bear one another's
burdens. We are also asked to bear our own. He writes such
astonishingly beautiful poetic lines about this – which could
have been written for a Pride service:

> So let us not grow weary in doing what is right, for we will
> reap at harvest time, if we do not give up. So then, when-
> ever we have an opportunity, let us work for the good of all.
> (Galatians 6.9–10)

What can make us weary of doing what is right? Or sometimes
not so much weary as fearful, of criticism or attack. Sometimes
it's fatigue – when you find it simply unbelievable that this
stuff still needs to be said. Sometimes isolation – when you feel
that other people don't really quite get it, even when they say
they do; even when they're saying they support you, you are
the only one who goes to your room and shuts the door and
reflects on your deep human need for both intimacy and mercy.

Because of the radical teaching of Paul in incredibly challenging circumstances, because the heart of the gospel of Christ
is love, it is not just possible, but vital, to say that you belong
here at this rainbow altar.

You belong here whether you identify as bisexual, lesbian,
trans gay, genderqueer, non-binary, or if you are not sure what
your label is or don't really want one. And so does every single
person who is straight: rich or poor, single, partnered, married,
curious. Every person belongs here who comes through the

door: on your legs, with sticks, in a wheelchair, carried in the arms of someone else – every person, whatever your age or ethnic background, the colour of your skin or your life experience. You belong at this rainbow altar when you are in work, out of work, grieving, glad, anxious, contented, despairing, if your mental health is robust, if your mental health is fragile, if you are in love, or pregnant or wish you were, or worry that you don't want to be, if you're worried about getting older or feeling that you're too young. It doesn't matter what you are wearing, or if you are thin or if you are big, or if you hate yourself or love the sound of your own voice. You belong here because you belong to God. *Every* person, whoever you are and whoever you are yet to be, is loved and accepted, forgiven and free.

As well as encouraging us in the manner of St Paul not to weary of doing what is right, I want to help resource us when we might grow weary of doing the right thing. And that is, in the manner of civil rights movements around the world, across time and across continents, by singing in praise of God and in solidarity with one another.

This song, to me, is a modern-day psalm; it echoes so many psalms which beg God to stay with me when I feel isolated. And it specifically says that however much money or comfort we have, these things will not fulfil us. This modern-day psalm reminds us that we can still feel isolated from God because of what we have been told in the past. But the Spirit of God is to lead us to freedom, to solidarity, to generosity and grace. To a place like this at this rainbow altar here today. To a place where no one stands alone.

Where no one stands alone

Once I stood in the night with my head bowed low
In the darkness as deep as the sea
And my heart felt afraid and I cried 'O Lord
Don't hide your face from me'.
Hold my hand all the way every hour every day
From here to the Great Unknown.
Take my hand, let me stand where no one stands alone.

Like a king I may live in a palace so tall
With great riches to call my own.
But I don't know a thing in this whole wide world
That's worse than feeling so alone.
Hold my hand all the way every hour every day
From here to the Great Unknown.
Take my hand, let me stand where no one stands alone.[3]

Notes

1 R. Wilchins, 'A Woman for Our Time', The Village Voice, www.villagevoice.com, 26 February 2002.

2 Wilchins, 'A Woman for Our Time'.

3 Lyrics and music by Mosie Lister, 1955; first recorded by Elvis Presley, RCA Studio B, Nashville TN, and released on *How Great Thou Art*, 1966.

23

Trinity 6

St Thomas

John 20.19–29

Thomas is often known as Doubting Thomas because of the story in today's gospel.

But I have always had a great affection for Thomas not least because I was ordained on this day, and it seemed to me at the time, and seems even more to me now, that it was a wonderful day to be ordained on: a day that asks us to meditate on faith and doubt in the person of Thomas.

At a time of deep questioning of identity – and especially I would suggest of Englishness even within Britishness – the divisions between people, geographically, economically and culturally, seem to be widening not closing. Doubt and uncertainty have been words used every day to describe profound questions of identity following the vote to leave the European Union and the chaotic political aftermath since.

At times like this, just as important and influential as the political, legal and economic arrangements are the stories and myths we tell ourselves: the hinterland full of emotion that asks us questions, not so much about what we earn or how we voted, but about who we are and who we trust. And this hinterland of stories, hopes and fears is where church, where Christianity, lives and breathes.

Whenever I am in situations where an audience or group is asking me questions, quite often someone will ask about doubt. I was with a group of sixth-formers recently and it came up there. 'Do you ever doubt?' And I'm always taken by surprise – because I can't believe they think I don't.

Doubt is a complex element of faith but it is how we view it that really determines how it plays out in our lives. And so, in the spirit of Thomas and in response to today's gospel, the question arises: what happens when we doubt what we believe?

This isn't just a religious question. When seemingly stable assumptions are thrown up in the air by a vote or by a diagnosis, this question is relevant politically and personally as well as spiritually.

I want to offer two possible scenarios. One is when we assume that doubt is the opposite of faith. The other is when doubt is part of faith.

If doubt is the opposite of faith, then doubt is the enemy of faith, threatens faith, and the story can go a little like this.

Doubt comes visiting. Oh no, we think, I don't think I'm supposed to let him in. Like the disciples in the gospel, we are hiding behind a locked door. So we resist for a bit. But then we think we could probably handle it – after all we're grown-ups – so we start to entertain Doubt. The conversation goes fine at first – well-put arguments, vigorous conversation. And we keep it all up in our heads, playing with the concepts and engaging with the challenge. We're proud of ourselves for being able to question ourselves. After a while, and as we are still feeling a bit naughty for even having Doubt in there, we start to notice that Doubt is niggling away at more core emotions, making us doubt more fundamental things: maybe she doesn't love me after all ... maybe I was wrong to leave that job ... maybe I didn't try hard enough to make him happy ... no one's really going to like me so I'll stop trying to make friends or go on dates. Bit by bit, we listen to the doubters in our head: maybe life isn't for love, maybe I can't do what I want, what have I done with my life?

Doubt like this is like acid thrown on a rose: inexorably burning away the flower, the bud, the scent of our best hopes and dreams.

And soon, Doubt invites round his best friend, Fear. They march into the living room, put their feet up and crack open a beer. Great, they say. Everything's fine as it is. Let's never sell this comfy sofa, let's never repaint the walls – it's all fine as it is. And every time you want to go into your own living room, and maybe suggest going out, or inviting someone round, or doing something different, there they are, colonizing your space, keeping you supplying them with crisps. You can't do it! they say triumphantly. You just can't! Stick with us!

And gradually you find that you have stopped hoping for anything else.

In this scenario, Doubt sniggers at our best hopes, chips away our confidence, makes us less willing to take any risk, and convinces us that the world is as it is and we are as we are because, well, deep down we've probably failed: we were fools, we were duped, and now we're stuck. And before we know it, the two of them, Doubt and Fear, with their other mate Despair, have made us belligerent like Thomas, encouraging us to lock the doors and demand a list.

'I don't believe you,' we say. 'I just don't believe you.' Because deep down we know that believing might change our life.

A second scenario is when we think of Doubt not as the enemy or opposite of Faith, but as part of Faith itself. A friend of Faith.

So Faith's friend Doubt has been coming round for years, knows you well, asks you sometimes quite awkward questions. Her style is bracing and frank. But you get the feeling she's standing up to you because she likes you.

Doubt, far from drawing the curtains and locking the doors, does quite the opposite. Doubt throws open the curtains and lets the light of Reason stream in through the windows. This light of Reason doesn't aim to destroy but tries rather to illuminate, make things clearer, with more depth of understanding. Questions are welcomed, laughter is heard as Doubt points out the absurdities and contradictions of life, and community is grown, nurtured and celebrated. Doubt and Faith invite their friends – How, What, When and the wisest friend of all, Why.

Friend Doubt is bracingly honest, insists not only on sitting in the living room where the teapot is still warm, but following you into the kitchen to see all the washing-up in the sink, simply disallowing you to maintain any fantasy about what you're like.

And in some areas of life, Doubt can save lives. Doubt might have saved the lives of the young men who died in the Battle of the Somme. Doubt in the diplomatic orthodoxies of the day might have let the light of reason shine on a set of unexamined political assumptions and perhaps avert the slaughter of the First World War. Who knows? But Doubt – defined as the willingness to question accepted orthodoxies – if given light and room to breathe, is one of the most precious abilities that humans can bring to bear when imagining and planning for the future.

If doubt is cast as the opposite of faith, if we think it's the enemy, it makes alliances with fear and despair to corrode and destroy our best selves. Group-think is not challenged because doubt is cast as disloyalty, and sometimes, as a result, catastrophic mistakes are made.

But if we cast doubt, not as the opposite of faith, but as part of faith, our inevitable doubts are honoured and welcomed as part of grown-up debate and creative conversation. 'I'm not sure what she said is right,' you might venture. 'Good point,' she says. 'Let's talk.'

Doubt as an integral part of faith is a commitment to open hearts and open minds. Not unlike coming to God as Jesus said, like a child, tirelessly and ceaselessly asking why.

This doubt doesn't destroy faith, but it does puncture our own hubris and it will winkle out any secret conviction we've got that, deep down, well, come on, we really do think we're right.

Doubt is important because it keeps us checking that the ground we're standing on is at least reasonably solid while we travel along.

And so a Christian spirituality begins to emerge from these two experiences of doubt, one that takes doubt seriously. And it's why it makes an appearance in the parish plan of St James's Piccadilly. We state as one of our core beliefs, 'Communal Christian life is marked by joyous celebration, forgiveness, doubting and discernment, sustained by friendship and prayer.'

Why would a church put doubting in our core value and belief statements? Because we will define doubt not as the opposite of faith but as part of faith.

And here's the thing ...

Doubt, when it's assumed to be the opposite of faith, is an isolating and frightening thing. It reeks of failure and makes us brittle. We learn this from the gospel. Thomas was isolated. He returned to the group and they told him something that had happened while he wasn't there. Out of this isolation, his reaction is fearful, maybe even a bit petulant, rigid, demanding proof. At least some of his reaction is surely simply wanting to belong – to have the same experience as the others.

But for those of us who Jesus refers to – the ones who have not seen, who have not had the chance to put our hands into his wounds – we're asked to share both our belief and our doubt, because again, as our parish plan says, this Christian life is 'sustained by friendship and prayer'.

One of the paradoxes of doubting is that, when it's shared, it often grows faith. Oh – thank goodness I'm not the only one sitting there thinking, 'Really? What does that mean?' When we share doubt, paradoxically this often helps us believe. And we stop being, in St Paul's words from our first reading today, 'strangers and aliens' to ourselves, to God and one another.

We become friends.

As the light of reason pours in through the clear-glassed seventeenth-century windows in this church, we bathe in its light, bringing our questions to the fore, acknowledging our uncertainties, and resolving that we will try to make friends with the questions themselves.

And so without proof and without seeing, sustained by prayer and friendship, we nevertheless stake ourselves on this path, praying, with the father of the boy Jesus healed in Mark's Gospel, in the words of the King James version: 'Lord, I believe. Help thou my unbelief.' This isn't a prayer to eliminate – the man doesn't say 'Destroy my unbelief'. He says 'help'. And the verb he uses is a continuous verb, carrying the meaning 'Please be helping, carry on helping, my unbelief which is always with me'.

Today, at the Eucharist, we offer our open hands: 'I believe,' we might say. 'Help thou my unbelief.'

And today we remember a towering voice in Europe whose death was announced this morning. Elie Wiesel, author of the Holocaust memoir *Night*,[1] spent his life after Auschwitz begging a continent so recently riven by war never to forget, always to challenge, never to let such toxic orthodoxy prevail again. In his memory, it is surely incumbent upon any European generation, now as then, to be comfortable with the importance of doubt, question, challenge and resistance to any orthodoxy that prevails against justice or peace. Doubt is a vital tool in the armoury of belief.

And so we come to the locked room, promising, with Thomas, not so much never to question again, as instead to remember Christ's insistence that his peace is with us. And we find that, without seeing, without looking even, we have been held all along in the wounded arms of Christ, who knows that we have never seen, and who asks us nonetheless to let go, and trust, and believe.

Note

1 E. Wiesel, *Night*, first English translation 1960, New York: Hill and Wang.

24

Trinity 10

Hebrews 12
Luke 13.10-17

I was fortunate enough to go to a performance of one of Handel's operas this week. *Rinaldo* includes one of the most famous arias ever written by Handel, a lament sung by a devastated lover who has been abandoned by the one she loves. *Lascia ch'io pianga.* Leave me to die alone. Her pain is corroding her in front of the audience's eyes – and it's an achingly beautiful tune.

Earlier in the week, St James's hosted a memorial service for a man who, by all accounts, had been a hugely energetic businessman, full of bonhomie and love of life. He loved coming to this church during the week, although he lived out of town, and his special request was that his funeral, which he knew was coming, would be held here. During that service, a clarinettist played the slow movement from Mozart's clarinet concerto. In the context, it was an expression not so much of the loud, hospitable, fun-loving man we had been hearing about in the eulogies, but of a quieter soul – a whispered expression of a person who loved and laughed his way through what had been a complicated life.

In both of these musical experiences, I found myself moved to tears, not only by the beauty of the music and the evident skill displayed but by the daring of the performers to play and sing incredibly quietly, and the ability of a large number of people in each case to be utterly silent as they, together, provided the wrap-around stillness for these tender melodies to be heard.

It takes enormous energy, skill, commitment and sheer guts to play the clarinet so very quietly, or for the soprano to control her top notes to the extent that we could hardly hear her.

It was almost unbelievable that this *pianissimo* was possible. In both cases, my eyes pricked and I just couldn't take my eyes off the musicians. Their daring and energy wrenched my heart open in a way that I think both of the scriptural stories this morning are describing.

Both of our Scripture readings today – mysterious as they are – are about what in theological terms are called 'theophanies'. A theophany is an appearance of God, a revelation of God, an evident manifestation of God. An obvious one you might think of is the bush that burst into flames in front of Moses, where the presence of God became unignorable, obvious, revealed.

Today's first reading comes from the very mysterious letter to the Hebrews. No one knows who wrote it. It used to be thought that St Paul wrote it, but not any more. It's full of what are often rather impenetrable phrases, and images that sometimes trouble thoughtful Christians. We had one of these in the reading this morning.

> But you have come to Mount Zion and to the city of the living God, the heavenly Jerusalem, and to innumerable angels in festal gathering, and to the assembly of the first-born who are enrolled in heaven, and to God the judge of all, and to the spirits of the righteous made perfect, and to Jesus, the mediator of a new covenant, and to the sprinkled blood that speaks a better word than the blood of Abel. (Hebrews 12.22–24)

Modern ears often struggle to hear the truths underneath this pre-modern imagery of enrolling the firstborn in heaven, and ritually sprinkled blood that somehow communicates more effectively than a man murdered by his brother, and so on.

But the thrust of this teaching is incredibly beautiful and offers both a comfort and a challenge to us who want to live lives attuned to the spiritual today.

The letter to the Hebrews is a poem in the form of a letter, written to encourage and challenge us; to build us up when we are struggling with faith. And so the imagery in today's reading is that of climbing a mountain; not just any mountain, but Mount Sinai where God dwells. In fact what the author is describing is our approach to God. The verb in Greek is *proserchesthai*, which means to approach, to move towards. In some part this is the instinct that prompts us to come to a church service. We've approached, we've got up and come out, we have approached the holy place, the place where we will meet God in bread and wine. The letter to the Hebrews encourages us to approach God, to move forward towards the spiritual reality at the heart of living; not just to stay put but to get up and go to the place where God is present both inside us and in the assembly. Here, God is named in the middle of a big city and in the middle of an ordinary August day. Here, prayer is expected and fundamental matters of life, death, truth and forgiveness are not embarrassing or shameful as they might feel on weekdays at work or at home – they are the whole point of coming. This is not to say that God lives in church and is not somewhere else, of course not; but there is value, says this letter, in getting up and going out and approaching the place where God dwells.

Coming to gather as church is, in this way, a physical expression of this inner journey.

It is a key principle in Hebrew theology that God's people are called back, called to return, called to renew, and to keep returning, keep renewing. For us listening to this scripture today, it is an invitation to keep approaching the place inside us, symbolized by this altar, that might feel quite dangerous to approach. This is where God dwells, where truth is told, where we know ourselves to be bracingly known by God, where we become painfully aware of our aching need to be loved, and where we trust, ever more deeply the more we do it, that our approach will be welcomed. We sometimes use the invitation at Communion that ends 'It is Christ who asks us to meet him here'. That's it. We are invited to dare to approach the place where God dwells in Christ, at the Eucharist, sacrificially as described in Hebrews, and inside us in the secrets of our own souls.

The second reading is a story that has many layers. Luke's Gospel is full of healing stories, and this one has as many meanings as the others.

A woman is in the synagogue. Jesus is there too, stirring things up as he often did. In the English translation, we lose some of the drama that Luke wants to convey. Jesus says '*Ide*', which means 'Behold!' Behold the woman! Echoes of Pilate's dramatic presentation of Jesus to the crowd – Behold the man!

This woman is someone to Luke, even though we don't learn her name and we know she is at the margins of her community. The story is unique to Luke – this woman doesn't appear in any of the other Gospels – and Luke tells us that she has what is somewhat mysteriously described as a 'spirit of weakness'. Later on, Luke interprets this as demonic possession.

The spirit of weakness causes her to be in the shadows, at the side, towards the back, and unable to stand tall. But before we get into the story of this woman, it's also important to see what happens around this encounter. Just previous to this conversation, Jesus has been asked about a local disaster in the news: a tower has fallen down, called the Tower of Siloam, and it had killed 18 people. So the crowd want to know from Jesus, were those people killed because they were sinners? Jesus has just spent some time in conversation with them contradicting this interpretation and saying that, no, they didn't die because they were sinners. The thrust of his own interpretation is that all of us live our lives closer to death than we think, and so of course we could die as the result of dodgy brickwork, or an illness, or anything else. Living in a spirit of repentance is really the key thing to take from this incident, not to wonder whether they died as a result of sin or not. But that's all by way of an aside – Jesus is embroiled in this conversation about the news when he notices this woman and he calls her over, and rather amazingly, she comes. Unlike some of the other Gospel characters, she isn't running after Jesus trying to get his attention. She's hiding at the back. It must have taken a lot of courage for her to come forwards when he asked. Clearly movement is not easy for her, she lives with physical limitations. The key movement in this encounter is from weakness to strength, from confinement to freedom. Her encounter with Jesus leaves her free and stronger than she was before. It has also involved movement from the side to the centre, from the shadows to the visible. Jesus' words are aimed directly at her: 'You have been freed.'

Some vivid detail follows. The religious leader who is there too is, in a wonderful description, *aganaktein* in Greek, a word

Luke only uses this once and which means really extremely irritated. (Incidentally, the other Gospel writers use it about Jesus himself. Mark likes to describe Jesus as irritated, and the disciples too.) But what does this religious leader do when he's really irritated by this happening in his jurisdiction, and on the Sabbath too? He doesn't confront Jesus directly but shouts at the crowd in a classic example of misdirected anger. He starts lecturing the crowd about what can and can't happen on the Sabbath. Jesus fights right back, saying, 'Well, if you can rescue an animal on the Sabbath or pick up an ox if it has fallen down, then you should be fine with a human being being set free, surely?' Jesus uses one of his most frequent and powerful accusations towards the religious leaders, that of hypocrisy.

It's Luke who interprets the woman's new-found freedom in terms of her previously being bound by Satan. Satan is the great accuser and divider. If she has been made whole, given her freedom, brought from the edge to the middle, from the side to the centre, then the forces of division and accusation are defeated in this beautiful theophany. The presence of God has brought unity and healing where there was division and discord.

And there's such energy in this story too. The woman is being given her freedom; the ruler of the synagogue is extremely irritated; then he shouts at the crowd because (perhaps) he's afraid to confront Jesus personally; then Jesus shouts back at him; and finally we have a contrast of reactions. Those opposed to Jesus are described as shamed, presumably not just by the woman's liberation but by the final detail in the story. But, rather brilliantly, the crowd, having been shouted at by their vicar, aren't shamed at all! They just ignore him and are full of delight, rejoicing and praising God.

What a contrast in reaction.

So some really important themes and questions emerge for us who want to take our spiritual lives seriously.

Theophany – the appearance of God in our midst in our real lives – is not confined to old stories and pre-modern ways of describing strange happenings. Every day is full of theophanies: small miracles, moments of God's appearing, sometimes dramatic, most often not very. How do we live our lives attuned to the theophanies around us? The clues are in these scriptures, and they raise questions that are both political and personal.

Politically, this woman is every human being who is creased up with distress or shame or economic exhaustion or political oppression. Structural injustices pervade our persistently unequal city; just this week it was reported that 200,000 children are vulnerably housed in the UK, some in converted shipping containers that are freezing in the winter and scorching in the summer.

The letter to the Hebrews reminds us that blood spilled on the streets, both Abel's blood and the blood of Jesus, cries out. In this city, too many young people are leaving their flats carrying knives. Mothers are washing the blood of their sons from the streets. Their blood cries out for a more just and humane society.

Where is it that you witness people who exercise religious or political power getting angry at a liberation that confronts them and starting to shout at the crowd? Wherever you see this, or do this, it points to a movement of the spirit that has challenged them: an everyday theophany.

Our calling as Christians in the name of this unnamed woman is to be an energetic participant in the political work in society with all those who are weighed down, that they might stand up, be seen and be set free.

And personal spiritual questions are framed in this story too.

Who is the unnamed part of you that is bent over, not able to be free, hiding at the back, at the side? It might be this part of you that is called to come to the middle and dare to approach the source of healing, forgiveness and liberation. An everyday personal theophany.

When in your life do you tremble like Moses because you know you're near something real or have seen something so true it hurts your eyes? Where is it that you touch the truth of what it is to be alive, and the possibility of what it could be to be free?

And like the pianissimo notes that I described at the beginning, these theophanies might not be in crashing signs or huge shoves or enormous events. They might be, as for that woman, in the middle of an ordinary day when she'd turned up as she always did to hide at the back.

Our work, our spiritual discipline is not to make everything dramatic or decisive, or to worry when it isn't. Our task is certainly not to fret or be permanently anxious about what we're doing and what God is up to. Our spiritual discipline and task is simply to return, and return, to keep approaching the sometimes rather frightening core realities of love, faith, forgiveness, justice and truth which are the hallmarks of the presence of God in the world. There we fall silent, and listen, listen hard, dare to listen for the sometimes pianissimo voice of Christ, who, as for that woman, calls us out of the shadows to approach God and be free.

25

Trinity 10

John 6.35–51

If you are a person who attends church services regularly, this might seem like an ordinary part of your routine. But as a way into our scripture today, I want to suggest to you that it is not at all routine for you to be here. Without overstating it, it's quite brave.

Our predecessors attending a church like St James's Piccadilly in almost every century but our own would be doing so at least partly because it was expected of them, it lent them some respectability.

Not now. Not in present-day London.

For many people – let's be honest, for most people, especially of a younger generation – the public practice of religion is somewhere on a spectrum from unfashionable, through unfathomable, and ending up at plain damaging. So those who choose to come are making a pretty strong choice. And there will be as many reasons as there are people here.

Some will come to find a sense of community in a huge and often lonely city. Some will come because it is a chance to contemplate and be contemplated by the mysterious presence of God. Some will come because they want to describe themselves as disciples of Jesus.

Why do you come? Why are you here?

Whatever has happened to you this week, whatever anxieties or troubles, whatever good times or scared times, whatever griefs or joys you are carrying, this is a place to return to. To remember your first love of living, and to be shown again that you are loved, you are loved so very much. That your life, just as it is, is held in the gaze of the One who created you.

And we do that remembering, contemplating, considering,

praying, in the context of a meal. The sacrament called Eucharist, which as you will know just means Thanksgiving. A unique event in the life of the church, unique every time but ancient as the earth itself. A place, a communal action, where time meets eternity; where we on earth are irreducibly close to the ones who have gone ahead of us into eternity. A touching place. A true place. And that's one of the reasons why it takes courage to come. Because here we face the truth of the world as it is, and God as God is, and we as we are.

You are brave to want to be fed with this bread and wine because it is broken bread and poured-out wine. This cup is not only the cup of salvation, as Christ has said, but, as he's also said, the cup of suffering.

Today I want to talk a little about vocation – partly because we are saying good bye to R and S, both of whom are moving house with their families in order to go to theological colleges in Birmingham and Oxford to train to be priests. But my purpose here today is, while celebrating these brave women, to make sure that we don't mistake or narrow a sense of vocation to the particular and specific ordination that they are going towards.

Vocation just means calling. You all have at least one, as do I. Many of us have more than one. We are bi-vocational, or tri-vocational. We are summoned into being by God, drawn up, called out, given a name and invited to live as fully and bravely as we dare. Everyone is called to be the person God creates you to be. And it's a lifelong task. Even for people who seem to have a comparatively visible vocation like being a priest, it's a lifelong task to grow into your vocation, see what it is, try it on, move around in it. And it changes over time.

I want to suggest that our vocations, as varied as they are, can find a home in the setting of a church community, rooted in what we are doing here this morning. So that whether your vocation is to be a friend, or a father, a sister, a carer, an artist, engineer or parent – whatever it is – we can be in solidarity with one another and hold one another in our lifelong learning about what our vocation is.

Our vocation is rooted in the Eucharist. This Eucharist, like every Eucharist, is a celebration. But it's a broken-hearted celebration because it is held the very night before Jesus died. And the night before someone dies is remembered with poignancy, their last words hung on to, their last actions given deeper meaning and edge. Knowing he was leaving, Jesus created a memory with the ones he loved that they would be bound to repeat and repeat over generations in order, as he said, to remember him. In today's gospel, we heard one of Jesus' mystical 'I am' sayings. 'I am the bread of life,' he says (John 6.35). In this mystical saying, we can find our vocation rooted in this living bread.

The Eucharist is not primarily a memorial service, despite the commandment of Jesus of Nazareth to repeat the ritual to remember him. Of course the Eucharist is rooted in the Gospel accounts of that Last Supper, but the fundamental trajectory of the sacrament of the Eucharist is forwards. It is a sacrament pointing towards the future. It is proclaiming a new future in the present which Jesus constantly referred to as the *basilea tou theou*, the kingdom of God. A future that we are invited to help build. A future where all are welcome, where everyone has enough to eat and drink. Where justice and mercy are kingdom principles to live by.

And the signs pointing towards that new future are right in front of us every week, because we say that, although we are many, we are one body because we all share in one bread.

We then return to the discovery that, both as a group and as individuals, we carry a eucharistic identity.

One way of understanding the Eucharist is to see that there are four liturgical actions, rooted in Christ's words 'I am the bread of life'. The bread is taken, blessed, broken and given.

And I want to suggest that this gives us our own pattern for living, as a community and as individual followers of Christ. We ourselves find our purpose in being taken, blessed, broken and given. It is in our spiritual DNA because we celebrate this together so often; because we learn this pattern of living, not only on a Sunday but on a Monday and Wednesday and Thursday; the sacrament of the Eucharist runs through us like a stick of rock. This sacrament only makes sense, only comes to life in the way it should, when it infuses the whole of our life, when it is our pattern for living in the world.

We ourselves are the body of Christ in the world today. And so it is we ourselves who are taken, blessed, broken and given.

We are taken

This is the mystical part of the human vocation. We are summoned into being by God, drawn into life by an unseen God whose creative life-force infuses every breath we take. We know ourselves to be taken into the life of the Spirit.

There are times in our lives when we might begin to see the outline of how a life taken up into the Spirit might be lived. You remember that in the Hebrew Scriptures Jacob sees it while he's half asleep. What an enticing prospect – a ladder to climb! Who knows where it leads, but step by step he might be able to commit himself to putting one foot in front of the other (Genesis 28.10–19). You remember too Jesus' creative and energizing conversation with Nicodemus. It's not a matter of climbing back into the womb to be all thin-skinned and new-born again. It's a matter of catching the Spirit where she is freely, wildly present. Many don't have a lot of time in modern life for this kind of spacious dreaming. In work and personal life, what is often valued most highly is decisiveness, purposeful achievement, even drivenness. While from time to time of course these things are important, they are usually detrimental to a lively and creative spiritual life. The movement of the Spirit is that of a wild and free energy that finds her way in through the cracks, sometimes the twilight moments of living, the in-between times. What are the in-between times of your day, of your life? What are they for us as a church? And do we have enough of them to be open to this kind of being taken up into God's purposes and God's presence? If there aren't enough of them, be brave and find some doing-nothing time when you simply put yourself at the disposal of the God who will take you up into the contemplative life of the Spirit.

We are blessed

The promise God makes to us is that we are blessed. Blessing does not translate into existence that is pain-free or smooth-running or easy. Blessing, in the tradition that Jesus inherited, was given to those who were elite, even godlike themselves. He adapted this in his Sermon on the Mount so that the blessed ones were the ones who hunger and thirst for righteousness, the ones who mourn, the ones who are poor. Blessing is the abundant, undeserved, outrageous, profligate love that is poured upon the world. Our task is to notice it and learn ever more deeply to live in the knowledge of it.

I was recently in Syria and I spent some time walking about in the utter, utter devastation of the bombed East Aleppo. Utterly shocking, total destruction. All around the debris of unimaginable slaughter. And in the wasteland of human destructiveness, the birds were singing for all they were worth. No human noise any more. Just the joyous, undefeated song of the blackbirds, and the swooping movement of the swallows. A moment of blessing in among the rubble of human destruction.

Without being simplistic or naïve about it, what are the true blessings you know about in your own life? For what do you want to give thanks today? And in the spirit of Matthew's beatitudes, know that it is where you are poorest in spirit that blessing emerges.

We are broken

I mentioned that the Eucharist is always, even on a day like Christmas Day or Easter Day, a broken-hearted celebration. That's because Christianity will always resist any attempts to sanitize life or construct a fantasy religion. The murkiness of our own mixed motives, our own capacity for jealousy, betrayal and violence are exposed in the story of Jesus' last days. We are confronted with this reality every time we celebrate the Eucharist together.

But there are many kinds of brokenness. As C. S. Lewis wrote on the death of his wife about grief, 'It has so many ways to hurt me ... I only learn them one by one.'[1] As the years go on, the wounds we carry inside us are not always visible to everyone else.

Our parish pilgrimage group recently returned from Berlin and Auschwitz. We were following in the steps of Dietrich Bonhoeffer, the Lutheran pastor murdered by the Nazis in 1945, just before the end of the war. He made incredibly difficult choices about what to do in the face of Nazi totalitarianism; and he has been lionized as a Christian martyr, even saint, because of his strength of faith and courage under fire. But his writing revealed a much less certain man, a person broken by anxiety and paradoxical searing worry. However confident or OK we might seem, as individuals or as a church, we in the church have to know how to be broken-hearted otherwise the broken-hearted people won't know that they belong here too.

There is no substitute in our church life for spending time face to face with the people who are destitute, addicted, grief-stricken – and for getting to know the destitute, desolate and addicted parts of ourselves, knowing that it is in this part of ourselves that God is most likely to be found. Staying close to this broken-hearted meal of the Eucharist will lead us, not to the sunny uplands of a false utopia, but to sorrow, to loss, to the violent and hubristic tendencies in ourselves and others. Sharing in this Eucharist takes us into the fiery furnace of grief. And it will give us the will and the depth of commitment to withstand the burning.

We are given

There is a lot of discussion in society, it seems to me, about self-help, self-fulfilment. If our Western, late capitalist, mature market economy has a mantra, then it might be 'You can achieve whatever you want if you work for it'. Self-definition and understanding are essential if society is to be just. But there is a danger in becoming too self-referential in the process.

Our vocation as church, and as part of the body of Christ in the world today, is not to become all that we can be for our own sake, or even primarily for our own happiness. Self-fulfilment, realizing our potential, are all fantastic aims on the road to a redeemed sense of service to other people, to society, to God. Our vocation is to become fully the person we are, so that we can give ourselves away.

How do we give ourselves away in a church community? It is important to note how counter-cultural this is, and to commit ourselves to doing it more, as the fourth distinctive element in this life that we have said we want to live. It was a former rector of St James's, William Temple, who said famously in the 1930s that the Church is the only institution that exists for the benefit of the people who do not belong to it. To retain that open-heartedness is very hard, especially when we are, inevitably, also in the business of keeping the show on the road. But to keep our own hearts and minds prised open, to keep the thresholds of our churches low, to keep our jargon to a minimum and our communities joinable by anyone who turns up, all of these things are practical ways for us to give ourselves away, even to the point of our own apparent failure.

We are Anglicans and so we believe in the priesthood of all believers. This eucharistic vocation is the vocation of every person gathered at this altar. We know the brokenness we each carry, we know the blessing and gift we each carry too.

There is much in modern life to resist and be worried about. Social media trolls, an uncertain economic future, the blandi-fication and, to some extent, the brutalization of our political culture, the pressure on young people, the housing crisis, the appalling rise in incendiary rhetoric towards migrants. There is much inequality and systemic prejudice to confront and continue to work to transform.

We celebrate this Eucharist, then, not in some religious fantasy world, but in this real world, remembering, for the sake of our own broken-heartedness and the broken-heartedness of all grown-up human living in the world, that we are church. For Christ's sake, we accept our calling to be taken, blessed, broken and given: a vibrant and adventurous vocation.

Note

1 C. S. Lewis, 1961, *A Grief Observed*, London: Faber and Faber, p. 33.

26

Trinity 14

*Preached from the outdoor pulpit in the courtyard of
St James's Piccadilly.*

Romans 14.1–12
Matthew 18.21–35

'Some judge one day to be better than another, while others
judge all days to be alike.'

There's an in-joke told among clergy about taking services
from the 1662 Book of Common Prayer. Of course the
poetry is wonderful, the vocabulary is beautiful, if challenging sometimes, and for many Church of England parishes and
cathedrals, apart from evensong, the main time it's used for
services is early in the morning on a Sunday – something like a
communion service at 8 o'clock.

With a busy day ahead, sometimes the vicar's concentration
isn't what it should be. The thing is that the Lord's Prayer
occurs twice in the Book of Common Prayer Communion Service, once at the very beginning and once near the end. If the
vicar knows the service well by heart, and isn't concentrating
– and this has happened more than once – they may think that
the second time they are saying it is actually the first, and so, as
the prayer ends, they set off to start the service all over again.
The helpless congregation can then be facing the prospect of
a kind of *Groundhog Day* loop communion service that they
can never escape. Church going round and round for ever …

One of the features of lockdown for many people has been
that we changed our relationship to time itself. For any working from home, the boundaries became blurred; it wasn't easy
to know when you were at work or not. For those on furlough,

or home-schooling, or shielding, or simply being more at home than they had ever been before, the usual markers of time, the ways that days used to be measured, were changed beyond recognition. If home itself was not safe, then this became a torture without end. Meanwhile, those who worked throughout found that work was harder, shifts longer, and the usual supermarket shop they did on their way home presented them with empty shelves. Time became so pressured because it became short.

And for some who struggled for breath in ICU wards, time became a torturous war against sickness that seemed never to end.

And, according to the current figures, for 917,000 people worldwide time became their path to eternity, as in one moment they slipped or fought their way through death to what was beyond.

The emergence of Covid-19, combined with our attempts to suppress it, has affected all of us in unforeseen ways. And one of these has been in our experience of, use of, attitude towards, time.

For Christian communities, such as the one Paul was writing to in Rome 2,000 years ago, understanding developed gradually that, while we live our lives in time, eternity isn't 'over there' somehow. Eternity is now and we live in the light of it now.

A service like the one we are taking part in today looks solid enough. Here we all are, the paving stones beneath our feet. Here we are, being church outside the church in this courtyard on a usually busy central London street, making a joyful noise in the centre of town. But this is a sacramental place, a liminal, creative boundary place, not just because we are quite literally between the street and the church but because we are present now in a sacrament where all time is present now.

This might feel too abstract to take in, but it's a perspective that can be made real by remembering so many stories and echoes, songs and conversations, held here, now, today. This sacrament, this communion takes place at the crossroads between time and eternity. Your life story is held here; and there are, here in this sacrament, layers and layers of stories and meaning.

We will hear the incomparable music from 900 years ago of Hildegard of Bingen; visionary writer of music like no other in her generation.[1] Her voice sings out here leaping across the centuries to this Eucharist where all days and all lives are present. Harry Emerson Fosdick, who wrote our first hymn,[2] preached such a powerful anti-war sermon in New York in 1933 that Dick Sheppard, the vicar of our neighbour St Martin-in-the-Fields, wrote to him and the Peace Pledge Union was formed. Martin Luther King Junior called Harry Fosdick 'the greatest preacher this century' and so when we hear this hymn later, our voices join with the civil rights movement and the Baptist inspiration of both those courageous men. When our singers sing our final song, '*siyahamba ekukenyenkwenkos*' in its English translation, we sing a Zulu folk song transcribed in the 1950s but whose language and rhythms link us to the history of Africa and the struggle against apartheid in South Africa. Jules Cunningham will dance today after this sermon in this courtyard space.[3] Jules's piece embodies Queer gesture – 'something we can't recognise' – in expressing that every moment of one life is lived in every moment; or to put it in a scriptural way – all time is here, we live not only on this day and in this hour but all hours are present here.

This perspective on time and eternity that Christianity offers an often fractious, often terrified, always complex society affects everything. We're not mired in trivialities here, or playing with philosophical niceties, we're trying to say something fundamental about human life in the context of all life for all time. 'All life is present in this death,' says St Paul.

Paradox is the mother tongue of religion.

And the parable – the short story or one-act play that Jesus created – which forms today's gospel is brilliant at expressing it. Of course the story is disturbing. At first glance it's the stuff of nightmares: an omnipotent and colossal God condemns a man who made a mistake to torture – which is against not only the Geneva convention but contemporary Jewish law – and death.

For critics of Christianity, it's a slam dunk. They have their man. That's why Christianity is not to be taken seriously. It's as we thought: God is, after all, omnipotent, mean and unpredictable, and that's borne out by the behaviour of actual people who actually go to church in diminishing numbers – because they're pretty judgemental themselves. If this is sacred Scripture, then it's right to say that this Christianity is not only untrue but deeply damaging.

For those of us listening to this troubling and disturbing parable, it's a challenge, of course. Our first mistake, admittedly led into it by the Gospel writer's final interpretative line, is our inability to do anything but anthropomorphize God.

Despite our best efforts (and to be honest, this particular story doesn't really help us with this), we probably really imagine that, when we're dealing with God, we're dealing with someone essentially like us, only bigger. We start from us, extrapolate and go up. We know about the vengeful feelings we have: anger, resentment, fury, violence, jealousy. We recognize the alarming and merciless destructive parts of ourselves, often towards ourselves if not others. And we imagine therefore that God's wrath is like that, only bigger – which makes it even more violent and more frightening.

And we end up with a God more to be feared than loved, whose capacity for cruelty is unlimited and ungovernable, and with the fearful recognition that we are at the mercy of that powerful, whimsical God.

But one of the most important things Christian theology wants to say about God is that God most certainly isn't like us only bigger. God is utterly other, utterly holy: God undefended and undefeated in the death and resurrection of Jesus that we celebrate in this Eucharist. And this perspective of God's utter otherness transforms what we might think of as God's wrath.

The American novelist Wendell Berry has written:

> To think of oneself as an agent of God's anger is exceedingly attractive ... there are certain intense pleasures in anger, especially if one's own anger can be presumed to coincide with God's, and also in the use of an angry self righteousness as a standard by which to condemn other people.[4]

The clue in taking this parable on is not primarily in the final sentence to torture, but in the first conversation between the king and the servant. Mercy, release, forgiveness: this is the action of God. And, crucially, all these conversations, events, judgements and mercies happen 'at the same time'.

Christianity invites us to encounter a God who is not distant, uninvolved, cool and uninterested, but a God who weeps with those who weep – including you and me. Who rejoices with those who rejoice – including you and me.

If I have learned to trust God, then I will not be afraid to encounter a God whose anger will not destroy me but will reveal to me – to us – the injustices we collude in, however shameful, the waste and cruelty I tolerate or promote. I am provoked and moved by an image of God whose incarnate self weeps with frustration and fury at my inability to grasp the depth and richness of living; who despairs at my reductionism, at our religiosity, more preoccupied with lists of things we believe or don't believe than with lament at our cruelty and neglect, towards ourselves, towards others, towards the planet itself.

This God longs for me to make even a tentative and joyful commitment, day after day after day, to love and forgive and be loved and forgiven for ever; and this God is faithful to me when I fail over and over again to live this out. This parable, discomforting and unsettling as it is, confronts us with timeless questions of what it is to be human.

Who among us does not recognize Jesus' brilliant storytelling – that when we are unable to let go of a long-held bitterness or resentment, when we hold on for what we think is dear life, we are in fact holding on to deathly resentment that sometimes can only be described, as in this parable, as torturous? This can be towards ourselves too: a relentless hammering away at ourselves, unable to forgive, unable to move on.

And this parable is so discomfiting because it holds within it the truth that the reason I constantly need mercy, from God, from other people and from myself, is that I make choices every day. I wouldn't need mercy if I didn't have power and agency in the world. It is in the exercise of our power and choice that we inevitably make mistakes, make bad choices, take a path that is perilous for us or for the ones we love.

And it's therefore, no wonder that I might become reluctant

to pray or find prayer difficult, because this parable faces me with a bracing truth: that God's mercy, as expressed in this parable, addresses me at the point of my power to act, and reveals to me my capacity for mistakes or betrayal or, to use the theological word, sin.

But if that weren't enough, it gets harder.

Not only are we addressed in this parable as people with power to act, and with the opportunity to forgive should we take it, but we are addressed as people in need of forgiveness ourselves.

We are addressed in this parable as human beings who are both powerful and needy. It's often hard for us to reconcile ourselves to being either of those things.

But if that weren't enough, it gets harder still.

Because, thirdly, when those two attributes operate together, our power and our need, we discover our own identity, not as victims – which is morally preferable to us, easier to inhabit – but as perpetrators. The things we have done and the things we have left undone.

Contemplating the mercy of God in this parable brings us into close proximity with our power, our need and our mistakes. Otherwise no mercy would be needed in the first place. No wonder we prefer our own illusions of God – either mean and cruel, with total and unpredictable power over us so we have no chance at all, or, on the other hand, the too-nice, placid God that we recruit to our own causes and opinions and who will never invite us to change. These fantasies of God are challenged by our encounter with this scripture, difficult and bemusing as it is.

As one commentator has put it, 'The gospel plays, according to Christians, the key part in the "long revolution" through which God makes and keeps human beings human.'[5]

In Psalm 85, the song is sung that 'mercy and truth are met together'. There is a deep wisdom in this that is the underlying faultline of this parable. Because for any human being, whenever real truth is told – by us or about us – mercy will be needed.

Another way of talking about the truth-telling that requires the operation of mercy for it to be bearable is to call it judgement.

Contemporary spirituality, especially in the liberal tradition, not to mention a contemporary cultural landscape reluctant to use the language of judgement, finds all this vocabulary difficult and challenging. And because the judgement in this parable has been so abused by church teaching, frightening people into submission, terrifying them with fear of torture and hell, the temptation has been, and still is, to ignore this difficult set of reflections, or to dismiss it, or to dissolve it.

It's important to be careful with this scripture; not all stories are the stories we need to hear at any one particular time. But if you're feeling up to it, jump in head first to this parable and, by doing that, reclaim some of that language in a compassionate, truthful and energizing way.

In letting this parable do its work in our lives, we submit ourselves to the judgement of a God we trust. This judgement will reveal us to be powerful, needy and mistake-makers. So listening to the story and letting it touch us isn't exactly a walk in the park. But it is at least imaginable, and survivable. Because the God we trust doesn't so much exercise judgement with mercy, as exercise mercy as judgement.

The eternal nature of God, who is at the centre of this parable, means that the events it describes are all present for all time in the nature of God: invitation, judgement, forgiveness, salvation.

The writer of John's Gospel made it clear that no book could possibly contain the extraordinary stories, events, teachings and possibilities of the life of Christ. And so, just as all time is present in this sacrament, so all time is present in this reading of Scripture.

In Jesus' story, the man ends up in a place that I recognize – and I wonder if you do too. That I am capable of grace and forgiveness, that I am able sometimes to let go of resentments and bitterness. But that also present in me – at the same time – is the capacity to exercise my power cruelly and selfishly, unaware of, or simply unable to accept, that I am loved and forgiven and free, created beautifully and wonderfully in the image and likeness of God.

All these moments take place at once. All of these possibilities coexist in me at the same time; and what this parable teaches me is that at the point at which I have power to choose – which you and I do in micro ways every day – God is with me, urging me to act justly, live gently, to forgive as I have been forgiven.

To comment too not just on the personal but on the political: you and I are living in the knowledge of extraordinary challenges that face us, living as we do in time in the light of eternity. The catastrophe that two-thirds of creatures have been made extinct in the last 50 years, combined with the catastrophe that because of climate change it's estimated that 1 billion people will become refugees by 2050.

It's important that the Church is engaged deeply with both these global issues, the emergency of the forced migration of people as refugees and the emergency of climate change. We sometimes make the mistake of thinking these challenges are separate and that some prefer to support one cause or issue over the other. But they are not separate; they are intimately connected. If our own actions continue to change the climate of the planet, we lay the foundations for a wholesale economy in the trafficking and exploitation of people trapped in desertification and poverty.

This parable lives today in reminding us that our own wilful neglect of climate change has, will have, is having, torturous consequences for people, not just creatures, and for the planet itself.

This parable lives today in confronting us with both our need and our power as human beings, and, in the light of this, with the judgement and mercy that in God's presence will surely come. And this parable invites us as a church into a faithful following of the joy we experience from one another, most especially across cultural differences, and from our astonishing planet. We are both tortured by grief at humanity's neglect and cruelty towards other people and towards the planet, while at the same time living in the light of utter freedom and the joy of being alive, today, under this sky, with these precious people.

This is the gospel we proclaim. All life, death and new life is bound up in this liminal, sacramental space – in you and me today. Every regret lives alongside every triumph; every act of love alongside our acts of wilful neglect. The wolf lies down with the lamb in the secret places of our hearts. In the light of this gospel, we thank God for the astonishing gift of life; God who knows our despair, who invites us into hope, as we celebrate this Eucharist, knowing that we are fearfully and wonderfully made in the span of our human life and in the light of all eternity.

Notes

1 O Virtus Sapientiae: *Antiphon for Divine Wisdom*.

2 'God of grace and God of glory', written in 1930 by Harry Fosdick when he was pastor of Riverside Church in New York City.

3 See http://www.juliecunninghamandcompany.co.uk/company.html.

4 W. Berry, in R. Shah-Kazemi, 2007, *My Mercy Encompasses All*, Berkeley, CA: Counterpoint, Introduction.

5 T. Gorringe, 2004, *Furthering Humanity: A Theology of Culture*, Farnham: Ashgate, p. 23.

27

Trinity 16

James 3.13 – 4.3, 7–8a
Mark 9.30–37

If you walk at high tide down the south bank of the Thames, past the Houses of Parliament, past Lambeth Bridge, and look over the wall, you begin to see an extraordinary sight as the tide goes out. As the water gradually subsides, you start to see the tops of the heads of four huge statues that have been placed on the stony beach.

The installation is called *The Rising Tide*.[1] Four life-sized shire horses are carrying four people, all of whom have their eyes shut. The horses' heads have been replaced by the so-called 'horse head' of an oil-well pump. For most of the time they are under water, and twice a day they emerge, only to be covered again by the tide that rises over their heads.

The British artist, Jason deCaires Taylor, says about his work: 'The Rising Tide is located within sight of the Houses of Parliament. I think we have to hold people accountable for what they're doing. And that needs to be documented in stone rather than in a few words in a newspaper column.'[2]

It is an art installation that serves also as an awareness-raising protest against climate change.

I visited the other evening and it was an eerie experience. You can clearly see the Houses of Parliament across the river and the amazing natural phenomenon that is the tidal Thames that relentlessly ebbs and flows. The suited and booted figures on the horses remain resolutely silent, faces turned up towards the sky, stone eyes wide shut.

Until earlier this year I was chair of governors of an all-through academy in North London educating boys and girls aged 4 to 18. Seventeen hundred students have just started another school year, the first one in its history that I have not been part of. But I can't help thinking about them, as the school motto was part of today's first reading: 'Show by a good life that your works are done by gentleness born of wisdom.'

James, the writer of the letter, is nicknamed 'James the Just' because the letter he writes – and he only has one in the Scriptures – is very down to earth, very practical, dealing with human life as it really is lived, each day.

'Show by a good life that your works are done by gentleness born of wisdom.'

Sometimes it's hard to make sense of the Bible – there is so much whispered allegory in its pages, so much nuance and so many stories. But sometimes we can use this opaqueness as a way of hiding away from what we deeply know is its wise truth. The American novelist Mark Twain is said to have remarked that it wasn't the parts of the Bible he didn't understand that gave him the most trouble, it was the parts he did understand.

Jesus was essentially a rural figure, but he spent time in towns like the small town of Capernaum we find him in this morning, and of course he travelled to the great city Jerusalem more than once in his recorded ministry. We sometimes say that our Scriptures begin in a garden – Eden – and end in a city – the new Jerusalem – and so the story of God and humanity can be traced too in the urbanization of the planet, the industrialization of human activity, the productivity and creativity that a diverse city seems to encourage and embody.

And what religion has to say about these activities – how, for example, we contribute to the creation, not just of a prosperous or flourishing city, but of a good city, is the stuff of many ethical and theological debates. The gospel today gives us a clue if we set it alongside the letter of James. In Mark's Gospel, once again the disciples are irascible, competitive, the equivalent of arguing on the bus on the way home. It's been a long day. Every day, they are witness to many amazing things – crowds and miracles – and they're listening to Jesus' often opaque and poetic turns of phrase with a mixture of awe and bewilderment, watching in wonder the healing and vivifying effect he seems to have on people. You can just imagine the scene. After another exciting day full of twists and turns, they are on their way home to Capernaum, and, after putting up with a bit of in-fighting, Jesus turns to them and perhaps rather irritatedly says, 'What are you arguing about?' The next detail is just brilliant and is the kind of detail that makes me love Mark's Gospel.

After Jesus turns on them and challenges them, Mark comments that they were silent because they'd been arguing about who was the greatest. I love this detail about the silence. It implies that their cheeks were burning a little, that they knew they'd been caught out squabbling.

This reaction reminds me of what has happened sometimes in the past if I have taken the wedding of a couple I don't know, and they have very kindly invited me to the reception. As I approach the table, the other people try not to look too horrified. Their thoughts are written all over their faces: 'Oh no, we've got the vicar – we won't be able to swear – dammit I wanted to get drunk' – and you realize that a table full of polite but rather wan smiles greets you as you sit down. And no one's very sure what to say.

So the disciples are a bit glum, expecting to get into trouble. But that's not what happens. Mark tells us that Jesus sat down, called the twelve, and said to them, 'Whoever wants to be first must be last of all and servant of all.' And then he took a little child in his arms: 'Whoever welcomes such a child in my name welcomes me.'

A lot has been written and said recently in the press about what welcoming really means in relation to the crisis unfolding on our continent regarding the large movement of people variously called a migrant crisis or a refugee crisis. What do you think about this and what does it mean for a Christian community to be hospitable, welcoming?

We come to eat and drink together at this Eucharist – and you will know that the word Eucharist comes from the Greek root meaning Thanksgiving. At this Eucharist, in a spirit of thankfulness for our lives, this sacrament embodies what a just future looks like: a future where all are fed, where no one is turned away, where, across society's divides, the balances of power are reconfigured and all are equal guests at the table. The very context for this meal is Jesus' meal with his friends the night before his unjust execution. And it is rooted in the Passover: it is our sharing in the unleavened bread first eaten by slaves escaping persecution. Our very sharing together at this Eucharist asks us to show hospitality to all who are in need, including one another.

And there are many ways we can put this into practice: we are asked to take the principles of hospitality that we receive at this holy meal and live them out the rest of the week.

If you live in London, register to give a spare room to an asylum-seeking family at www.housingjustice.org.uk.

Join the Winter Shelter training. St James's, in partnership with our churches, with the synagogue and the mosque, will welcome people going through homelessness to sleep here in the church, here in the sanctuary, with a hot meal and break-fast the next day through the winter. There's so much that you can get involved with, so please do.

Join me in sleeping outside overnight in central London to raise funds for people who will come to the shelter this winter.

Hospitality is at the core of the Christian vocation. Not a hospitality that means doing something 'to' others, but a mutual hospitable stance in a world where we are all guests and Christ is our host. This hospitality means too sharing lunch together with anyone who comes on Christmas Day, a mixture of congregation, homeless guests, tourists and visitors. Anyone who comes.

Our identity as guests at Christ's ritual table is only really fulfilled when it finds expression at Christ's weekday meal table. The ritual Eucharist doesn't make sense unless it finds expression in the way we live. Join us for Sunday, or Monday, or Tuesday, or Thursday overnight or Christmas Day. So our gathering here this morning to break bread together and to share wine from one cup is in itself an expression of God's hospitality to us that we are asked to show to others.

The writer and doctor Sheila Cassidy sums it up well:

Jesus did not say that we would be known as his disciples by our purity or by our piety. He did not say that we would be recognised as Christians by our beautiful liturgy, our distinctive dress or by our rote recitation of the creed.

Christians would be known as disciples of Jesus Christ by our love.[3]

'Show by a good life that your works are done by gentleness born of wisdom,' said James in his letter. Your acting in the world can be characterized by gentleness – I would want to say – to yourself and to others. And this is in turn rooted in the Wisdom of God who, as we learn from the book of Proverbs, is the female personification of God who stands at the crossroads and calls for justice (Proverbs 8). We can join her call.

In sympathy with the stone figures I mentioned at the beginning, it's easy to feel that, what with the troubles of the world, the colossal challenge of climate change, the millions of people displaced by war, the irreducible need that human beings seem to have for selling and buying, even each other, the water gets very high sometimes. We are in over our head, and we can start to feel a combination of helpless and hopeless.

And reminding ourselves of the truth that we have no power of ourselves to help ourselves, not fundamentally anyway, can if we're not careful lead to our being too afraid to act at all. And our differences and arguments about what to do can sometimes become part of that problem too.

So let's not just go red and stop talking as the disciples did. It is arrogant of us as human beings to believe that we can solve all the injustices in the world, and that if only we tried a bit harder or gave a bit more or strained a bit more we could do it. This kind of belief might sound as if it's rooted in justice and love, but often it's rooted in anxiety, a sense that we must endlessly make up for something. It is unredeemed anxiety and, at root, is a denial of the presence of God. It is functional atheism, acting and living as if God didn't exist.

But there is another path we can take which is somehow, mysteriously, expressed in the poem with which I will close this sermon.

It is published in the book *Good Friday People* by Sheila Cassidy, the doctor I quoted earlier. It's written by Sister Carol Bialock RSCJ, one of Sheila Cassidy's Good Friday people herself. Although it is not absolutely clear what all the metaphors in this poem mean, for me it is, to quote James's letter, a wise and gentle use of the language of neighbours and suffering, welcome and hospitality. For me, it is an encouragement to trust that, while we know we can never do enough, we are asked by our celebration of the Eucharist to practise what I hope we can call 'fearless hospitality', rooted in our trust that God expresses such fearless hospitality to us.

I built my house by the sea.
Not on the sands mind you
Not on the shifting sand.
And I built it of rock.
A strong house
By a strong sea.

And we got well acquainted, the sea and I.
Good neighbours,
Not that we spoke much.
We met in silences,
Respectful, keeping our distance
But looking our thoughts across the fence of sand.
Always the fence of sand our barrier,
Always the sand between.
And then one day
(and I still don't know how it happened)
The sea came.
Without warning.
Without welcome even.
Not sudden and swift, but a shifting across the sand
    like wine
Less like the flow of water than the flow of blood,
Slow but flowing, like an open wound.

And I thought of flight, and I thought of drowning, and I
    thought of death.
But while I thought the sea crept higher till it reached
    my door.
And I knew that there was neither flight nor death nor
    drowning.

That when the sea comes calling you stop being good
   neighbours,
Well acquainted, friendly from a distance neighbours.
And you give your house for a coral castle
And you learn to breathe under water.[4]

Notes

1 *The Rising Tide*: Edition 1, River Thames, Vauxhall, London.
Tidal sculpture 0–8m. Installation date 2015.

2 Jason deCaires Taylor, quoted on https://www.underwatersculp
ture.com/projects/rising-tide-thames/.

3 S. Cassidy, 1991, *Good Friday People*, London: Darton, Longman
and Todd, p. 63.

4 Cassidy, *Good Friday People*, pp. 108–9.

28

Trinity 17

Acts 6.7–end
Mark 9.30–37

Last Saturday it was sunny. Hot. I spent the day in a beautiful garden in Cambridge with a group of people from different faith backgrounds, most of whom I didn't know, who had been convened by Rowan Williams to listen to a conversation. The day was so beautiful, and Cambridge so tranquil, that the exchanges we were listening to seemed almost other-worldly, incongruous to our placid surroundings.

A young woman called S was talking to an older man called J P. J P is a Tutsi survivor of the Rwandan genocide: his parents, family and many friends were hacked to death during 100 days in the summer of 1994 when a million Tutsis were murdered in a killing spree by Hutus.

S is the daughter of a Hutu general, who was jailed for his part in the oversight of the massacre of Tutsis, although she protests his innocence. She now lives in Belgium, in some kind of exile from her homeland, working with young Rwandans on reconciliation and peace projects.

The gathering was part of a series of dialogues called the Inspire Dialogues, whose conviction is that, while we often rush to judgement about saying 'What can we do?' in the face of atrocities, sometimes what we actually can do is listen, talk, dare to engage, try to speak.

Its conviction therefore is that talking is not cheap, it is costly. And that honest conversation is a place to start.

S and J P spoke slowly, both speaking in their second or third language, but deliberately and with emotion that neither of them could conceal or reduce. It was hard to listen; harder still to think of something to say, something to ask; As I listened, I felt as if I was drawing near a burning building; the heat of it threatened to burn my face, and the people inside were looking out at me, an accused bystander, as well as trying to speak to each other.

This summer a group went from St James's Piccadilly on pilgrimage to Berlin, Krakow and Nuremberg. Although 29 people went, it was a whole-church endeavour and many others came to the preparation meetings without coming on the trip itself. As a group, we went to Auschwitz, Birkenau, Berlin and Nuremberg and tried to face together the horror, the bleakness, the nihilism of Nazi ideology that caused one set of human beings to murder 6 million other human beings with an industrialized killing machinery that left many of us feeling disorientated, sick.

Earlier this year I visited Syria for eight days, travelling through the desert on a bus with armed guards to the front and back, knowing that, at one point, ISIS strongholds were on one side and Jabat al Nusra were on the other. Over the eight days, Syria and cities we were in were bombed by no fewer than six countries: UK, US, France, Israel, Russia and the Syrian government. I listened to the stories of former residents of Eastern Ghouta, the intense trauma and mess of a population in the middle of a war, with very little hope, with trust destroyed. And now, back in London, I listen to the news and think that President Bashar al Asaad is about to commit a further atrocity, with Russian assistance, in the province of Idlib. And there is nothing anyone is going to do to stop it. I have myself struggled to find words for that experience, visiting a society and a country which is in the middle of its own nightmare, with an exhausted population and a generation of brutalized young people.

Rwanda, Auschwitz, Syria. Names that in our generation are freighted with a toxic symbolism that will linger for as long as we are alive, and beyond.

Chemical weapons, gas chambers, machetes. It is hard to face the depravity to which human beings can sink. To which, I have to face, perhaps I could sink.

I am speaking about bleak subjects in this sermon – and sermons are supposed to be about preaching good news. But the gospel does not, in its proclamation of good news, offer bland assurances that everything will be all right, because it patently isn't.

But I think I can offer, rooted in this same gospel, a sense of hope.

In today's scriptures we had a dose of realism and a refusal to over-spiritualize what are the truths about human life in the world.

In the passage from Acts we heard the beginnings of a conspiracy against Stephen, who was clearly an astonishing person: kind, full of the Spirit, brave. He was a leader of a group of seven who were specifically tasked with serving the poorest people in first-century Jerusalem; women whose husbands had died and who were themselves destitute. We hear the religious leaders beginning to plot his destruction. They 'stirred up the people'. Then they suddenly confronted him, seized him and brought him before the council.

This is a familiar story. It was told in the years before World War Two, when the people were 'stirred up' with disgusting anti-Semitic propaganda through newspapers, Nazi leaflets, book burnings and most famously Kristallnacht in 1938. In 1994, incitement against Tutsis was 'stirred up' among Hutus by a dedicated radio station, broadcasting filth and lies about Tutsis, calling them cockroaches and declaring them subhuman. And while in Syria I watched a propaganda film made by the Deputy Speaker of the Syrian Parliament which left me feeling physically sick. Public executions, chemical weapons attacks, the dehumanizing of a whole generation reminded me again that the first casualty of war is truth.

In the gospel for today Jesus tries to explain that he will be killed for what he is teaching. Despite his being as plain as this, the reaction of his closest followers is still to be arguing along the way about who is the most important among themselves.

T. S. Eliot had it right when he commented that 'human kind cannot bear very much reality'.[1]

And in the face of this reality, is this gospel really adequate? Is it really adequate in the face of the torture and cruelty of Auschwitz, Rwanda, Syria? Jesus gets a child and puts the child in front of the crowd and says to the rest of us – you have to accept the kingdom of God like a child.

Really?

Surely these toxic places are no places for children. And yet.

One million children under 16 were murdered in the Holocaust. Young ones were sent to the gas chambers holding their mothers' hands so they didn't cry.

In the 100 days of the Rwandan genocide, 53.7% of the million killed were children and young people under 24. It is difficult to establish the proportion of boys to girls, but it is known that there were orders to kill boys, to the point that some dressed up as girls to try and survive.

And in Syria, the use of barrel bombs by the regime and Russia has led to estimates that, from 2013 onwards, 1 in 4 civilian deaths have been and continue to be of children under 16.

These places are no places for children. But in one of the appalling barrack rooms in Birkenau, paintings survive from adults waiting to be sent to the gas chamber, of large-scale figures of children on their way to school. Ordinary children, painted by their parents trying to humanize an inhumane environment, trying to comfort and entertain children who were similarly about to die.

One of the common threads between these experiences of Syria, Auschwitz and Rwanda when placed next to the gospel is that of imagination, and how human imagination can serve God when placed at the service of the gospel, searching for hope in a bleak world.

Our group that went to Auschwitz did so for as many reasons as there were people. Everyone who went went as an individual and I wouldn't presume to speak for any of them. Why we went as part of St James's Church, though, I can speak about. And some of it is rooted in the church's historic vocation, based in the gospel, to be witnesses. And to take steps, in the manner of Christ's ministry, to create witnesses. That requires two things.

First, that you are willing to travel. You are willing to put your body into a different place; you are willing to go there, stand there, move yourself to be there, so that you see a different perspective and bear witness to what you see.

And second, that you are willing to try to imagine the experience of the other.

We are rightly schooled these days not to commit the cardinal sin of uttering platitudes to suffering people. When you are in the middle of your own suffering almost the worst thing anyone can say is 'I know how you feel'. On a personal level, this platitude often elicits a rage: how can you possibly know?

That's really true and important.

But an exchange last Saturday in Cambridge made me think about this a bit differently. One person in our group was being very careful to say to the Rwandan guests, I can't possibly imagine how you feel, how it was. And to this everyone nodded. Because that's what you're supposed to say.

But one of the youngest people there – a theatre director in his 20s – challenged this. 'I don't think that's good enough,' he said. 'Maybe we can't imagine what it was like. But I really think we should try.'

And I felt that he had taught me something by saying this.

One of the themes of our trip to Germany and Poland was reflecting on the very difficult decisions we have to make about how to remember; how not to forget the lessons; how to work now to try to prevent such cruelty again.

Of course it was hard to look at the piles of shoes and suitcases at Auschwitz. But as one commentator has said:

In a perversely ironic twist, these artefacts – collected as evidence of the crimes – were forcing us to recall the victims as the Nazis have remembered them to us: in the collected debris of a destroyed civilisation. Armless sleeves, eyeless lenses, headless caps, footless shoes: victims are known only by their absence, by the moment of their destruction. In great loose piles, these remnants remind us not of the lives once animating them, so much as the brokenness of lives now scattered in pieces.[2]

Important debates will continue about how to remember the dead, especially the dead from genocide and state-sponsored criminality. But from the gospel point of view, if Jesus is saying anything approaching what we think he might be saying, then he is valuing the childlike (not childish but childlike) capacity for two things: imagination and asking questions.

Of course it's not possible really to know another person's experience – either joyful or desolate. And so we can't claim that knowledge.

But even to travel to Auschwitz-Birkenau, or to sit in courtroom 600 in Nuremberg, means that those who went and those who supported them were part of a commitment to create witnesses; to face something hard together. And to be willing to try to imagine now what the real human beings experienced then. And in doing that, to face our own capacity for both depravity and honour.

And, like a child, to keep asking questions, especially the question that all young children ask a lot: Why?

Too many of us practise our faith mostly in our heads; we easily get stuck there. But finding some aspect of faith 'interesting' is not to explore a theological category or a spiritual discipline. Christianity is not primarily a matter of intellectual assent, although this way of knowing is a noble endeavour. As a practised religion, Christianity is not primarily a set of doctrines, but a life to be lived. Messily, full of mistakes, getting a lot wrong, often desperate for forgiveness, often longing for love.

In fulfilling our vocation as a community that is willing to create witnesses, to deploy our imaginations in the service of justice, we might ask ourselves the following questions.

Where are the places that you can go to – actually physically travel to – that will change your perspective, and fertilize your imagination? Where is it that you can put your body so that you witness a different reality, learn more about what it's like to be human and learn more about where God is in the world?

And are you prepared to keep asking, for your whole life, keep asking *why?* without giving in to despair?

Are you willing to try to imagine another's experience, not just that of the victims but that of the perpetrators? Not just the Jews but the Nazis? Not just the Tutsis but the Hutus? Not just the civilians but the men in the forces suppressing Syria's population in the name of the regime of Bashar al Assad?

Because if we stay away, trying to convince ourselves in some way that by doing that we can stay out of it, stay pure, then we are not able to live the gospel we proclaim. Our own shame is the necessary seedbed for our redemption. Our own shame is precisely the place where God meets us in the crucified Christ, murdered by frightened politicians and religious elites, the roots of whose fear is in every one of us.

And so we commit ourselves to listen, to imagine, to pray. Because in all these crucibles of suffering, past and present, truly listening and imagining is not primarily about us. It is a gift, perhaps the only gift at this distance, that we can give to the ones who died and are dying. That they remain, and will always be for us, mysterious, precious souls, not statistics, whom we have tried to meet, tried to hear. And that they are precious to us because they are precious to God. And that we will remain forever shocked, forever stricken, that this cruelty is part of our humanity. Part of us.

And, like a child, we will live the lives we have been given, attentive to the possibilities of justice offered in the kingdom of God, playfully, joyfully, quick to cry tears of solidarity, but always asking *why*. And acting every day, every minute of every day, to help make the world more just, more kind, more shaped like the life of Christ.

Let us pray.

Eternal God, hold us quiet through the age-long minute. When you are silent and the wind is shrill.[3]

Amen.

Notes

1 T. S. Eliot, 1979, 'Burnt Norton I', *Four Quartets*, London: Faber and Faber.

2 James E. Young in Ann Weiss, 2001, *The Last Album: Eyes from the Ashes of Auschwitz-Birkenau*, New York: W.W. Norton & Company, pp. 16–18.

3 Prayer attributed to Amy Carmichael (1867–1951).

29

Trinity 18

2 Timothy 3.14−4.5
Luke 18.1−8

Last weekend I took part in a day of what are called Thinkins.
This device is used by all sorts of organizations – arts organizations, businesses and, in this case, a new journalism startup
called Tortoise Media. The idea is to get away from a panel
event where a few speakers debate in front of an audience, and
to gather a group of people who say what they think about an
issue. The point is to try to make the participation rate high; no
questions are allowed, regular straw polls are taken, and your
opinion is allowed to change and develop but you must express
it if you want to speak. The overall aim of the startup is to
practise 'slow news', less knee-jerk, less driven by a voracious
news cycle, and, like a tortoise, to take some time to reflect
and move more slowly. To go deeper into an issue by first of
all taking time to listen.

I was speaking at a Thinkin that was looking at the clash,
or perceived clash, between religious and secular rights. Two
scenarios were cited. The first was the current protests outside
primary schools in Birmingham led by some Muslim cam-
paigners and parents unhappy that their children are being
introduced to the 'No Outsiders' programme, where families
of different makeup, including parents of the same sex, feature
as characters.

The other issue was of an actor who had been cast in a
dramatization of *The Color Purple* to play a character that is
portrayed as a lesbian character, although this is not explicitly
stated in the book. A Facebook post was researched from 2014
where she said that, based on her own Christian faith, 'I do not

believe homosexuality is right.' The theatre have sacked the actor. The actor is now suing the theatre.

Some very challenging opinions were aired by people who identified as religious, and also by those who had been very hurt by religion.

What interested me as part of this event was something that happened right at the beginning. The Thinkins are often held in the newsroom of Tortoise in London, although sometimes they go on the road – in fact, we've held one at St James's Piccadilly on the relevance of the Church in modern society. In the newsroom, it's a bustling place, and there are cameras everywhere – everything is streamed live, and also recorded, packaged for later transmission.

This was the only Thinkin of the day where the cameras were switched off. And it's because the secular news editors judged the theme of religion to be too sensitive to stream live. I was really struck by this sensitivity, and thought more than ever how important it is to gather together to practise our religion in an open and transparent way. And that the practice of religion can never be allowed to be privatized, to become disconnected from the light of debate and scrutiny by others. The discussion I was involved in got very heated and, as the only public representative of the Church there, I was rightly put under pressure about what was perceived to be the Church's attitude towards sexuality, assisted dying, abortion and equality.

Afterwards, the editors offered this reflection about our society, in the light of these heated discussions. And I thought it was so well expressed, I wanted to repeat it here.

> We heard that ... society has become more complex, creating more points of abrasion; because digital technology has driven us deeper into our echo chambers and made possible an ugly culture of anonymised abuse; and because interacting more and more by digital device, rather than face to face, we are forgetting the art of social negotiation and trust-building.
>
> There is no right not to be offended. And we must have the right to speak our minds. But there is no obligation to offend, either. We should, as the social psychologist Jonathan Haidt has said, seek both to give and to take less offence.[1]

This secular journalistic reflection put me in mind of Scripture's definition of love as love that 'does not take offence'. But this teaching is lost in an atmosphere where religion is often seen, and of course often is, more part of the problem than part of the solution. Siloed ourselves, guilty of group-think, we fight for our rights before taking the time to listen hard to what others feel so deeply. It is a persistent paradox that in the twenty-first century, with all the scientific and philosophical knowledge at our disposal, the world seems more tumultuously religious than ever.

And it's simply no longer credible for the Church to stick its fingers in its ears and pretend that we don't know things now that the writers of our Scripture couldn't possibly know. But it's also not a credible option for the Church to roll over in the face of the immense challenges of post-modernity and become just another single-issue campaign group, or another self-help programme.

The vocation of the Church is to point away from itself to Christ: the spacious, infinitely creative, generative, forgiving presence of God in the world – in your inner soul and in mine – and in the universe we call our home.

To be part of church in contemporary society is exciting, because here we are asked to look at the deepest of themes in the most honest of ways. Church in contemporary society has the potential to be hugely energizing in finding ever more vivid ways to point away from ourselves towards the mystery of the God of the universe. Of course church as a human community at times is infuriating and you might wish it were different from how it is and the people in it were easier to like. But in terms of our vision of a just and beautiful society, we persistently gather, we physically gather, to imagine a better world together – which is more counter-cultural than we might think.

Scripture too, with its intensely perplexing and creative stories, faces us with truths we have forgotten or don't dare to say. Scripture is thoroughly relevant when we take the time to wrestle with it – not just to read it but to grapple with it, learn to love it and listen deeply for its truth. And the spiritual muscles we exercise in grappling with its wisdom are essential for deepening not just our knowledge but our wisdom as we work out how to live in the world.

We heard some incredible encouragement in the first lesson today which energizes me.

> In the presence of God and of Christ Jesus, who is to judge the living and the dead, and in view of his appearing and his kingdom, I solemnly urge you: proclaim the message; be persistent whether the time is favourable or unfavourable; convince, rebuke, and encourage, with the utmost patience … (2 Timothy 4.1–2)

'Whether the time is favourable or unfavourable' – also translated sometimes as 'in season or out of season'. Never give up. And I love the thought of being 'solemnly urged' not to give up. It sounds like something we should say more. And it is a message for our own day, when religion should not be trying – ever – to coerce or force, but is always in the mode that St Paul describes here, the mode of persuasion, debate, encouragement. Wrestling with Scripture is expecting to be convinced, or rebuked when necessary – and all with the utmost patience.

And the brilliant parable that we heard in Luke's Gospel again reminds us that Jesus is incredibly creative as he writes his characters. In this one, he starts with a widow and a judge. Immediately a contemporary audience would understand the huge disparity between these characters. In any patriarchal agriculturally based society, like first-century Palestine, the widow is extremely vulnerable, socially and economically. She is one of the most powerless people in society. But she absolutely refuses to be cast as that powerless person that everyone might expect her to be. She consistently and persistently speaks up for justice. And the judge – what a great character he is! He's a bit supercilious, pleased with himself, probably enjoys a bit too much the fact that people give him respect in the street or want him at their house. He doesn't properly respect people and has given up on God. He doesn't need God.

This woman, this apparently powerless, voiceless woman, is so persistent that she makes justice happen, ultimately in collaboration with this reluctant judge. Jesus' teaching methods are inventive here. He's painting an unattractive picture of this man, albeit one that perhaps his audience can relate to; but then he says, as he does elsewhere, 'Well, if her persistence is effective with this very unattractive character, then just think how praying to a God who is loving and just – think what a difference that could make.'

These scriptures – the story told by Jesus and the advice written by Paul – carry a theme consonant today for us as people who are trying to make our way in the world as people of faith.

With the themes of patience and persistence, both Jesus and St Paul urge us to pray, as a way of addressing the injustices of the world and the building of community.

And in a society where we are siloed and where we make God's love and mercy too narrow to suit our own purposes, we turn a corner if we persist along the road of prayer – and suddenly emerge into a huge love like the ocean or the night sky, within which the torturous anxieties and sickening worries that occupy our minds most days can be put down and given over.

I spent some time recently with a man who earns his living by being paid for sex. He can make good money in a day, but if he does do a day of this, working from a rented flat, advertised on a website, then he needs time to recover afterwards. In some ways, he says, he feels very lost. Used. Addicted – although never to drugs. It became apparent that, being also a Muslim and a transvestite – although he is clear that he is not transgender – his vulnerability, economically and socially, is of a similar level to that of the widow described in Jesus' story. I was incredibly moved by the kindness and humour of this man, and heard in his conversation his persistence in wanting to make something of his life, trying to find someone to love; his persistence in wanting to connect, wanting to make friends, wanting to help other people. From deep within his incredibly precarious circumstances, I met someone who was indescribably alive. I heard in his conversation a persistent voice wanting connection and love – a voive that would not be silenced or put down. And in his kind eyes, I learned something about what it might be like to pray persistently like the widow. Time spent with him encouraged me to pray in a way I can't quite explain.

Given so much division and fractiousness, given the prejudice that is dressed up as passionate free speech, given the wreckage left by some religious practice in the lives of people who identify as lesbian or gay or trans or bisexual, for example, or the damage done to people whose lives turn out to be complicated through divorce or abortion or prison or debilitating illness, it's really easy to want to give up on faith or God. Or to say that the inner troll we all carry around should just be allowed to carry on abusing and yelling and standing up for its right to say what it likes, whoever it hurts, whatever the cost.

As the Tortoise editors reflected further:

> It has become orthodox to interpret the present state of the nation in terms of inevitable decline and discord. That polarisation is here to stay. That the digital public square is nasty. That we're in for more trolls and more bots, peddling fakery and hatred.
>
> But only if we let it. This is not our first re-thinking of mass communication, political organisation or personal dignity.[2]

Persistently, courageously, we will continue to say in season and out of season that we turn to Christ. And that cosmic eternal Christ that we turn to, rooted in the prophet and poet Jesus, is an inexhaustible source of love, acceptance and a call to peace. The more we need, the more we can have. And that this deep love of justice and compassion, rooted in Christ, will give us the energy not to retreat into a privatized Christian silo of self-congratulation, or a sense that we should just give up because frankly it's too hard.

This prayerful persistence, which we must continue to articulate publicly, is not easy for a community where a lot of us don't really want to be tub thumpers or thought of as proselytizing, trying to convert others to our point of view.

But we must, like the widow, be persistent, patient, relentless and energetic.

And just in case there is any doubt, it's so important to keep saying publicly, persistently, without fear, and with love, in among all the noise of trolls and competing rights, that you and I are made, beautifully made and loved as we are – whatever our sexuality, ethnicity, gender fluidity or non-binary identity, whatever our emotional, mental or physical health.

And that, while of course we will want to find ways to disagree well, and to love without limits, we are called by this gospel to confront and challenge any view, within ourselves or within another Christian community, that diminishes the dignity of a person who identifies as LGBTQ+. Tolerance is not enough. An engaged commitment to love, mercy and justice is more reflective of the energy of the gospel.

In today's polarized world, we have no option but to keep looking energetically for ways to say that this persistent, emotionally intelligent – yes, tolerant, creative, merciful and inclusive – Christian faith is possible; that our Scriptures are beautiful and challenging and that we love them; that the Eucharist gives us a vision of the future where all are welcome and all are fed; and that, as in the gospel, the poorest among us are the ones who teach us that kind of persistence, because the poorest among us know what it is to have to have that kind of persistence in a life that is often too precarious. Persistence both in prayer and in life.

Let us place our energy, persistence and patience, in the manner of the widow, at the service of justice and, like her, never give up.

Notes

1 Tortoise Media editors, 19 October 2019.
2 Tortoise Media editors, 19 October 2019.

30

Harvest

Job 12.7–10
Luke 12.22–31

This week is a pertinent one in which to be celebrating a Harvest festival. On Monday the news was full of the Intergovernmental Panel on Climate Change report which effectively called for nothing less than a revolution in the way we are living to avoid catastrophic damage: not only damage to the poorest people in the world, whose livelihoods will be destroyed by flooding and drought, but a drastic reduction in biodiversity and an increase in the rate of extinction of creatures. And for Christians this isn't just an ecological issue but a spiritual one, as it is God the Creator we celebrate, the one who made us and all that is seen and unseen.

And two days later, after the IPCC report was published, the Church remembered the seventeenth-century nature mystic Thomas Traherne, whose writings from the 1660s and 1670s, were undiscovered until the twentieth century.

Thomas Traherne was a parish priest in Herefordshire. He was born during the English Civil War, grew up under siege, was ordained during the Protectorate of Oliver Cromwell and was a prolific writer of poetry.

He was a Puritan by training although he didn't really write like a Puritan. There's not much austerity or commitment to ascetism in his sometimes rather overblown imagery and language.

Traherne seems to have moved from Puritanism towards a religious sensibility that allowed enormous enjoyment of nature, receiving all the world has to offer as a gift from a loving God. His writing was emotional, passionate, poetic, mostly about the natural world and how we as human beings, made in the image of God, should live in it. He's prolific, over-whelmingly joyful, childlike, exuberant in his love of the sky, and the trees and the creatures and the birds.

> The sun is but a little spark of His infinite Love. The sea is but one drop of his goodness. But what flames of Love ought that spark to kindle in your soul; what seas of affection ought to flow for that drop in your bosom ...[1]

Let me transport you forward from seventeenth-century Here-fordshire to twenty-first-century London. A man in a high-vis jacket is picking up litter in a London park. It's early in the morning, misty, late summer, and last night's pizza boxes and cans of lager are clustered under the trees. Not many people are there. But the wildfowl are there, gathered in groups by the Serpentine. Among them are the colourful, often noisy, Egyptian geese. A group of ten or twelve of them are lying down on the grass under one of the larger London plane trees. And as the man in the high vis approaches, they don't move away – and so he starts to talk to them. I wonder what he's saying. He's speaking to them in his native Bulgarian and the talk seems friendly enough. He's smiling at them. His litter picker continues to spear bits of paper, plastic wrappings, crisp packets. And as he picks up the litter, he is helping to save their lives. As he speaks to them, perhaps they are saving his. The conversation goes on for some time, until all the plastic is removed from their vicinity and he waves them goodbye.

This is a really typical scene in a London park early in the morning. Hyde Park was first opened to the public in 1637, the year Thomas Traherne was born. And since then, these inter-actions between people and creatures have happened every day. Every hour of every day.

Back in the twenty-first century, this encounter between the man and the geese seems to encapsulate the relationship between human beings and our fellow creatures that is needed in the light of the IPCC report and in the light of the invitation of mystics like Thomas Traherne to love the natural world, delight in it, enjoy it, luxuriate in it. The beauty of the Egyptian goose doesn't seem to be lost on the man. Their feathers

– black, brown, cream, green, orange and white, with their distinctive dark brown eye patches – contrast with their pink legs and black, brown and red beaks. Impressive when they fly, with a wingspan of up to 1.3 metres, they are 2kg in weight, keeping themselves well fed on the seeds and grass that is plentiful in the park. The man is, on behalf of urban humans, cleaning the environment in which the ducks are living, removing human detritus, saving them from the city waste with which they are surrounded. And he talks to them in his native language; he is far from home, working a low-paid job. I have no idea of his circumstances but am struck by his humour and gentleness as he jokes with the geese.

There is some sort of mutual saving going on here. But a sort of love too, in this tiny, fleeting personal encounter between humans and creatures in the middle of the city at the break of the day.

Thomas Traherne, in writing so exuberantly and joyously about the natural world, invites us human beings to notice, to remain attentive, even in the middle of our working day in the middle of a city, like that man picking up litter in the early morning in London. To love the gifts with which we are always surrounded, and to take part in nothing less than the fundamental change of attitude that is so urgently needed. A distinctively Christian contribution to this contemporary debate will be to celebrate a faith in God that is rooted in our sensual experience of the world, that is, in that sense, thoroughly incarnational. God's presence is at the centre of the materiality of life and death, and resurrection is at the heart of it.

One aspect of Thomas Traherne's spirituality that I recognize is that he seems always to be reaching for something. Not just waiting for it, but yearning, stretching, almost straining for a deeper unity, a more profound union with the divine, and therefore a greater and more satisfying happiness, which was one of his preoccupations.

Thomas Traherne teaches us a habitual stance towards creation that is not fundamentally human-centric. Despite one of his goals seeming to be individual happiness – which could seem too self-serving – he defines that happiness as union with the divine, bound by the cords of love, as embodied by Christ on the cross. And so in the end it is more of a self-giving than a self-actualization.

> That Cross is a tree set on fire with invisible flame, that illuminateth all the world. The flame is Love, the Love in his bosom who died on it. In the light of which we see how to possess all the things in Heaven and Earth after his similitude.[2]

And so, despite Traherne's yearning for and emphasizing of happiness for an individual person, there is for me, in his focus on the central presence of the cross at the heart of creation, a de-centring of the human experience which lies underneath all his quests for happiness.

And, in a fundamental way, a de-centring of the human experience is what is needed in our attitude towards the current ecological crisis.

Of course there are real and urgent concerns about the effects of climate change on some of the poorest people in the world. At St James's a couple of years ago we heard first hand from peanut farmers from the Philippines whose land is flooded much more often and whose livelihoods are endangered by the rise in global temperatures. We have only last week been hosting an exhibition of photographs of women farmers in Kenya. And there are many more examples. The unequal and unjust impacts felt by different populations around the world are a matter of shame for those of us in developed nations, who have exported our carbon-emitting progress to poorer nations, who now, not unreasonably, challenge us back. The politics are not straightforward.

But, fundamentally, do we not require a revolution to de-centre the human from how we look at the planet, which is a God's-eye view of creation? It is our habitual stance to view the planet's ecosystems as constituting 'resources' which we can benefit from. We have, since industrialization especially, viewed the natural minerals, water, animals and plants as resources – sometimes resources that we've worked to make sustainable, but resources nonetheless. At the Climate Change marches that regularly move down Piccadilly, often the chants and banners read 'Leave it in the ground'. That is, stop viewing the earth as a natural version of a supermarket shelf, full of choices and goodies for us to eat and use.

Perhaps the spirituality of Thomas Traherne can help us here in two ways. First, for Traherne, the relationship between humanity and the natural world is characterized by the gaze of a lover towards the beloved. And, second, he helps us recover a doxological stance towards nature. Love and Praise.

Just as a lover gazes on their beloved, caught between the desire to possess and the desire freely to adore, Traherne offers us language and energy simply to love the environment we are in. Just love it. And in loving it, weep for it too.

> ... you never enjoy the world aright until the sea itself floweth in your veins ... till every morning you awake in Heaven: see yourself in your Father's Palace: and look upon the Skies and the Earth and the Air as Celestial joys.[3]

It is because we love God, who loves us, that we are no longer the centre of our own universe. It is Christ who is the active centre of all creation, and, as Denise Inge comments, the created world is therefore mysteriously 'God's body'.[4] Traherne insists that it is in the cross that we 'enter into the heart of the universe'.[5] For Traherne, God is disclosed in creation and we are to be enjoyers of that creation, therefore enjoyers and participators in the life of God.

To lay aside our androcentric language can make us playful again, in Traherne's language, more childlike (another of his main themes).

Playing with the scene I described in the park means that we realize afresh that the bird doesn't know it's called a bird. It doesn't know it's called an Egyptian goose. It doesn't even know there is an Egypt. It is gloriously and unaffectedly itself. It's very beingness is in itself part of God's love letter written into creation, more eloquent than any word.

This is rooted in the Hebrew theology of Job, who, daringly, isn't interested in defining and possessing nature so much as in asking it for wisdom.

But ask the animals, and they will teach you;
the birds of the air, and they will tell you;
ask the plants of the earth, and they will teach you;
and the fish of the sea will declare to you.
Who among all these does not know
that the hand of the LORD has done this?
In his hand is the life of every living thing
and the breath of every human being.
(Job 12.7–10)

The language of the earth, in which the creatures speak with us if we ask authentically, is not necessarily conventional religious language. But there it is in the theology of Job, and in the 'otherness' of the creative act in Genesis, which doesn't at all depend on human intervention to make it happen. It is God's action and God's business. Many who are not speaking from a Christian perspective at all would say we are in the current ecological crisis because we have lost the ability to hear and speak the language of the earth, of the natural world. This kind of assertion isn't usually one that finds a Christian response, but there are theological and spiritual resources to help us take part in this conversation.

And that in itself then asks the question, what will we hear if we really listen?

This brings us to Traherne's second helpful approach, that of Praise. Not only are creatures and plants getting on with life without reference to our naming or defining them, they are themselves constantly praising their Creator. And all of our liturgy, celebrated as it is at the crossroads between time and eternity, is offered, not as something we have created or put together, but as a moment in time when we simply join in the eternal praise offered by the created order visible and invisible. Like listening to the angels and archangels in the book of Revelation, whenever we gather to pray, we 'lift the lid' on what is a constant cacophony of praise and prayer and exultant beingness – our prayers simply join this praise, which is always happening, for a few short hours a week.

On Easter Day this year, I had an experience of this myself, which for me was an embodiment of the vision of Revelation and the singing of praise and the declaration of holiness contained in the Sanctus we sing every Eucharist.

It was 5am. I was preparing for the Dawn service at which I was going to sing the Exultet. One of the most ancient songs of the Church, the Exultet announces the astonishing news of the resurrection of Christ. It is sung to ancient plainchant and so I was outside our central London church at 5am on Easter Sunday morning. The clubs had disgorged most of their revellers, and the deafening sound of thousands of glass bottles being tipped into bin trucks was punctuating the early morning. There were a number of people sleeping in the church overnight keeping vigil, and so I went into the church garden so as not to disturb them. It was still technically dark before dawn, although because of light pollution it's never really dark. I began singing: 'Rejoice heavenly powers! Sing choirs of angels!'

As I sang, I realized I wasn't singing alone.

Just feet away from me, a blackbird was singing at the top of his lungs – much, much more beautifully than any human voice. Just because he could. Just because he was a blackbird. I found it hard to continue my practice as I realized my voice of praise was simply joining in what was already going on every morning, making every morning Easter morning, a day of resurrection and exultant joy at being alive. *(At this point, a recording of a blackbird was played and the Exultet was sung as a duet as part of the sermon.)*

> Rejoice heavenly powers! Sing choirs of angels! O Universe, dance around God's throne! Jesus Christ our King is risen! Rejoice O earth in glory, revealing the splendour of your creation ...

I remembered research I had read about city birds, discovering that their lung capacity has increased over years because they have to sing more loudly over the traffic. I remembered reading also that birds, like this stunning blackbird, were being fooled by the night lights of the city and singing way before they should. But despite my curated music perhaps being out of kilter with the blackbird's natural timing, still, my feeble attempt at praise was enveloped, held, cherished even, within the love letter that God was writing even at that very moment – to me and to all of us with ears to hear.

Hildegard of Bingen, the Christian writer and mystic, wrote in the twelfth century as an accompanying text to much of her plainchant music:

> Underneath all the texts, all the sacred psalms and canticles, these watery varieties of sounds and silences, terrifying, mysterious, whirling and sometimes gestating and gentle must somehow be felt in the pulse, ebb, and flow of the music that sings in me. My new song must float like a feather on the breath of God.[6]

For Christians from the twelfth century or the seventeenth century, and for twenty-first-century Christians today, at the centre of the universe is the resurrection energy of Christ risen: the deathly powers of nihilism, human hubris, pollution of motive, abuse of power, all the themes of Christ's death, are dissolved by the miracle of resurrected life after such destruction. Which is why, even in the face of the stark details of the IPCC report, we will want to act not only decisively but joyfully, with a playfulness of spirit as part of the living world God has made and is remaking even today.

All we are doing here, in this service, is joining in the worship of all creation of their Creator. Our song joins the songs of the blackbird. Our words join the cries of the foxes, our prayers join the praise of all living things, as we say in the Eucharistic Prayer – with angels and archangels and all the company of heaven. There is one reality; heaven and earth are joined, we are in union with all that lives and with all that has died and yet lives. If creation is God's love letter, then we gaze on it with love and thankfulness, and we must act decisively and comprehensively to make real change in the way we live in the beautiful, beloved, living world that God has given us to delight in.

I give the last word to Thomas Traherne: 'It was God's wisdom made you need the Sun. It was God's goodness made you need the sea. Be sensible of what you need, or enjoy neither.'[7]

Notes

1 T. Traherne, 2020, *Centuries of Meditations* II, New York: Angelico Press, p. 14.

2 Traherne, *Centuries* II, p. 20.

3 Traherne, *Centuries* I, p. 156.

4 D. Inge, 2008, *Happiness and Holiness: The Writings of Thomas Traherne*, London: Canterbury Press, p. 57.

5 Traherne, *Centuries* I, p. 56.

6 Hildegard of Bingen to Odo of Paris, 1148–1149, Epistolarium, 40R.

7 Traherne, *Centuries* I, p. 15.

31

All Saints

Revelation 7.9–17
Matthew 5.1–12

Our public conversation, in the ongoing Covid-19 pandemic, is littered with words like 'bleak', 'foreboding', 'catastrophe', 'mental health crisis'. The prospect of another four weeks of severe restrictions, commonly known as a lockdown, has settled like a blanket over life today; a background count of worry, a realization that we must keep away from one another. Our energy is at risk of being suffocated, dampened down. Our spirits are dulled. And our feelings of being afraid – perhaps of being periodically gripped by fear but more commonly a dull thump of remaining afraid – are debilitating. Our eyes – my eyes – if I'm not careful, remain fixed, not on the far horizon or a blue autumn sky, but on the city pavement, fearful, cold, wet, grey. And on lifeless computer screens, on graphs I barely understand but which I know are going in the wrong direction.

This is a tough moment.

I won't make assumptions about how you are doing, but I know that many people are struggling, and that some have been brave enough to say that they are. Which is why I make no apology for repeating what is important, yet again, to say to yourselves and to anyone else who will listen: it is OK not to be OK.

Alongside the proper recognition of this hard day, here on this festival of All Saints, something else absolutely astonishing is also true, simultaneously and irreducibly: it is deeply baked into the life of church and society, even during a pandemic.

This irreducible truth is that, into this tough week, into this tough winter bursts a riot of colour, noise, chatter, robes, bravery beyond belief, courage beyond measure – the Communion of Saints. Their stories are of human lives lived to the full, the awkward squad, the outspoken lot, the colossally unwise-if-you-want-to-stay-alive crowd.

They burst on to the scene today with their stories of battles fought and won, justice called for, conversion of heart and mind that sometimes baffled even them at the time and propelled them into an unknown future with their hands firmly grasping the hand of God.

Banish from your minds any thought of carefully crafted stained glass with saints captured and ossified, pious and still. From the contemplatives comes a message for our lockdown times: even the Trappists, even the isolated scholars knew what it was to be fully alive, to want somehow to go to the heart of things, not to waste their time in displacement activity but to keep returning to the deepest meaning of living and the hardest truth of dying.

Here they come, the Communion of Saints, rattling through their pandemic prayers with us at this Eucharist, with stories from their own times of plagues and wars, persecutions and healings – and inviting us to live, to live, *to live* as friends and followers of Christ who knew such suffering and glory as they.

It's sometimes said that a saint isn't someone really pious whose life makes you think that it all looks a bit too much like hard work, weighed down with the knowledge of God. Saints are human beings who live their lives in such a way that you think 'I'll have what she's having'. Saints are somehow intensely alive. Many of them suffered terribly of course, and many die for what they believe in, but the manner of their death is set in a deeper perspective because the Christian tradition will always insist that life in abundance is our calling: the saints are simply the ones who've said yes.

Saints are companions who reassure us that the path we tread, however challenging or alarming, is one that's been trodden before. In this vast and unknowable universe, we are never alone.

Sometimes courageous or foolhardy, awkward as well as inspiring, saints are human beings who somehow have an irreducible desire to travel towards the centre of things, close to the dwelling place of God. Like a journey to the centre of the earth, saints will come close to the heat and the dust of living at the core.

I don't know about you, but I need their energy today. I need their example, their persistence, their awkwardness. I need their gold leaf and singing and playful defiance in the face of grim urban grey, and sickness and death.

Because somehow, in this sacrament, I know their presence. It's not an intellectual knowing; it's not a thought-out theological argument for a category of humanity called 'saint' which is a kind of upper-class Christian. It's not based in either a pre-Reformation piety or a post-Reformation squeamishness about the saints.

It's a different kind of knowledge, a different kind of knowing. It's a felt knowledge that in this sacrament breaks my heart, and breaks it open, and leaves me, in communion with the saints, both undefended and undefeated.

Much of what we know about life and living, about death and dying, is not what we understand intellectually. Of course thinking things through is important, as is taking account of our broken hearts. But often the most important decisions we take, or directions we decide upon, come first not from our head or our heart, but from our gut. We live by felt knowledge.

This is the kind of knowing that roots us here in the fusion of eternity and time that we know characterizes this sacrament. And it roots us in a new form of communion with the online community who join us now in this moment, or later. That's what makes this sacrament a liminal sacred space – for us physically, boundaried by the prayer-soaked walls of this church building, the air thick with music and the smell of wine for the banquet of the kingdom rehearsed here every Sunday, every time.

This sacramental communion of saints gathers whatever the restrictions, whatever the constraints. We will be here making church, being church, not gathered but dispersed yet no less present, no less bound by our baptism, whatever comes.

Come with me then on this day to this altar. Not to argue for some kind of intellectual assent as to the existence of saints – of God even – but to do some deep, felt theology together by sharing in Christ's body and blood which is mysteriously present in the same way for us now as it was for them then.

To celebrate All Saints this year is to determinedly throw a party in a pandemic, but it's not a frivolous party; it has the depth of a wake. Our company is with people who know what it is to live life on the edge. They invite us to come to the edge and look over into the choices they made, choices made not knowing if they would lead to oblivion or to the eternal life on which they staked their lives.

And as we face another four weeks at least of physical confinement, let our spirits remain unconfined. As our bodies are governed by the law that will keep us at home, let our spirits remain in tune with the Holy Spirit of God – ungovernable and free.

To accompany us in this next season, let us call on the saints to travel with us with two things in mind: a search for holiness and an appreciation of eternity.

Holiness is a way of living that focuses on our inner life; the word comes from an old English word meaning wholeness. To learn holiness is to learn we are holistic beings. Even while we affirm that God alone is holy, we are asked to make decisions, to practise the kind of spiritual yielding, that bring us closer to God in the ordinariness of each day. And it is precisely in the ordinariness of holiness and in the ordinary holiness of saints that their beauty and example are to be found.

One of the most damaging mistakes we can make in our spiritual lives is to surround ourselves with fantasies: if only I were a better person, or if only I hadn't had the family I had, if only I hadn't got married to them, if only I had more money or a different job or more friends or fewer relatives or a different house.

It is part of the human condition from time to time to believe that everything would be better if we weren't us and this wasn't it and they weren't there ...

But men and women and children who live lives of holiness are somehow free from this level of 'if only'. The original people who were called saints were simply those who had remained faithful through death, often at the hands of others, and who went freely to their death, accepting that this was, at that moment, simply who they were and where they were.

It is in our generation that we are living through this pandemic. Holiness in the midst of this isn't a quietist philosophy that means we have to take everything lying down – quite the opposite if you look at the feisty saints. But it does mean a fundamental starting from where we are and finding depth here, not wishing we were somewhere else.

Holiness does not require a special set of circumstances or a particular preparation. There is no work, no set of circumstances that cannot be hallowed, that cannot serve as a path to God or a setting for prayer. And, to be honest, our own anxiety that we are not doing enough or not living enough of a holy life has precisely the opposite effect: that is, that anxiety keeps us confined, gets us stuck, and change is much less likely.

For all our study of their methods and speeches, it is in our gut that we are asked to let the saints accompany us, not our heads.

Because the freedom and holiness of the saints is rooted in their conviction that they are simply singing a different song: a music that finds its home in eternity.

And this is the second lesson from the saints: that the fear of death is dissolved by their freedom to accept it. Saints live thoroughly ordinary, recognizable lives but are somehow marching to a different beat, dancing to a different rhythm that has its origin in the eternal dance of God. We're invited to listen for, and find, that beat in our everyday life, not in a life we wish we had or thought we would have by now.

The saints invite us to imagine a world of joyful, beautiful resistance to the forces of destruction and death: a place where our damaging fantasies are overwhelmed by our equally strong desire to love, by the compulsion to forgive and by the instinct to praise, to give deep thanks for all that has been, and, for the future, to give in to our aching desire simply to say yes.

The next weeks and months will be hard, but the saints are with us – the ordinary people who loved the life they knew they would lose, but loved it anyway.

In this kind of living, we are not alone; our inner life has hidden within it the seeds of holiness that remind us we are loved, forgiven and free. We are broken-hearted but open-spirited, and our hope is irrigated by both the suffering and the glory of the saints in light.

One of the saints we remember today, Julian of Norwich, assured us that, in the end, all shall be well.

Yes, in the end, all shall be well. But it's vital to remember, too, that if it is not well with you today, then what that means is that it's not yet the end.

32

All Souls

John 6

The sculptor Cornelia Parker placed dynamite in a garden shed and blew it up. She then collected the mutilated fragments and suspended them from the ceiling of the Tate art gallery, freezing in time the moment the explosion happened. All the jagged parts of wooden walls and roof, the contents – the domestic debris of a life collected in a garden shed – are exploded and held in suspension around a single bare light bulb at the centre of the fragments hanging in the air. The display of this sculpture, entitled *Cold Dark Matter*, in 1991, has become an iconic moment in the history of the Tate galleries, so powerful was its impact on those who saw it.

Commentators interpreted it in many different ways – a vision of the cosmos, reminiscent of a galaxy far away, a comment on modern fragmented society, and so on.

For me, it is a powerful picture of grief.

The garden shed was full of objects that illustrate and accompany a life – magazines, a chair to relax in, a radio tuned to a favourite station. The explosion was real, and destructive. All the fragments of building and contents were gathered, and then reassembled. Now, it is not a solid earthbound shed but a semblance of a shed, with air and light and jagged edges. A shattered building before the pieces fall to earth.

When we experience the death of someone we love, our lives can feel as if they have exploded.

The violence of our reaction can surprise and scare us. The pieces of our life are strangely familiar still, but they are all in the wrong place. There is space where there used to be solid walls, and we can't trust our own eyes.

It can take years for the pieces to settle – they are suspended, we are suspended. We hold our breath, it seems for days; we can't believe that the person we knew has really gone, and we wait in a state of suspended animation for them to come back, even though we know they won't.

Today, All Souls' Day, when we thank God for the people we love who have died, is an emotive day that calls for truthful and strengthening words, honest prayers and permission to cry.

Death is a mystery to us. For all of us, it has only ever happened to someone else. What we see is that the person we love becomes still and silent. After that, it is a matter for belief.

The promise that Jesus makes in the sixth chapter of John's Gospel is that it is the will of God that nothing and no one should be lost. The phrase he uses is that all will be gathered together. There is a promise enshrined here too: that 'anyone who comes to me I will never drive away' (John 6.37). *Anyone*.

The fragmentation that comes with grief, the heart-stopping stillness of the moment after you realize the explosion has happened – it is this jagged intervention into a human life that Christ describes in this gospel and seeks to heal.

This healing is not unlike the mending dynamic of the Kontakion for the Dead. This ancient song is 1,500 years old and comes from the Eastern Christian tradition. Unlike Western tendencies to try to neaten and explain everything, it uses spare language and is full of paradox. The name 'Kontakion' comes from the word for a scroll. To sing this ancient song is really to unfurl the scroll. There is something deeply wise in this. We learn more and more about what it is to live and to die as life goes on – as the scroll unfurls.

We learn, as we travel further through life towards death, that, without trying to make anything better when someone dies, there is a truth in the paradox that, even as we go weeping to the grave, alleluia is sung still by humanity, by creation, in the abundance of the earth which has received the body of the one we loved.

Our fears of what happens when we die are carried by the knowledge that somewhere, some time, in Christ the battle is over, the storm has ceased; alleluia can be sung, even though we think we will never sing it again.

God's promise in John's Gospel is that all will be gathered. The fragments of our lives lived over years, the sharp edges that have cut us and hurt us, unlike the exploded shed, will fall to earth in the end, like the grain of wheat, and be held in the darkness there; and will find new life growing in Christ. This promise is beautiful and good and true.

And like the basket of fragments collected after the feeding of the five thousand, there is a miraculous abundance in this gathering: the fulfilment of a promise made long ago that nothing and no one would be lost.

A promise never fully understood, but on this day, in this dark night, one in which we can place our trust.

33

Remembrance Sunday

Isaiah 2.1–4

It's striking that the way we mark each year the terrible reality of war and its cost is by keeping silence.

Silence is a commodity rare in war. A lasting peace, let alone a just peace, requires much more than the laying down of weapons or the renunciation of violence. The silence that comes after a battle can be simply the silence of the silenced, the silence of the dead. Any imbalance of power, residual resentment, will provide the environment for re-igniting the war – and we are more than capable at the drop of a hat of retreating to our own trenches and shouting slogans across no man's land.

Making peace, maintaining peace is very, very hard work. When Jesus says in the Sermon on the Mount 'Blessed are the peacemakers', he hasn't said 'Blessed are the ones who wish for peace or hope for peace or talk articulately about the importance of peace'. It's people who actually make peace who are the subject of his blessing. Making peace requires a level of confidence and security, because creating a lasting peace involves having your own assumptions and prejudices challenged and transformed.

It was my privilege during my last role at St Paul's Cathedral to be responsible for the liturgy to mark the end of British deployment in the Iraq war. In such a conflicted and controversial atmosphere, prayers were hard to say. Bereaved families, injured service personnel, politicians, journalists and senior military leaders were all under the same roof. But at that service the then Archbishop of Canterbury, Rowan Williams, was impressively independent in his challenge to everyone there, including the ranks of politicians in front of him. He spoke about the period leading up to British intervention in Iraq in these terms:

> ... there were those among both policy makers and commentators who were able to talk about [the conflict] without really measuring the price ... Perhaps we have learned something – if only that there is 'a time to keep silence', a time to let go of the satisfyingly overblown language that is so tempting for human beings when war is in the air.[1]

War is only possible when we have started to believe that the 'other' is fundamentally not like us. And this 'othering' language starts innocuously enough, with comments about different cultures or customs. And making lasting and just peace requires the wilful and deliberate dismantling of this tendency to 'other' people who are more like us than we think.

Making peace involves a very difficult logical path which goes something like this. You are different from me. You want different things, you may speak a different language. Your life is unrecognizable to me, to the extent that you are fundamentally different from me. Sometimes I don't like what you say and I don't agree with what you want. And sometimes territorial ambition or wilful violence towards another in order to gain more power makes it very hard to want to make peace.

The ending of war in order not to sow the seeds of the next one – as happened at the Treaty of Versailles in 1918 – requires some surprising pragmatic skills and is not an event that can be measured by the laying down of weapons or the cessation of physical violence.

It is human beings who make war. And it is human beings who can broker peace. It's not some alien over-arching philosophical blueprint to which everyone is enthralled. The ending of a war, or the prevention of a war, is full of provisionality, ordinary daily decision-making, not divorced from the realities of the personalities in the room at the time. And it grows in the earth of ordinary day-to-day peace-making about which every one of us has choices every day.

And so the work of ending war, of making peace, of recognizing the power-broking and the harmful language that can provide the environment for war in the first place, is a daily task for everyone in this room, not just the professional diplomats, soldiers and MPs.

Today we honour the willingness of the mostly young men and women who will go where they are sent and risk injury or death in the service of their country. And we especially honour the ones who went and did not return.

But the wider context for war and peace is not 'over there' or 'decided by someone else'; the environment in which war breaks out is a lot more ordinary than we think.

I end with the words of Etty Hillesum, who died aged 29 in Auschwitz, in 1943:

> All disasters stem from us. Why is there a war? Perhaps because now and then I might be inclined to snap at my neighbour.
>
> Because I and my neighbour and everyone else do not have enough love. Yet we could fight war and all its excrescences by releasing each day, the love which is shackled inside us, and giving it a chance to live.[2]

Notes

1 Sermon preached by Rowan Williams at the service to mark the end of hostilities in Iraq, 9 October 2009 at St Paul's Cathedral.

2 E. Hillesum, 1996, *An Interrupted Life: The Diaries, 1941–1943; and Letters from Westerbork*, London: Owl Books, p. 6.

34

Varnishing Day

Preached at the St James's Church Piccadilly annual service to mark Varnishing Day at the Royal Academy of Arts.

Colossians 1.15–29

On Varnishing Day, perhaps it is appropriate to quote a painter. It is, accordingly, a letter written by Vincent Van Gogh that provides me with my starting point in considering what a priest might say to a church full of artists. In it he commented: 'I want to paint man and woman with that something of the eternal which the halo used to symbolise, but which we now seek to confer through the actual radiance of our colour vibrations.'[1]

For the most part, contemporary artists have left halos behind as a way of expressing the divine presence in humanity – indeed there are some who would want to suggest that art departs from illustrative or figurative attempts altogether. Similarly, reflective Christians respect the theological equivalent of halos – pre-modern expressions of doctrine and belief – but now look for ways to express the mysterious presence of God for a post-Enlightenment society in new and imaginative ways. Just as some might ask why we still paint landscapes when we have photography, Christian faith wants to ask questions not just about what is seen, but about the quality of seeing, and to explore the assertion that we ourselves are seen by the unseen God.

It's a fundamental question but not one that people ask every day, or even very often in this generation: is there a God, and if so, what is God like? The orthodox Christian answers to these questions are Yes and The Trinity. In fact we celebrated

Trinity Sunday only yesterday so we are in the season. Well, you might say, that's the Church doing what it does best – answering questions nobody's really asking and still answering questions people used to ask but have moved on from. Fair point, but Christian faith, the communal life of this church, lively in its services, political engagement and social commitment, is expressed not in a list of beliefs to be memorized, but in a language to be learned and a life to be lived.

It's in places like this on days like this that the deeper questions can emerge if we let them: what about God, what about the spiritual mysterious presence that underpins the universe and somehow interacts with us to call us beyond ourselves? And from time to time our presence in a building like this on a day like today invites us to ask that perplexing and fundamental question: is there God? What's God like? This question has had one answer in Christian history that was in its time new and fresh, imaginative and quite amazing. The nature of God, said the fourth-century Council of Nicea, is not a remote sitting-on-a-throne king, ruling in a despotic way, unaccountable and alone. The nature of God, they posited, is dynamic. There is one whole God, but there are three 'persons' of the Trinity, as they came to call them: Holy Spirit, the one who inspires and moves now; Christ, who in Jesus was a particular person at a particular time but who expressed the nature of God in a new way on earth before returning; and Creator of the Universe, called Father especially when we're relating God to Jesus. Not three separate gods – but three ways of being God that we discovered in the whole story of Jesus of Nazareth.

Of course the philosophers started to describe this mystery in philosophical language to make the point that this was a very particular way of experiencing God. So we end up with rather beautiful words like 'consubstantial, coeternal' and so on. Words which, however beautiful, can make this Trinity sound like a complex Rubik's cube formula and keep us ordinary mortals at a distance. And, of course, the Trinity became a doctrine over which blood was shed and division enshrined – did the Son Jesus proceed from the Father alone, or from the Father and the Spirit? Over this precise point the Eastern and Western churches divided. The language and doctrine of faith was professionalized and – rather as now when many of us have learned to call our bodies with which we are intimate and familiar by medical names, my tibia instead of my shin bone, my patella instead of my kneecap, and so on – so the language around the Trinity was professionalized and we became alienated from this most beautiful and imaginative of images of God.

And imagination is the key to this. There have been thousands of ways in which people have tried to explain what the Trinity means: difference in unity, relationship in aloneness, clover leaves with three parts, candles with three wicks. St Augustine, that most profound of thinkers and most humane of Christians, came up with steam, ice and water, all different ways of expressing the same element.

It's hard to imagine something that is so undefinable. And so all our reflections begin in the recognition that all the words we find are totally inadequate, that language is completely useless, although we can't stop ourselves trying.

But I shared a platform with a professional astronomer once. He talked about the birth and death of stars in space and the creation of black holes, describing what he thought was the energy that bound and shaped the universe. As he showed astonishing pictures from the Hubble telescope, he started to talk about the scientific fact that the universe itself is expanding, and that the rate of expansion is itself increasing. The universe is growing now, and the rate of growth is accelerating. As his studies led him to see the movement and energy, the life and death of stars, the spectacular supernova images from light years away, the best description he said he could come up with of this fundamental energy that he observed in the universe was 'dynamic love'.

There is no better way to describe what the Trinity is trying to get at. Is there God, if so what's God like? In contemplating this question, the Trinitarian answer imagines the energy that is God – the energy that underpins the universe, that breathes life into the mystery of humanity and that holds and sustains all that is – in another technical word that theologians use, and that's *pericoresis*. Which means an eternal dance. God is the three persons of the Trinity; God is a noun of course. But also

God is a verb, God is the movement between the persons. God is Godself, interrelational, flowing, 'dancing'.

The more we learn about the interdependence of the planet, the more we learn about the way humans depend on other parts of creation and how we are all vulnerable to one another, the more this pericoresis, this eternal dance makes sense to me when I try to put my brain into gear and think about God as well as pray to God.

God is not 'three bits on top of one another', Father at the top, Son a bit further down and Spirit swirling about somewhere underneath. Neither is God – as feminist theologians sometimes rather disparagingly put it, based on the common image of the Spirit as a dove – 'two blokes and a bird'. God in Trinity is a dynamic, creative, mutually interdependent, wholly beautiful, ultimate presence.

Ruth Fainlight's poem 'The Angel', which made our second reading,[2] has something about it that to my mind expresses the paradoxes that Christian theology deals in all the time. The intuitive language of molten glow, sudden wind, sunlight, music somehow rests, as she puts it, on her bruised shoulders. Her effort is somehow necessary, as she attempts the futile task of moving the rock herself, of releasing Christ herself. And the relationship between her futile and bruising effort and the givenness of the sunlight, the odour, the feathered quill, is that of the believer, who struggles to maintain belief in what she knows to be true – the astonishing gift of life itself, the invigorating presence of God – but whose brain and body strain to remember from whom we have come and to whom we will return. The struggle is always present, and is necessary even in the context of the gifts within which we live.

St Paul in his letter to the Colossians, which we heard in our first reading, gives the scriptural basis for religious artistic endeavour. As Christianity is an incarnational religion, Christ becomes, in Greek, the *ikon* of the invisible God: the image, the depiction, the expression of beauty that points only away from itself to the originator of the beauty.

When the theological ground on which we stand is that, before we start contemplating God, God contemplates us, it results in a reversal of our expectations that it is up to us to debate and decide what God is like. It reverses the looking. God gazes at us before we gaze on God. We become the one who is gazed upon, appreciated, loved. And in this contemplative space, it is possible to hear an irresistible invitation to live, and to join in the dance, to let go of the tightly held, rigid, point-scoring exchanges with which we fill our week, to release ourselves from our focus on what I can get out of you and how I can get on, independently from you; and to allow ourselves to fall into this dynamic, loving, interdependent way of living. And as we fall, we hear the words of the mystic Teresa of Avila who assured us that we cannot fall out of the everlasting arms of God – we can only fall into them.

The famous Rublev ikon of God in three persons depicts a circular mutual gaze with enough space for us, who are looking upon it, to join the group. Artists, priests, care workers, scientists, whoever you are and whatever your past, all are invited to live this spiritually alive life rooted in the dynamic love of this mysterious God. A hugely challenging way of life, in that it makes us vulnerable to one another, and encourages us to commit ourselves to a way of life that rests on love: that will not insist on its own way, that will not be boastful or arrogant or rude; a way of life that rejoices in the truth and will not delight in wrongs or keep score (see 1 Corinthians 13). A Trinitarian life is a life that is contemplative and peaceful but not static; a life that is energized and irrigated by love. We might pray even for the will to want this way of life, or, if we can't do that, pray to want to want to live this way. It is a risky prayer, not a particularly safe way to live. But I suggest that, whatever language you use, and however doctrinal our attempts to describe it, it is the life for which we were made: a just and beautiful life made for love.

Notes

1 M. Roskill (ed.), 1972, *The Letters of Van Gogh*, London: Penguin, p. 151.

2 R. Fainlight, 2011, 'The Angel', in *The Heart's Time*, ed. Janet Morley, London: SPCK.

35

St James's Day

Preached in the courtyard of St James's Church on Piccadilly from the stone pulpit attached to the north wall of the church.

Let me transport you back 100 years or so. It is 1904. The Rector of St James's Church has been for the last four years Joseph McCormick, always known as Joe. A keen sportsman, a particularly good cricketer, Joe stood six foot three in his stockinged feet and had, they said, a powerful Irish voice. Friends of his got together with the churchwardens and in 1904 built this outside pulpit to their church in the hope that his strong voice would carry on to the crowds on Piccadilly.

For your information, I'm standing on a box.

Sometimes on a Sunday afternoon they would hold services outside. Joe or one of his sons would preach from this pulpit and over 100 musicians would form an orchestra grouped nearby. We don't quite have 100 ukeleles today in the St James ukulele orchestra but … you never know … next year maybe …

Contemporary reports, however, say that the sound of horses' hooves and carriage wheels on the cobble stones of Piccadilly just outside the gates drowned out the sound of his voice.

There aren't many churches with a pulpit outside. And pulpits have a chequered reputation, especially in today's society, much less deferential than Edwardian Piccadilly when this one was built. In broadcasting our message from this outside pulpit, we might stand accused of spoiling the Sunday morning of a capital city still recovering from last night. We might be joining in the doom-laden shouts of the Oxford Circus prophets who use tannoys and leaflets to tell us that the End is Nigh. But, for good or ill, we have this pulpit attached to the outside wall of our church. And to everyone who sees it, it says that at some point in its history, this congregation of St James's wanted to talk to all the people who were outside the church, not just wait for them to come inside the building.

Churches aren't the only places where pulpits are part of the furniture. On the front of many sailing boats, particularly fishing boats, there is what's known as a pulpit right out on the bow – a raised platform right at the front of the boat. If you stand on it, you are in a lookout position. This kind of pulpit is used in order to weigh anchor safely. Sailors use this pulpit to lean right out – to drop anchor safely or to tend to the sails.

And so, on St James's Day, taking our own cue from our architecture, perhaps we can see this outside pulpit not so much as a desire to talk down to the people of Piccadilly, six feet above contradiction, but, by contrast, as a signal that we want to be people who are leaning right out – on the lookout, scanning the horizon, remembering where we are anchored and being willing to plumb the depths of our life experience before God. Willing to drop the anchor deeper down and to look beyond the immediate issues of the day. To be attentive to the Holy Spirit which blows where it wills, and to tend our sails accordingly.

We are named for James. And James the Apostle himself had a nickname, Son of Thunder. A difficult nickname to celebrate in these days when religious fervour is viewed with such suspicion.

St James's Church is named after a disciple who was hot-headed, got things properly wrong, was unattractively competitive, and clearly (in Matthew's Gospel) had a complicated relationship with his mother. If you have ever got things really wrong, if you have ever made a mistake, if you have ever had a complicated relationship with your family, James is a saint for you.

Set as we are in central London, we know, because we're human beings, that being part of this church of St James's does not inoculate us to, or protect us from, the competitive, anxious, money-driven instincts that we find in ourselves and everyone else if we look hard enough. Churches are not full of perfect people – quite the opposite: churches are full of people who have somehow recognized that they need God.

We are not by any means perfect, but what we have said is that we want to be on the lookout – not for the next big thing or the next global star or the next economic trend, but leaning out, on the lookout for the deepest truths about God and about us. And to help us keep ourselves anchored and looking towards the far horizon, we try to do some important things together.

In a noisy city we want to offer silence.
In a relentless city we want to offer rest.
In a competitive and unequal city, we want to offer a vision of utter acceptance and forgiveness offered by Christ to everyone who comes.

In a city where many are lost, we invite you to be found.
In a city where many are lonely, we invite you to build community across different ages and backgrounds, and find friends.
In a city full of distractions, we invite you to pray.

And when you have nothing left, when the fear that you feel seems to have won, when all seems lost and you are quietly despairing, we say that there is no more authentic way to come to God; you are most of all welcome if you arrive like that.

And, you know, although it's really important to listen – and Christians should surely spend much more time listening than speaking – it is sometimes important to speak up. To say clearly, publicly and without equivocation that our faith in Christ persuades us that there is no barrier between you and God so don't let the Church or anyone else try to build one.

We are gay, we are straight, we are trans, we are wealthy, we are poor. We are vulnerably housed, some of us have our own homes, some of us have jobs we're not sure about, some of us love our work and some of us are pretty desperate to find some. Some of us have retired.

Some of us are not that well.

Some of us struggle with our mental health, some of us struggle with our weakening bodies, even though our spirits are strong. Some of us have almost given up on life, some of us are bursting with energy to make the world a better place. We are Brown, we are white, we are Black. What binds us is that we have said we are willing to go deeper, go ever deeper, looking for the depths and trying to face the truths that we know are within us and that connect us to God.

So to our central London parish we say, because we are Londoners ourselves: we know that you are working hard, in the coffee shops around here or in the hotels. We know that it's really hard to make the rent, and that some of you live in situations that make you really miserable. We know that you are working hard in the offices here – and we know too that some of you are making an eye-watering amount of money. We also know that for some of you these streets and this church building are the only home you know.

We also want to say from our lookout position, from our anchored faith, that we believe you matter – immensely – and that the gospel is good news for all of us. A gospel of healing and peace.

The tradition of this parish being active in this city goes right back to the foundation of the church itself. In 1688, the year of the last Roman Catholic king in England and four years after this church was opened, the parish decided to establish a workhouse for people who at that time were known as the 'able-bodied poor'. By 1776, the workhouse in Poland Street, Soho, a stone's throw from this building, had grown into one of the largest in the country. In the 1881 census this workhouse had over 600 people living there.

One famous nineteenth-century song, derived from an English folk song called 'The Unfortunate Rake', was called 'The St James's Infirmary Blues'. It was recorded by, no less, Louis Armstrong, Joe Cocker, Van Morrison, Hugh Laurie, and more recently the band White Stripes. It's a powerful lament for a young man or woman, cut down by disease – and it tells the story of one of the young people of this parish. This story and this song have now been sung all over the world, and will be sung later in this service. Although it is not a usual song to sing during a service, and it is not directly addressed to God, it tells powerfully the story of one of God's people in this parish, and reminds us of the absolute imperative to confront injustice in our own lives and in the life of this city.

We are simply the latest generation of people to be the St James's church; and there will be others here in the future who call this courtyard theirs – whose names we will never know – after every one of us here has died.

And so, leaning out from our lookout perspective, with James as our companion in Christ, let us now sit for a moment in silence and listen to the sounds of the city, and to the sound of our own beating heart as part of it, and know that here, even here, even now, God is with us.

36

Women's Vocations Day

London Diocese

Luke 10.38–42

I was taking a workshop not long ago for a mixed audience of women and men – a mixture of people from church and non-church contexts. I asked them to say what came into their head when they heard the phrase 'Christian woman'. There was quite a silence. Nothing good obviously, I thought.

After a while, someone said, 'The Queen.'

Then they got going: Ann Widdecombe, Dot Cotton from *EastEnders*, Britney Spears when she was young and took a virginity vow, but not any more. Some remembered the young lesbian character Sophie from Coronation Street, others the Vicar of Dibley or Janet from *The Archers*.

Several of these, I pointed out, didn't actually exist. Could they think of actual Christian women?

Mother Theresa then made an appearance, as did the art critic Sister Wendy. A white audience had come up with all white women, quite a number of whom were fictional and most over 70. As a snapshot of European twenty-first-century Christianity, which has not yet many prominent female leaders of the profile, say, of the Pope or the Archbishop of Canterbury, and for an ageing Church of England population, maybe this wasn't too surprising. A Black-majority or more mixed audience might perhaps have come up earlier with other names associated with the Civil Rights movement, such as Coretta King. The intersectionality of invisibility was on display here.

With this audience, we then talked about what they thought of the phrase 'Christian woman', and pejorative descriptions emerged: bossy, probably quite kind but in a judgemental sort of way, a bit dumpy, maybe quite practical but ultimately bland.

This conversation was instructive, because we as women don't discern our vocation in a vacuum, but in relation to our own contexts and stories. And it's quite easy for us to get stuck in, to internalize, if we're not careful, some of these stereotypes or the self-limiting beliefs we ourselves carry around. We in this generation are discerning vocation in the context of the Me Too movement, the Time's Up campaign, the equal pay controversies. We as women have multiple vocations, most potently of all to be the person God created us to be. And I have news for those of you who are thinking, praying, those of you who have turned up to a day like today. If you are looking at those of us with dog collars on, assuming that we discerned our vocation long ago and that was that, you're mistaken. Our discernment is an every-day discernment that will, please God, continue for the rest of our lives. Our task as women, as men, is to keep listening, keep discerning, to recognize the multi-vocational lives we lead, then have the courage to follow these calls.

I chose for us to hear the Gospel of Luke today, and his story of the two sisters, Martha and Mary. For me, this story captures the incredibly creative opportunities for us as women to follow Christ and to live Christ-shaped lives – but it also doesn't shirk away from some of our challenges.

You know the story. Martha's cross because she's doing the work while Mary sits meekly and listens to what Jesus is saying. This little family – Martha, Mary and their brother Lazarus – live at Bethany, a small village just outside Jerusalem. By all accounts, Jesus was really very friendly with them, visiting them often. When Lazarus died, Jesus was distraught, as John's Gospel tells us. And this little vignette of their life and Jesus' visit has become famous over the years for Martha getting told off by Jesus. She has got stuck there over the years, and often from preachers, mostly male, she gets a bad press.

For those of you who like art, there is a wonderful picture of this scene in the National Gallery in London. It's *Christ in the House of Martha and Mary* by the seventeenth-century Spanish painter Diego Velasquez. Mary, with her long blond hair, is sitting rather wanly in the background listening to Jesus talking. Martha is in the foreground with forearms that wouldn't be out of place in a professional rugby team, hacking the heads off fish. She looks furious.

And so she is locked into this story as the one who got told off for being too busy. In church conversations, we can get so fixed on this aspect of Martha that women sometimes say, 'I'm a Martha not a Mary', rather negatively describing themselves as more practical, more active. Of course there's something here about not allowing ourselves to be distracted by our 'many tasks' so that we forget to pray, but that's true of women and men alike. The fundamental problem is one that is repeated over and over again when we hear, read or preach Scripture. We have allowed Martha to become ossified, stuck, one-dimensional, whereas in fact she is one of the most inspiring, holistically described characters of them all.

What else do we know about Martha? We know that when her brother dies, she is furious with Jesus for staying where he was for two days. She leaves her seemingly more placid sister in the village and goes out to meet Jesus before he gets there. And what she says to him there is, in some ways, terrible. 'If you'd been here, my brother wouldn't have died' (John 11.21). It's raw, honest and emotional. Martha is an example of how to address Christ in prayer, how to tell the truth about the most precious, the most painful parts of our lives and our experience. In Martha I find a courageous woman, able to tell Christ the unvarnished truth about her life. She doesn't dress it up or make it sound better than it is. In this exchange, she lets out her grief and distress, just as the Psalms would have taught her to do.

When Jesus comes to the grave of her brother, and orders the stone to be rolled away, Martha is thoroughly practical. The body has been there for four days and so she protests that this is a very bad idea. She challenges Jesus publicly. In front of the crowd, she is challenging, fearless, prophetic. She names what is stinking.

Sometimes, like Martha, we are called to say out loud what is stinking. To stand up with people who are voiceless, suffering; not to be afraid of the crowd and their murmuring to keep it down. Martha names what is stinking, and sometimes, so should we.

And right in the middle of John's story, there is the most remarkable exchange between Jesus and Martha. Because this is yet another side of Martha. She contemplates Jesus and confesses that she believes. This is Martha filled with faith and contemplative energy, saying what she believes about God, to God. And her confession of Jesus as Messiah is very different from the more famous one which is Peter's. Peter says almost exactly the same thing – and then immediately gets into a fight with Jesus which results in Jesus saying, 'Get behind me, Satan.' No such tussle with Martha. She is steady, truthful, strong.

In discerning our own vocations to be the people God has created and is calling us to be, we can take from the example of Martha and Christ a set of questions.

Where do you think you might be a bit stuck, like Martha, in a one-dimensional view of yourself, and what are those other talents, strengths, abilities and characteristics that could be set free? Where is it that you discern the crowd are murmuring for you to keep quiet? How honest are you in your prayers to God? Do you protect God from your griefs and furies or, like Martha, do you let God have it face to face?

In this service we will sing a hymn by a woman who found a way to fulfil her vocation at a time when women in the UK were much more constrained in their roles than now. Charlotte Elliott wrote the hymn 'Just as I am' in the first half of the nineteenth century. She was, in some ways, the Billy Graham of her day: there are accounts of thousands of people coming forward and coming to faith precisely during the singing of this hymn. She found a voice to shape and teach the faith at a time when women were not able to take part in any of the decision-making of the Church. She wrote her own words, sometimes wrote her own music, and raised her voice as a poet. She also wrote from her own experience. As a lifelong user of a wheelchair, she wrote frankly from her own life. And so I hope that we can honour her today as a disabled woman who leads us in worship 100 years after her death, without being ordained or part of the official structures of the Church in any way.

Our task, as women considering the direction of our own

lives, is to listen, continually to discern, and not to allow anyone at all, especially not ourselves, to confine or limit the movement of the Spirit who blows where she wills.

Martha is much more than the woman who was cross about doing the washing-up. We're real experts, as women, at honing, guarding and protecting our own self-limiting beliefs. These are fed by, shored up by, sometimes enforced by societal, cultural or church expectations that are sometimes rooted in false teaching of Scripture.

But the gospel according to Martha is that our vocations are holistic, engaging all of us: our emotion, our practicality, our intellect, our prophetic courage. These vocations are expressed in as many ways as there are women, not just in ordination.

I pray that as Christian women we will become ever more adventurous, curious and courageous, never afraid of expressing our emotions or stretching our intellect, never afraid to be thoroughly practical, and never afraid to look around us in society and name what is stinking.

We can hear this good news for Martha because it's good news for us.

What is the gospel according to you? Christ's love and grace will draw it out of you. I pray to God that, in your life and words, you will preach it too.